Flight Lessons 4: Leadership & Command

How Eddie Learned to Lead

James Albright

Copyright © 2017 James Albright
All rights reserved.
ISBN-10: 0-9862630-7-9
ISBN-13: 978-0-9862630-7-1

Acknowledgments

Thanks to Chris Manno for over thirty years of trading aviation stories, writing techniques, and for permitting my blatant grand larceny of his artwork without complaint. Thanks also to Chris Parker for all the fact checking, sense of grammar, and style pointers. If he's told me once, he's told me a thousand times to avoid hyperbole. (This book makes a thousand and four.)

Thank you especially to Grace (*The Lovely Mrs. Haskel*) for proofreading this five times and living through it the first time. We've witnessed our share of death through my Air Force career but the deaths chronicled in these pages were the ones that hit the hardest. I lost six squadron mates on the hills of Dubrovnik, Croatia on April 3, 1996. We both lost six friends.

James' Lawyer Advises:

Always remember that James, when you get right down to it, is just a pilot. He tries to give you the facts from the source materials but maybe he got it wrong, maybe he is out of date. Sure, he warns you when he is giving you his personal techniques, but you should always follow your primary guidance (aircraft manuals, government regulations, etc.) before listening to James.

In Memory of:
Captain Ashley "AJ" Davis
Captain Timothy Shafer
Technical Sergeant Shelly Kelly
Technical Sergeant Cheryl Turnage
Staff Sergeant Gerald Aldrich II
Staff Sergeant Robert Farrington, Jr.
The Crew of IFO 21

Contents

US Air Force Rank Structure (1995)	8
86 Airlift Wing Chain of Command	9
Acronyms	10
Prelude: The Prediction	13
1: Remington's Secret	25
2: The Politics of Command	41
3: The New Sheriff	65
4: Blind Spots	101
5: Go Along to Get Along	125
6: Team Ramstein	147
7: Transformation	167
8: The Prince	199
9: The Process	223
10: What Really Happened	243
Postscript	249
A Few Thoughts	277
Appendix: Accident Report Extracts	279

James Albright

US Air Force Rank Structure (1995)

Leadership is immersed in politics and in the military the politics are structured by military rank. The U.S. Air Force rank system is derived from the U.S. Army. A higher ranking officer is automatically given deference by officers of a lower rank and by all enlisted members. Enlisted members include those who are "enlisted" and those that are Non-Commissioned Officers (NCOs). NCOs are those of rank sergeant or higher.

While not technically correct, some in the military refer to others by pay grade because it makes the translation between services easier. Enlisted pay grades are from E-1 to E-9. Officer pay grades are from O-1 to O-10. This can be useful when understanding how an officer from one service relates to another. In the Air Force, for example, a captain is an O-3. In the Navy, a captain is an O-6. The Air Force captain owes the Navy captain a salute.

Promotion is never guaranteed and officer ranks are "capped" at certain numbers. The number of lieutenant colonels, for example, is limited. You cannot promote a major to lieutenant colonel until another lieutenant colonel is promoted, retires, or is otherwise eliminated. Officers are given two tries at each promotion, and if they fail on the second try, they are normally forced out. If this happens after 20 years, they are allowed to retire. Otherwise, they are simply shown the door.

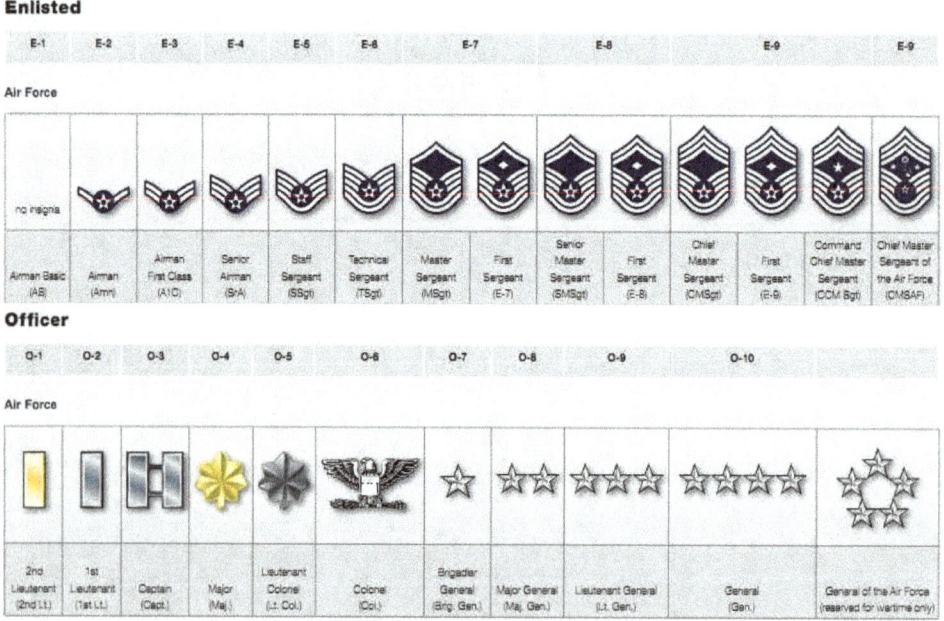

Flight Lessons 4: Leadership & Command

86 Airlift Wing Chain of Command

In the early nineties, the USAF embraced the concept of OBOWOB, "One Base, One Wing, One Boss." You can draw a line from commander to commander up and down and clearly see who reports to who.

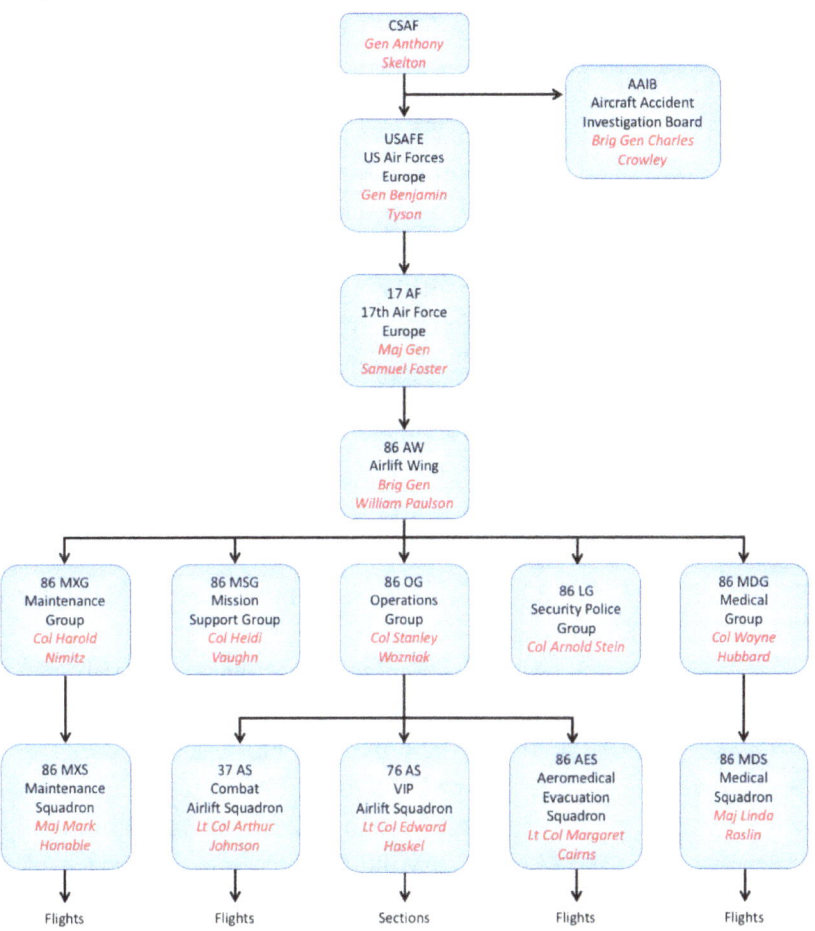

I've only shown those entities that have an impact on the story, there are many others. More than one wing reports to the 17 AF, for example. Each group has more than the squadrons shown but these are the ones that impact the story. At the bottom level, each squadron has between two and six flights or sections.

In the words of Bob Dylan, "you got to serve somebody" – everybody has a boss.

Acronyms

The United States Air Force (USAF) loves its acronyms and is only bested in this fetish by the Unites States Navy (USN). It is a part of the culture and while I've tried to minimize it somewhat, you may find yourself needing a secret decoder ring. Here it is:

17 AF	17th Air Force
37 AS	37th Combat Airflift Squadron
76 AS	76th Airlift Squadron
86 AES	86th Aeromedical Evacuation Squadron
86 AW	86th Airlift Wing
86 MDG	86th Medical Group
86 MDS	86th Medical Squadron
86 MSG	86th Mission Support Group
86 MXG	86th Maintenance Group
86 MXS	86th Maintenance Squadron
86 OG	86th Operations Group
86 SPG	86th Security Police Group
89 AW	89th Airlift Wing (Andrews AFB, MD near Washington, DC)
AAIB	Aircraft Accident Investigation Board
AC	Aircraft Commander
ADF	Automatic Direction Finder
ADO	Assistant Director of Operations
AFIIS	Air Force Instrument Instructor School
AFMPC	Air Force Military Personnel Center
AMC	Air Mobility Command (which replaced MAC)
Article 15	Administrative punishment, just short of a courts martial
ATC	Air Traffic Control
AWACS	Airborne Warning And Control System aircraft
C-130	Lockheed "Hercules" aircraft
C-141	Lockheed "Starlifter" aircraft
C-20	Gulfstream III aircraft
C-21	Learjet 35 aircraft
C-9	Douglas DC-9 aircraft

Flight Lessons 4: Leadership & Command

CAVU	Ceiling and Visibility Unlimited
CC	Commander
CINC	Commander in Chief
CP	Copilot
CSAF	Chief of Staff, United States Air Force
CT-43	Boeing 737 aircraft
DNP	Do Not Promote (Recommendation)
DO	Director of Operations
DP	Definitely Promote (Recommendation)
E-3A	Boeing 707 configured as AWACS
E-4B	Boeing 747 configured for USAF
ECM	Electronic Counter Measure
EP	Evaluator Pilot
ER	Effectiveness Report
FAA	Federal Aviation Administration
flak	Fl(ieger) a(bwehr) k(anone) antiaircraft gun; has turned into the word "flak" to denote any antiaircraft fire from the ground
FOD	Foreign Object Damage
GIII	Gulfstream III aircraft
HQ	Headquarters
IG	Inspector General
IOE	Initial Operating Experience flight (or trip)
IP	Instructor Pilot
LR-35	Learjet 35 aircraft
MAC	Military Airlift Command
MC Rate	Mission Capable Rate
MDA	Minimum Descent Altitude
MSA	Minimum Sector Altitude
NATO	North Atlantic Treaty Organization
NCO	Non-Commissioned Officer
NDB	Non-Directional Beacon
OTTO	On-Time Take Off
OUI	Operating Under the Influence
P	Promote (Recommendation)
PANS OPS	Procedures for Air Navigation Services / Aircraft Operations
PAR	Precision Approach Radar

POW	Prisoner of War
RO	Radio Operator
SAC	Strategic Air Command
SAM	Surface-to-Air Missile
SECDEF	Secretary of Defense
TAC	Tactical Air Command
TACAN	Tactical Air Navigation system
TERPS	U.S. Standard for Terminal Instrument Procedures
USAF	United States Air Force
USAFE	United States Air Force Europe
USN	United States Navy
USTRANSCOM	United States Transportation Command

Prelude: The Prediction

The Summer of 1989

E-4B 3-1676, (USAF Photo)

"Are these the nuclear 'go' codes?" I asked.

"I can neither confirm nor deny that, major," the colonel said. "You know that."

"If you want to be on the ground by 1900, I'm going to need to know why," I said. "I can push air traffic control around, but only for the right reasons." I leaned against the metal railing that lined the hallway as he thought about his secrecy requirements versus his need to update those secrets. The blue carpet beneath our feet was lined with thin wires to dampen static electricity and the windows appeared to be covered in mosquito netting, but the metal grid was there to absorb any electromagnetic pulse from a nuclear bomb explosion. The airplane was a flying power plant and radio station, oozing with electrons. I knew that taking my hand off the rail for only a few seconds would subject me to a small jolt of static electricity. Keeping in contact was a habit.

"Let me put it to you this way," he said, looking over his shoulder. We were alone in the long hallway that stretched the distance from tail to nose of our

Boeing 747, but he held his voice to a whisper. "If we don't have that bag on the airplane after 1900, and we have to go to war, the President of the United States will not be able to direct his bombers, missiles, or subs."

If the guy representing the White House was worried enough about bombers, missiles, or subs, then my decision was clear.

"Got it," I said. "I'll do my best and pass along an ETA when I have it." I spun on my heels without waiting for his reaction; time was fleeting. Our E-4B looked like a generic Boeing 747, except maybe the "United States of America" emblazoned on the length of the fuselage may have given away our real role in life. I picked up the nearest phone and dialed zero, one.

"Flight deck." I recognized the flight engineer's Texas drawl.

"Pete, this is Eddie. Tell Dave to push it up to Mach nine two and descend to thirty thousand. Then hand the phone to the nav."

"Sure thing," he said. After ten seconds, there was another voice.

"Captain Marks," he said.

"Paul, we are headed for thirty thousand feet at Mach nine two. I need an ETA for Offutt by the time I get back to the cockpit."

"Yes, sir," he said. "Are you descending to improve our true airspeed?" he asked.

"Exactly," I said. "And you don't have to 'sir' me."

"You got it, sir," he said. Among all our pilots and engineers rank didn't seem to matter unless someone from outside the flight crew was present. For some reason our navigators didn't play that game; I would always be Major Haskel to Captain Paul Marks.

I ducked into the radio operator's compartment and found the lead RO. "Sergeant Saterwhite, please get me the Offutt Air Force Base weather shop." As he dialed I stood by his console with my back to the windows opposite his station. The walls on his side were perfectly square and if it were not for the sounds I could have mistaken his cubicle for a ground-based radio operator's cubicle. I heard the sound of the air around the fuselage increase in volume and pitch, telling me we had accelerated past Mach 0.90. I wondered why the deck angle of the aircraft hadn't decreased yet; we should have begun the descent. "Here you go," Saterwhite said, handing me a phone.

"I am a hundred nautical miles west of Casper, Wyoming headed for you,"

Flight Lessons 4: Leadership & Command

I said. "I need the best winds between twenty and thirty thousand. Over." I didn't often use the 'over' called for by the manual on these half-duplex phones, but many non-aviators didn't seem to know when to talk without it. He could only talk once I released the transmit button. The weather officer simply said, "standby."

The radio operator gave me a look while twirling a pencil between his thumb and forefinger. The arc of the pink eraser seemed to describe the top of a question mark. "This is me, standing by," I explained.

In another minute, I had my answers and headed forward and up the spiral staircase to my own office. I opened the cockpit door and looked at the navigator at his rearward facing desk. "Midnight, ten," he said. That would be 1910, local time.

"What if I gave you another fifty knots in tailwinds?" I asked.

"Lemme see," he said.

I returned to my waiting seat, row one, left, top floor of our flying office building. The "T" of my flight instruments told me we were flying at Mach 0.92, wings level with a 3 degree nose up pitch, Flight Level 350, and headed almost perfectly due east. "Why aren't we descending?"

"ATC is working on it," Dave said. "We have traffic below us."

"Declare priority and move them out of the way," I said. Our airplane's special status allowed us to do that, but I would need to make a phone call to the Federal Aviation Administration after we landed.

"Really?" he said.

"Yeah," I said. "I've got the airplane."

"Pilot, nav," I heard over the interphone.

"Yes."

"You give me fifty knots and I'll get you on the runway on the hour," he said. "But not to the chocks."

"Are you using the standard descent schedule?" I asked.

"That's all I got," he said. I knew his squadron manual gave him a higher speed schedule for this situation, but we didn't have time for that kind of pilot-to-navigator instruction.

"Okay," I said. "Call the base and find out what runway they are on. If they are on three zero and the winds give us less than a ten-knot tailwind on one two, tell them that's what we're using. And tell them we want the pattern empty by the time we get there."

"You don't want much, do you?" he said. It was humor from the captain. That was a positive sign. I was starting to think this might work.

Dave spun the altitude selector to 300, meaning 30,000 feet.

"I see thirty," I said. "Ask for twenty-seven." I thought about that some more. I dialed the autopilot's vertical speed function and set 1,000 feet per minute. I pulled just enough of the four throttles to keep the speed at Mach 0.92, our limiting speed at these altitudes.

In a moment, Dave reset the altitude selector to 270. Once we got there I pushed the throttles forward by the same amount I had pulled, plus a little more. "Pete, you have the throttles. Keep us at nine two."

The cockpit of the Boeing 747, even our military version, is eerily quiet at most speeds. But once the speed crept over Mach 0.88 the air started to separate behind the iconic 747 hump and became noticeable in the cockpit. By the time we got to Mach 0.92, it became noisy enough in the cockpit that we had to raise our voices to be heard.

"Pilot, nav," I heard.

"Yes."

"The base says the pattern belongs to you," Paul said. "You can expect a left quartering tailwind, but only five knots."

"Okay," I said. "I'm going to fly 300 knots below 10,000 feet until I don't have to. Let me know when we are on the normal speed schedule to make the chocks on the hour."

"You got it, sir," he said. The FAA requires all airplanes to fly slower than 250 knots when below 10,000 feet except for a few military exceptions. Some fighters, for example, are allowed 300 knots until configuring for landing. The speed limit made sense of course, it gave everyone a better chance spotting each other and avoiding a midair collision. We almost always abided by the rule, but could grant ourselves a waiver if we needed it. I wanted to get rid of that extra speed sooner than later. Getting back on the speed schedule would eliminate having to guess when I needed to slow down to get the landing gear and flaps extended. If I was too fast to land, I would have to go around and our timing would be out the window.

Flight Lessons 4: Leadership & Command

At 27,000 feet we would normally begin our descent when 90 nautical miles away. That would provide a nice 3-degree descent, but it also resulted in decreasing true airspeed. I knew we could make a 4-degree descent work and that would improve our forward speed.

"We'll start down at 80 miles," I said to Dave. "Don't let me break anything."

The weather was "clear and a million," meaning the visibility was unlimited and there was no ceiling. Offutt Air Force Base sits ten miles south of Omaha just west of the Missouri River. The base hosts the headquarters of the Strategic Air Command, a squadron of spy planes, and the infamous "Looking Glass" birds that had been standing airborne alert since 1961. But none of those missions outranked ours and I knew there would be a uniformed officer with a black brief case flanked by two armed guards waiting for us. As I waited for the distance indicator to wind its way to 80, I thought that the secrets people on the airplane must have done something seriously wrong to find themselves without the secrets needed to go to war simply because the calendar had advanced to the next month. These secret codes were normally published in monthly books that had to be replaced by the end of the last day every month, at midnight Greenwich Mean Time. That would be 1900 in the Midwest today.

As the distance closed to 85, Dave requested and was granted our initial descent. I tapped the throttles, telling Pete they again belonged to me. I pulled a little, and did some math. Our ground speed was 540 knots, exactly nine miles every minute. A 4-degree descent should take about 3,600 feet per minute. That's a lot. But our maximum speed would decrease with altitude and, with that, so would the required descent rate. "I think you got this," Dave said.

By the time we got to 10,000 feet things were starting to look normal, except we were way too fast. We were lined up with the runway 30 miles away, still doing 320 knots. "That's all I can take," I said. I pulled all four throttles to idle and pulled the speed brake handle. "Dave extend each setting of flaps when we have the limiting speed. When we get to the gear speed I'll bring the speed brakes in."

After the second notch of flaps the navigator finally said what I had been waiting for. "On a normal descent schedule to make the chocks, pilot."

I pushed the speed brake handle in and pointed to the gear handle. "Gear," I said. Three minutes later we were back to normal.

"Fully configured, on speed," Pete said. "The before landing checklist is complete."

A minute later we were on the ground and a minute after that we spotted an Army Colonel with a black brief case standing next to our normal parking spot. At 1858, the air stairs hit the ground three stories below us.

After a week of operational duty, our flight crew was replaced and spread to the winds, each with their own lives to return to. As the crew commander, I had one final task to complete: paperwork. After combining the various logs and forms from the rest of the crew, I added my trip report. That report was usually a sterile, one-paragraph summary of the week's events. Being an aspiring author, I normally handed in four or five pages, written in whatever style that amused me at the time. "The Case of the Missing Black Bag" was written ala Hunter S. Thompson. "Zounds," I wrote, "fifteen minutes short with no supply of minutes in sight!"

"That's damned funny," Alton Gee said as he signed off on the report. As our head scheduler, Lieutenant Colonel Gee's initials would be the last step before the paperwork hit the commander's desk. "I bet you even get a chuckle out of Rodney P."

Alton was the only person in the squadron who could get away with calling the commander by his first name. The boss was Lieutenant Colonel Rodney P. Larson and Alton called many people by first name and initial. But he tended to invent pet names for his favorite pets and it was the highest honor in the squadron to be granted such a name.

"Maybe you ought to give up this flying thing, Ed-you-el. Maybe you can be a writer instead."

"All I want to do is fly," I said. "Anything else is a distraction."

A young sergeant dropped a stack of new paperwork on Alton's desk and stood. Alton found another stack, placed my report on top, and handed the bundle to the waiting orderly. Alton read the top line of each new sheet of paper and dealt them onto his desk like a deck of cards. Two or three ended up in the trash. Alton got up and started to talk as he added flights to our scheduling board.

Flight Lessons 4: Leadership & Command

"The Pentagon boys are running a midnight exercise tomorrow night," he said as the flight started to take shape with his grease pencil marks. It was a ten-hour sortie from eight pm to six am, one of our least favorite flights. "Drill some holes in the sky," he continued. "Well, nothing to be done about it. Let the whining begin." His board looked back two months and forward two months. I was happy to see that I had done the trip within recent memory and would probably escape it this time. A crowd started to collect outside his office, knowing that fates were about to be decided. Alton scanned the fourteen listed pilots and selected Majors Jesse Smith and Bob Wilson as pilots for the overnighter. Almost on cue, Wilson entered.

"Alton," he said. "I really can't do this tomorrow night. I promise I'll do the next one."

"You're up in the batting rotation," Alton said. "Fair's fair."

"But my wife and I have tickets to a show," he said. "Please."

"You are either an aircraft commander or you aren't," Alton said.

Bob looked at me for support, but I didn't want to do the flight either. "Eddie?" he said. Alton tended to put any pilot he didn't like in the whiner category and that may have been unfair in this case. Bob wasn't the strongest pilot in our arsenal, but he was competent and not bad company at any bar. "Let me think about it," I said. Bob left.

Alton looked at me and the empty spot along the row of the schedule next to my name. "I don't know why you want to help him out. He hasn't done one of these in a while and you did the last one."

"He's going through a rough patch with his wife," I said. "They've only been married a few years and she still hasn't got the hang of having a part time husband. Let's cut him some slack, Alton."

"Okay, Ed-you-el," he said. He erased the "AC" from the intersection of the flight and Bob's name and redrew it on the line with my name.

"Haskel!" I heard yelled from across the hallway from the commander's office. "Get your ass in here now!"

From outside the scheduling office I saw a sea of eyes turned my way. The commander was unhappy and broadcasted his displeasure for all to hear. I got up and tried to walk as casually as I could under the circumstances without appearing disrespectful. I appeared at Lieutenant Colonel Rodney P. Larson's office doorway in a pose halfway between "attention" and "parade rest."

"Sir?" I said.

"It says here you flew at Mach nine two to make this block time," he said, veins bulging through the thin blonde hair of his pale scalp. "Tell me that's not what you really did and that this is some kind of exaggeration of your so-called writing style."

"That's exactly what I did, sir," I said. "I flew as fast as I could and lower than economical all to maximize true airspeed. I exceeded two-fifty below ten for a few thousand feet too. We landed on speed and made it with two minutes to spare."

None of that did anything to soothe the savage beast. "Well that's the last time anyone does anything like that," he said. "Dismissed."

I returned to the mission planning room, just outside of Alton's office. The crowd left a seat at the table for me, which I took. All eyes in the room shifted from me to the door behind me. I turned to see our angry commander.

"The next pilot who exceeds Mach eight six in this squadron is fired," Lieutenant Colonel Larson said. "Does everyone understand that?"

"Yes, sir," every pilot in the room said. Every pilot except me. Larson left and the eyes returned to me.

"Why Mach eight six?" someone finally said.

"I don't know," I said. Mach 0.86 was our usual cruise speed and we taught our pilots to vary that plus or minus Mach 0.04 under normal circumstances if needed to make our timing work. But when the mission dictated it, we allowed pilots to go as slow as the airplane's maneuvering speed or as high as the maximum operating speed. At higher altitudes, that was Mach 0.92.

And so began the month of missed block times. We always had one airplane on operational duty for our White House and Pentagon masters who rarely complained about block times unless we were late. None of this should have mattered except the normal schedule was based on Mach 0.86 as a starting condition. Now that it became a maximum, block times became almost impossible to make.

Larson exploded with rage at each late report. The non-pilots wondered how the pilots had lost the ability to land on time while the pilots counted the days until Lieutenant Colonel Rodney P. Larson had to fly the operational bird. When that day came, he managed to land on time. Slowly but surely word got out, Lieutenant Colonel Larson flew faster than Mach 0.86. It was no longer a maximum speed.

A month later I had orders to upgrade. It would be my second time as an Air Force instructor pilot and was what I had been hoping for secretly. Sometimes the best way to get something in any bureaucracy is to pretend you don't care if it happens or not. But I cared. I sat in the scheduling office, opposite Alton's desk, never mentioning the schedule or even casting an eye to the board.

"Well I might as well get to some real Air Force scheduling," Alton said, picking up his grease pencil. "I hear that young Ed-you-el is going to be a real Boeing 747 instructor pilot. Ahead of the pack, as they say."

"Somebody's looking out for me," I said. "I wasn't expecting this for another year."

"That somebody, believe it or not," he said, "is one Rodney P. Larson."

"I guess he's forgotten the Month of Missed Block Times," I said. "Even a blind squirrel finds a nut now and then. It's just the law of averages."

Alton gave me a half laugh and half of a wry look. He retreated from the scheduling board and sat down. "Maybe this is Rodney P's way of apologizing to you for that bit of nastiness. He isn't the best squadron commander we've ever had around here. But he isn't the worst."

"He swims in an elite pool of scum," I said. "He isn't the worst squadron commander, but he is in the running for the title."

Alton gave me a pained look. "You want my prediction for you, young Ed-you-el?"

"Sure," I said.

"I predict that one day this man's Air Force is going to elevate you to commander of a squadron of your very own," he said. "It is inevitable. You are smart, you are a good pilot, and you manage to collect supporters wherever you go."

"That's good to hear," I said.

"But I also predict you will fail as a squadron commander," he said. Alton had a way of hurling insults but he usually did so with an audience for comedic effect. We were alone in his office and I was an audience of one.

"You are a terrible judge of people," he continued. "You think very highly of your peers and you turn a blind eye to the faults of anyone who works for you. Ordinarily those are fine traits, but not so fine in a commander."

"I'm not so sure that's right," I said.

"It is," he said. "Take your support of our worst pilot, that whiner Bob Wilson. He busted his qualification check, he busted his first upgrade check, and he is the first pilot in here to complain about unfair treatment. And yet you do nothing but defend him."

"He's not that bad," I said.

"But he isn't the only one," Alton said. "You have the same blindness for half the engineers, navigators, and flight attendants." I let his words hang. It was hard to tell when Alton was serious or setting up the world's biggest punch line. Patience always paid dividends in his office. "It seems to me that whole block time mess could have been avoided if you politely closed the door with the boss and explained to him what the real maximum speed of the airplane is. He was a fine line pilot before he went to headquarters for three years. When he came back he didn't know the numbers as well as he should have. You secretly wanted him to make a fool of himself because you secretly think all superior officers are stupid."

"I suppose," I started but ended, running out of words.

"Young Ed-you-el, I really like you," he said after my awkward pause. "I really do. But you have to realize that just because somebody makes colonel around here doesn't make them a bad person. You don't seem to understand that just because someone doesn't have SAT scores like yours or can perform differential calculus in their heads like you can, that doesn't make them stupid. I will grant you that most Air Force commanders get to their lofty positions because of political connections and other such nonsense. But that doesn't make every one of them evil."

I thought of a retort but it ended up sounding foolish in my head so I squelched the thought. Lieutenant Colonel Alton Gee befriended me on my first day in the squadron and I thought we enjoyed each other's company for our almost daily discussions about engineering, history, or anything else that struck his fancy. But now I feared our friendship was coming to an end.

"So you will one day be a squadron commander, young Ed-you-el," he finally continued. "And I hope the best for you, I really do. But I think the die may have already been cast. You are who you are."

In six years, the first half of his prediction came true, I was selected to command an Air Force squadron in Germany.

> *"Leaders aren't born, they are made. And they are made just like anything else, through hard work. And that's the price we'll have to pay to achieve that goal, or any goal."*
> —Vince Lombardi

> *"We are what we pretend to be, so we must be careful about what we pretend to be."*
> —Kurt Vonnegut

The Air Force is an interesting laboratory for growing leaders, often at very young ages. A twenty-two-year-old second lieutenant security officer, for example, can find him or herself in charge of fifty armed men and women with licenses to use deadly force. For pilots, things are a bit different. A clear majority of pilots will lead no one, except perhaps an aircrew, which is a challenge in its own right.

I was thirty-eight years old when I took command of a flying squadron in 1995. By then I had attended three courses designed to teach leadership: Squadron Officer School (three months), Air Command and Staff College (one year), and the Squadron Commander's Course (five days). But the best lessons by far were taught by those I was charged with following. By then I had been a member of six flying squadrons and subject to the leadership of thirteen commanders. Of the thirteen, I considered only two worthy of emulation. The rest varied from mostly harmless to bordering on mostly harmful. By the time I showed up for my turn at bat, I had learned from the worst. Of course, that left me with a very large question: could I do any better?

The Mach 0.86 incident really happened, as did much of what is to follow. I've changed some of the locations, reordered and changed some of the events, and combined many of the characters. You cannot assume any of the characters in the story that follows are faithful representations of actual people. All this is an effort to focus on the lessons of leadership and to protect the identities of some very fine men and women.

Leadership is not easy, as most who have had their try can attest. But military officers have a few extra challenges along the way. We also have the burden of command, which, as we will see, complicates things greatly.

Oh yes. All of the names have been changed. Even my own.

1: Remington's Secret
The First Week of April, 1995

Ramstein Air Base F-16, 22 Sep 1989 (USAF Photo)

Traveling at 200 kph steels your focus. In the United States driving an Opel meant you were driving an ancient piece of trash, but here in Germany this machine was a magnificent thoroughbred. The rental car agent confirmed that there are still stretches of the *bundesautobahn* that had no speed limits and the two-page guide she gave me showed that a round sign with black circle and five thin diagonal lines meant no speed limit. "Of course, it is advised you should observe 130," she said.

"Of course it is," I agreed. I held onto that advisory until I was passed by a BMW doing double that. Then we got to see V_{MO} – velocity maximum operating – as the rightmost of the three pedals at my feet met the floor. The airline promised me a midnight arrival but they had lied; we made it to the German tarmac before sunrise and with a little extra speed I could make it to my 0800 meeting with the new boss.

I was making good time leaving Flughafen Frankfurt. The predawn, Friday traffic was light and whenever I blasted onto a slower moving car in the left lane, they dutifully pulled over to the right. I'm going to like this country. But just as the sun began to peek into my rear-view mirror I was forced back to reality: a red circle around the number 100. What's that come to in dog years? If a 10K race is 6.2 miles, 100 kph must be 62 mph. I could do better on the New Jersey turnpike. Oh well, it wouldn't do to get a speeding ticket on the first day of my newest assignment. Especially not this assignment. "Don't blow this," I said to myself.

In less than two hours I saw the Anschlussstelle Ramstein-Miesenbach sign and two minutes later I presented my identification card and orders to the guard at the west gate of Ramstein Air Base, Germany. He returned my papers, saluted, and wished me a *guten tag*.

Ramstein would be assignment number nine for me but it was hardly just another assignment. This was the one most Air Force pilots would fantasize about, few would have even a remote possibility of being considered for, and fewer still would attain. Command. "Don't blow this," I said again as I crosschecked the base map against the mixture of German and U.S. signage. My first stop was to Visiting Officer's Quarters to change into my flight suit, and then to report to the new boss, the commander of the 86th Operations Group. Maybe skip the uniform and just show up? No, uniform first.

The Ops Group headquarters was collocated with the 86th Air Wing headquarters, in a building right across the street from the flight line. It was a drab building painted in standard Air Force light brown with only a building number painted in darker brown and a sterile sign over the door. The sign read, very simply, HQ 86 AW. A directory behind a glass plate led me to a stairwell lined with airplane pictures. As I took the steps by twos I caught the wing's lineage: the P-47 Thunderbolt, the F-86 Sabre, the F-101 Voodoo, the F-102 Delta Dagger, the F-4 Phantom II, and finally the F-16 Falcon. The last Falcon, I heard, left the base earlier in the year.

The outer office was open but empty. It was 0815 on a Friday, there should have been someone there. There were two inner offices, the larger of the two was also empty. I was late. Maybe they all gave up on me. I peered into the smaller office, the one marked "86 OG Director of Operations - Lieutenant Colonel Dillon May," and found a lieutenant colonel sitting behind a desk with his feet propped on an open drawer and an unlit cigar perched between two pale lips.

"What can I do for you?" he said, causing the cigar to bounce with each syllable.

"I'm Lieutenant Colonel Eddie Haskel," I said. "Reporting for duty."

"Eddie!" he said, getting up and offering a hand. "Welcome to Germany. I'm Mayhem."

"Of course you are," I said. "It says so right under your wings." Where my flight suit name tag patch had my wings and "Lt Col Haskel," his were simply his wings and the word "Mayhem."

"The boss is on an early morning flight," he said. "He told me to send you on to the wing commander and back here when you are done with that. Woz should be in here by the time you are done."

"Woz?" I asked.

"Colonel Wozniak," he said. "I'm sure you heard of him." Of course, I knew who my new boss was, but there were rules about us lieutenant colonels addressing full colonels by slang names.

"This is a fighter base," he continued. "Well, this was a fighter base. Everyone has a call sign. What's yours?"

"I don't have one," I said.

"What do we call you?" he asked.

"Eddie," I said.

"That's not much of a call sign," he said. "I'll come up with something for you. Have a seat, we need to get you briefed before you see the man himself."

Mayhem explained that he was the last F-16 squadron commander in Ramstein history and moved over to be Colonel Stanley Wozniak's deputy. General Lesley Remington was the last fighter wing commander in Ramstein history and was ordered to hang around until his replacement showed up in another month.

"The general isn't doing so well," Mayhem said, lowering his voice. "He lost his mojo after the shoot down and after the Air Force pinned the blame on him, well . . ." Mayhem didn't complete his thought, but he didn't have to. The story was well known, even outside of the Air Force. A year prior the general was deployed as the commander of a Combined Task Force Operation in Turkey, charged with enforcing the combat air patrol over Northern Iraq. Two of his F-15 pilots misidentified two U.S. Army UH-60 Black Hawk helicopters as hostile and fired on both, destroying them and killing all 26 military and civilian personnel aboard. A military investigation faulted the pilots, members of a controlling AWACS aircraft, and the failure to adequately integrate Air Force and Army elements. Remington, as the commander, was given an administrative reprimand and his career was pretty much over.

"It seems to me General Remington was just the ceremonial scapegoat," I said. "I'm not sure what he could have done short of flying every sortie himself."

"Maybe," Mayhem said. "Remmy showed up here a hero and remains so to everyone who knows him. But he was in a different element in Turkey. Those air-to-air boys all dream of being the next Steve Richie."

"There will never be another," I said. "Air combat has changed."

"Hold that thought," Mayhem said. "Let me see if he's ready for you."

Sitting alone I studied the photos on Mayhem's walls. They were all of ground support aircraft, like the F-16. The so-called "air-to-mud" mission was what combat purists would say is the purpose of the Air Force: to help the ground warfighter seize and hold territory. The F-15 Eagle, on the other hand, was designed to seize airspace. Every Eagle driver wanted to be the next Steve Richie, the last combat ace in Air Force history. But air combat changed since the Vietnam War; it was now air-to-air missiles that seized the sky without all that yanking and banking. There would be no more aces.

"Remmy is waiting for you," Mayhem said. "Just down the hall, last door on the right. Let him pontificate for as long, or as short, as he wants and come back here."

The long, carpeted hallway was bordered on one side by tall cabinets filled with model airplanes and awards and the other wall by large paintings of more airplanes. Everything spoke of fighter aircraft and warfighting, save a solitary photo of a C-130 dispensing chaff. Each painting of each fighter drew your eye to the beauty of the aircraft or the drama of the actions depicted. There are few things more engaging than the look of one fighter on its back, pulling its nose down to an unsuspecting adversary. In stark contrast, the photo of the C-130 was notable only in that it was poorly composed with the airplane in a haphazard angle to the frame.

General Remington's office was fronted by a large reception area, complete with fine German furniture and more photos of the wing's history. A large credenza was lined with more model airplanes, all fighters. The secretary, seated behind a desk and peering over a P-47 Thunderbolt model read the name under my wings and gestured me to the General's office.

"General," she said, "this is Colonel Haskel."

I walked in, stood at attention and saluted. General Remington peered above a blue manual I recognized immediately from my own collection, returned my salute and gestured for me to sit. "I'm just doing some pleasure reading," he said. "But I always have time to speak to a fellow commander."

"Your copy of the Aerial Attack Study looks even more worn than mine, general," I said.

He looked at me, startled. "I didn't know you were a fighter jock."

"I'm not," I said. "But I am a big fan of Colonel Boyd."

"Me too," he said. "Did you ever meet him?"

"No, sir," I said. "He was long retired before I got to the Pentagon but I managed to set eyes on him when he came to accept an award from the SECDEF. I was struck that more Marines attended the ceremony than Air Force."

"What got you interested in him in the first place?" he asked.

"I worked aircraft acquisition and read about Colonel Boyd's opposition to the F-15 and the B-1. I figured any acquisition officer with that much testosterone was worth emulating."

"Damned right," he said. "Did you know he revolutionized fighter combat?"

"Yes, sir," I said. "My undergraduate degree is in engineering and Colonel Boyd's energy maneuverability theories should be required reading for any Air Force pilot."

"Well, I suppose that is true," he said. "At least for a fighter pilot. Perhaps you ended up flying the wrong airplanes, Colonel."

"Any airplane can be flown with precision," I said.

"Eddie, I can talk airplanes all day long. But you have things to do and places to be. So how about I give you my standard new commander briefing?"

"I'd like that, General."

"Command is different," he said. "You know that. In the official eyes of the military, a commander has vested upon him a special power that no other human being will ever know. But, between you and me, in the Air Force it is different. And that is doubly true for a commander of a flying squadron. So let me ask you, Eddie. What is the difference between command and leadership?"

I didn't spend a lot of time thinking such philosophical thoughts, but this particular question had vexed me since the only thing on my shoulders were solitary gold bars. I knew the answer instinctively. "A commander has the additional power to order people to their deaths," I said. "A leader has to convince subordinates the plan of attack is in their best interest. A commander should do that if possible. But even if it isn't in their best interests, a commander can tell the troops, 'take that hill.' And if taking that hill means certain death, so be it."

"That nails it, Eddie. So a commander also leads. So, final question. What is the most important aspect of leadership?"

"Taking care of one's people," I said. "Period. We are all motivated to get the job done. If you take care of your people, your people will take care of the mission."

"That's definitely true," he said. "You have to remember that as a commander. So far your focus has been on airplanes, on the pointy end of the spear. But all that changes now. You focus on your people and let the operations officer handle operations."

"I can do that," I said.

He sat back in his chair, holding his copy of Colonel Boyd's Aerial Attack Study. I hadn't noticed that the general never put it down. He caught my eyes and drew his own back to the blue booklet. "You know I did meet Colonel Boyd once in the Pentagon," Remington continued. "He had already retired and worked as a consultant in acquisition. The word was every blue suiter that ever went to work for him got the same lecture about integrity. You ever hear that?"

"No, sir."

"Well let me give you the same lecture, it is as important as anything you ever heard in any leadership school. It goes something like this. 'If your boss demands loyalty, give him integrity. If he demands integrity, give him loyalty.' I can never get that out of my head."

"From what I read," I said, "he conducted his career that way."

"I think you are going to do fine here, Eddie," he said, getting up from his desk. He extended his right hand, which I shook. "There is a secret to command that I wish I could give you right now, before you begin. But that would rob you of the journey and the chance to truly learn it. But I have no doubt you will learn it." He released my hand and stared into my eyes, willing me to blink. I blinked.

"Welcome to the brotherhood of commanders."

"The boss just landed," Mayhem said as I returned to his office. "He should be here in a few minutes. So what did you think of the general?"

"He seems to be a fine officer," I said. "It seems the good ones are the first to be thrown overboard."

"I don't know about that," Mayhem said. "He always took care of his people, no doubt about that. But he should have known those Eagle drivers were bloodthirsty killers."

"Isn't that part of the job description?" I asked.

"Yeah," he said. "I suppose it is. You seem like you have a little killer blood in you, Eddie. What are you doing here leading a VIP squadron?"

"I'm here to take care of my people," I said. "That way they can take care of the mission."

"There's more to it than that," he said. "Let me tell you a little something about commanding a squadron in a wing this size. First . . ." His words were interrupted as the outer office came to life. I turned in my seat to see the youngest full colonel I had ever set eyes upon outside of a Hollywood movie. Colonel Stanley Wozniak's hair was jet black, his pale skin free of age spots of any kind, and his boyish grin seemed more suited to a teenage pal. It certainly wasn't the face of someone I would now call my boss.

"You must be Eddie," he said as he peered into Mayhem's office. He looked at his deputy. "Is he the real deal, Mayhem?"

"As real as they get," Mayhem said. "He's done his time with Remmy and me. You are up next."

"Come this way," Wozniak said. "We have some business to attend to."

I followed Wozniak to his office, a larger version of Mayhem's with a large picture window facing the flight line. I could see three lines of C-130 Hercules, now the top aircraft on base. On any other base these dirty, noisy aircraft would be known as "four-fan, trash cans" and their crews would slink around the base as second class citizens. But now that the fighters were gone, the "Hercs" were the only combat aircraft on base. The wing owned eighteen of the old birds. My squadron's thirteen aircraft were nowhere to be seen.

"You come highly recommended, Eddie," Wozniak said while pointing to a chair opposite his desk. I sat as he fumbled with the lock on one of his desk drawers. "Your boss at the Pentagon said you have a knack for fixing things. We got something for you to fix." He found what he was looking for and pulled a sealed manila folder from a larger envelope. He tossed it to me.

Two words on the envelope immediately caught my eye: EYES ONLY. They were handwritten in what was probably an extra wide Sharpie pen, red of course. Below those words were three more: Lt. Col. Haskel.

"Take this someplace private, Eddie," he said. "Read it, don't copy anything, and then burn everything. You cannot tell anyone about its contents and certainly not that you got them from me."

"Cloak and dagger?" I asked.

"Something like that," he said. "Do you know Clevis Haney?"

"I've met him once or twice," I said. "He was in our sister squadron at Andrews. About the only thing I remember about him is his accent. Kentucky, I'm guessing."

"Tennessee, actually," he said. "Well, Clevis got himself into a bit of trouble. A lot, actually. His squadron – well, your squadron pretty soon – members of the 76th Airlift Squadron filed nine complaints with the inspector general. All nine were corroborated and turned into Article 15 charges. You know the problem with that?"

"I imagine it would be hard to prosecute nine Article 15's without elevating the whole thing into a Courts Martial," I said.

"You got it," he said. "One Article 15 is pretty serious business for an officer. For a lieutenant colonel, it would probably end up with some paperwork with the remote chance of redemption. Two Article 15's, perhaps they could farm him out to some meaningless job. But nine? That's Courts Martial territory."

"Maybe jail time?" I asked.

Flight Lessons 4: Leadership & Command

"It depends on the charges," he said. "In this particular case, probably. So we offered him early retirement, which he took. The problem is you are walking into a bad situation. He beat the troops into submission so now the morale is low, performance is low, and expectations are even lower. So get smart on what went wrong and fix it."

"I can do that," I said.

"I hope so," he said. "You going to the squadron today?"

"Yes, sir," I said. "I'm meeting Clevis in an hour."

"Okay, but," he started to say but paused. "Maybe you should meet him before you read these. He can't know that you have these. Put these away until after you meet." He got up, signaling our first meeting was over. "Welcome to Ramstein. And, by the way, I was serious about 'burn after reading.' Do I have your word?"

"Yes, sir," I said. "You have it."

Most of the base sits north of the single east-west runway, including the main ramp where the 37th Airlift Squadron's eighteen C-130s are parked. The north ramp also serves as home to the 86th Aeromedical Evacuation Squadron's four C-9 Nightingales, the transient cargo ramp, and the passenger terminal. The 76th Airlift Squadron – my squadron – is found south of the runways in the fighter revetments once home to the base's long lineage of bomb droppers. It was about a fifteen-minute drive around the runways.

If it were not for the single tail of our CT-43 Boeing 737 and three T-tails of our C-20 Gulfstreams peeking over the tree tops, you could drive right up to the squadron and miss it. The buildings and ramps were cut out of the German forest and even the nine fighter revetments used to house our C-21 Learjets were painted to blend into the surroundings. We often joked that in the Air Force world of VIP transport we would be best to camouflage our comings and goings; this squadron seemed to have done just that.

The double doors led into a short hallway flanked by two offices. I picked the one with the waiting secretary, ready to make the all-important first impression. But before I could utter a syllable she was on her feet. "Good morning Colonel Haskel," she said. "I am Susan and I will be your secretary three days from today. The current boss is expecting you." With that, she turned on her heels and I followed her into the next office.

I remembered Clevis from our days together at Andrews Air Force Base, Maryland, just outside of Washington, D.C. There he flew the Boeing 707 under what I was told was close supervision. He was only a fair pilot which put him in the bottom of the pecking order at the 89th Airlift Wing. I flew the Gulfstream IIIs in another squadron and only once or twice had to deal with him. We were both lieutenant colonels but he was six years my senior in rank and age. I was not yet 38. Clevis looked 58.

"How ya' doing, buddy?" he asked as I approached. He remained seated and pointed to a chair opposite his desk. "You ready?"

"I think so," I said. "I was hoping to learn from one with experience, as we used to say at Andrews."

"Nothing to learn, buddy," he said. "This is pretty low key compared to the 89th. Besides, the squadron runs itself. All you have to do is fly, show your face at a weekly meeting, and make sure Felix is on top of things."

"Felix?" I asked.

"Felix Henderson is your DO," he explained. "He keeps watch on the inmates. He's a pretty good writer so I have him do all the ERs."

"You have your director of operations write all the effectiveness reports?" I asked.

"Sure," he said. "None of these kids know how to write. And I sure as hell ain't going to do it." I let his words hang. "Give you a piece of advice, Eddie. If you don't know how to delegate, this job will eat you alive."

"How are the people?" I asked.

"The best," he said. "No worries."

"Any troublemakers I need to know about?" I asked.

"Hell yes!" he said. "You got a bunch of crybabies that can't wipe their own noses without permission. They will make your life hell."

"Any names?" I asked.

"No need for that," he said. "Basically, all of them."

"How about an example?" I asked. "Just one."

"Nah," he said. There was a knock at his office door and a young captain stood, waiting. "What?" Clevis said. "Can't you tell I'm busy?"

Flight Lessons 4: Leadership & Command

"Sorry, sir," the captain said. "I thought you wanted to know immediately when another flight engineer busted a check ride. Well, Sergeant Wells just busted his check ride."

"Okay," he said. "Next week Monday it won't be my problem anymore." He looked at me. "It will be yours."

The captain left and I looked at Clevis. "Are you having problems keeping crewmembers trained?"

"Yeah," he said. "I think people just aren't as smart as they used to be. We never had these problems when we were their age, did we?" He got up. "Make yourself at home. I gotta go."

With that, he was gone, leaving me to stare at the walls of his, soon to be my, office. Susan entered with a cup of coffee and a pamphlet. "We printed the biography you provided on the change of command program. It looks pretty good. Colonel Henderson gets back from a trip late tonight but was wondering if you would like to join him and his family for a Volksmarch on Sunday.

"That would be great," I said. "Thanks."

My bio read just as I had typed it before faxing it from the Pentagon. It was my fourteen-year career summarized in three paragraphs. My officemates suggested I add whatever medals I had accumulated over those years along with a few of the citations I had earned in the five-sided puzzle palace. But I had declined, opting for short and sweet. Reading Clevis' bio I started to regret that decision. His nine-paragraphs detailed every single medal, award, and citation. I wondered if the members of the squadron would think their new commander was a slacker.

I knew the squadron officer corps was bottom heavy, with nearly thirty lieutenants, as many captains, no majors, and just Clevis and Felix the only lieutenant colonels. I didn't want my introduction to be me wandering alone in the halls, so I retreated to my rental car and back to my temporary quarters. It wasn't much of a first day.

Armed with an order of schnitzel take away and a six pack of Bitburger Premium Pils, I unsealed the eyes-only envelope with a mixture of dread and excitement. If nine members of the squadron took the extraordinary steps needed to file inspector general complaints, how many more were too timid or afraid to speak up? Could Clevis really be that bad or was I stepping into a squadron of crybabies, as he put it. Inside the envelope, I found nine individual reports, each about ten stapled pages topped by the IG's initial findings. Each cover sheet said the same thing: "complaint appears valid, recommend judge advocate coordination prior to further investigation."

I considered taking select pages from each complaint before fulfilling my promise to burn after reading. I pulled out my notebook and opened to a blank page and stared at the nine reports. This was serious business and I needed to arm myself. But Colonel Wozniak's order rang in my ears. "Do I have your word?" I closed my notebook.

The Visiting Officers Quarters provided me with a book of matches and I found an outdoor grill suitable for the task. All nine reports incinerated for good, I spent the next day looking for off base housing. I had two months before the kids were out of school in Virginia and we could then be a nuclear family again.

Felix Henderson's note included a map to a Dorfgemeinschaftshaus in Seibersbach with instructions to bring a coat and shoes I didn't mind getting dirty. "A little hilly, scenic, and good beer at the end of the 10 kms. Meet you 15 mins before the 0700 start."

I had been a frequent traveler to Ramstein Air Base over the years but rarely left the beaten path between the base and a few well known bars in nearby towns. Seibersbach is a small village ready made for a postcard, quaint high-pitched roofed houses lined with even quainter stone streets. I pulled into a dirt parking lot with a "Seibersbach Volksmarch" sign and spotted a tall American with an even taller wife and three very tall children.

"Felix?" I asked.

"Eddie!" he said. "Thanks for coming out. I thought maybe we could get to know each other before the change of command."

"Thanks for thinking of it," I said. "I've been feeling a bit cooped up."

"If you can walk ten clicks up and down these hills, we can cure you of that," he said with a grin that exposed two missing teeth. "I can gar-ran-tee it!"

"Cajun?" I guessed.

"To the bone," he said. Felix introduced me to his family with decreasing levels of accent commensurate with age. The youngest son, probably ten, led the way. We filed through a gate and each child delighted in handing a ticket to the gate keeper. "This one's on me," he said. "I don't suppose you have a lot of Deustche Marks on you."

Flight Lessons 4: Leadership & Command

"Thanks," I said. "So my task today is to keep up with a ten year old without wheezing."

"Me too," he said. "They usually blaze the trail in front so we old guys can talk." The morning began with a cool fog that I suspect would become bone chilling as we climbed the first hill. Walking through a forest was not something many Americans do for a weekend activity but, judging by the number of people ahead and behind us, it was a favorite German pastime. The clear skies and crisp air encouraged talk of our host country.

"Best assignment you will ever have," Felix said. "In fact, the only turnover we have is with the pilots. Nobody else wants to leave."

"Why do the pilots want to leave?" I asked.

"Well you got a mixture of problems here," he said. "Half your Learjet pilots graduated number one or two from their pilot training classes and part of the deal is that after three years here they have to go to a major weapon system. The other half are just like your Boeing and Gulfstream pilots. They all came here as seasoned instructor pilots from a major weapon system and are coming up on ten years."

"Is that the current commitment level?" I asked.

"It sure is," he answered. "So your lieutenants are leaving to other airplanes because they got no choice and your captains are heading for the airlines. And the wing makes that decision easy because nobody in this squadron ever gets promoted to major."

"Why don't we have any majors?" I asked. "The standard Air Force squadron manpower template says we should have four," I said.

"We can't hire any majors because they know they can't make lieutenant colonel here," he said. "Eddie, you ever serve in a fighter wing before?"

"Yeah," I said. "My 707 squadron in Hawaii was one of only two big airplane squadrons in the entire command. But we got guys promoted all the time."

"Well we don't," Felix said. "This wing is famous for eating its young."

"That's surprising," I said. "General Remington seems to have the right attitude about these things."

"Remington makes a good first impression," Felix said. "But he doesn't wear well."

"Well he impressed me," I said. "We talked for about thirty minutes and people seemed to be his priority."

"Oh I believe that," Felix said. "The general is one of those guys who tells a good story at the bar and knows how to capitalize on history."

"History?"

"Personal history," Felix explained. "See he was in the same squadron as Steve Richie back in Thailand. Only he showed up after Richie already left."

"But he was in Vietnam," I said. "There weren't a lot of airplanes to shoot down at the end of the war, you can't fault the guy for being too young for the fight."

"No I ain't blaming him," Felix said. "I guess my point is that General Remington is one of our last connections with the bad old days, he was in the last really big fight. Wherever he goes his reputation goes first. He's a likeable general, his fighter pilots want to be just like him."

"You still haven't told me anything bad about him," I said.

"Well I'm not sure there is anything bad about him," Felix said. "But he lives in a world where people just follow him because of who he is and nobody gives him any bad news. They know he doesn't want any, so they never give him any. And that's why we live in a wing where the group commanders can do as they please, the squadron commanders have to deal with the group commanders, and everyone pays the price."

"So we are at the mercy of Colonel Wozniak then?" I asked.

"Colonel Woz just showed up last month," Felix said. "I think he is just treading water until the new wing commander gets here. That's just a month from your change of command tomorrow. We're pretty much cleaning house in this wing."

"How so?"

"The combat airlift squadron got a new boss in January," he said while touching his left index finger with his right. "The aeromedical squadron in February, the operations group in March, and now us VIP airlift guys in April." He held up four fingers. "In May we get a new wing king. Who in this man's Air Force thinks it is a good idea to change out every commander who deals with airplanes in only five months? Things were bad, I agree. But it sounds like the Air Force is desperate to change things around here."

"Desperate times call for desperate measures," I said.

Flight Lesson: Celebrity Leadership

I believe there are four steps in the path from beginning to true leadership:

1) Job Title (Followers follow the leader because they have to)

2) Operational Advantage (Followers follow because the leader knows how to "get it done")

3) Personal Growth (Followers follow because the leader offers them a chance to grow)

4) Loyalty (Followers follow because they want to)

Leaders will normally progress from Step 1 to Step 4 but much of this depends on the followers. Leaders may have to use different steps for different followers and may have to start over in a new environment. Celebrity leaders can often skip some of the steps, but doing so can leave the leader in a tenuous situation.

Celebrity Leadership Defined

ce•leb•ri•ty

- A famous person.
- The state of being well known.

Fame, of course, is relative. In a finite community, a person can become well known by deed or title. In a community of Gulfstream pilots, for example, developing a reputation is possible through social and professional associations. Within a company fame can be simply bestowed by awarding a title, such as "chief pilot."

The Advantages of Celebrity Leadership

A celebrity leader can have a great advantage. An Air Force commander, for example, assumes office with Step 1 completed by virtue of the assignment. The commander's reputation can convey to followers that Steps 2 and 3 will be assured. That can generate instant loyalty if used properly. But if the commander falls short along the way, the loyalty may be found to be only temporary.

A well-known chief pilot or director of aviation can generate similar levels of instant loyalty which translates to early smooth sailing. Followers will want the leader to succeed and can be especially tolerant of any missteps early in the leader's tenure.

The Pitfalls of Celebrity Leadership

Leaders can mistake the early smooth sailing and instant acceptance as a level of loyalty they have not yet earned. This can blind the leader's normal instincts to establish the necessary political connections, to get to know the people better, and to learn the mission more fully.

2: The Politics of Command
The Rest of April, 1995

Ramstein Air Base C-20A Gulfstream III (Photo: Matt Birch)

As Lieutenant Colonel Clevis Haney spoke behind the podium, I scanned the assembled troops. In a squadron of a hundred and fifty we had managed to assemble nearly a hundred, which meant I was looking at two-thirds of the squadron. Most stared vacantly forward, few made eye contact with their outgoing commander. Was that significant?

Members of the audience, by contrast, hung on every syllable thrown their way in that folksy Tennessee dialect. They were mostly dignitaries from the wing with a few spouses thrown in for good measure. You could see there was a bond there, Clevis was one of them, a part of the wing's leadership. I couldn't help but critique his performance from a public speaking instructor's point of view. He spoke as if reading, a nervous stammer creeping into every other sentence. Clevis turned a page in his notes and I thought, "how many more pages?" I could see General Remington shift uneasily in his seat, two to my left. Colonel Wozniak, on my immediate left, was motionless. Another page turn and then, "Thanks, y'all." The audience applauded, the troops remained in their parade rest, and Clevis returned to his seat.

"Thank you, Colonel Haney," Colonel Wozniak said with a smile. "Ladies and gentlemen, please stand for the national anthem."

As we stood I studied the faces of the command I was about to assume. The vast majority were officers and all but one of those junior to me. Lieutenant Colonel Felix Henderson, standing in front of the formation of troops, had just turned 43, five years my senior. There were sixty pilots, mostly male. Of the ten flight engineers, all were male and half of those probably five to ten years older. All but two of the fifteen flight attendants were female and all but two of the seven radio operators were male. The crewmembers were all dressed in flight suits while the ground support personnel were dressed in fatigues. All our maintenance personnel were civilian contractors and sat in the audience with the dignitaries. It was quite a mix, this squadron.

"Please take your seats for the change of command," Wozniak said as the last note of the national anthem finished. General Remington smiled and looked to Clevis and me and said, "shall we?" I followed the general and Clevis to stage center. We three stood at attention with the general on the right, Clevis to his left, and me further left. Chief Master Sergeant Calvin Trenchard, the squadron first sergeant, stood behind us, between Remington and Clevis, holding the squadron flag. Colonel Wozniak issued the command, "Officers, center."

General Remington executed a left face turn while Clevis and I made a right face turn. This placed Clevis eye-to-eye with the general and me behind Clevis. Clevis saluted the general and said, "Sir, I relinquish command." Remington returned the salute. Chief Trenchard stepped forward and presented the squadron colors, a flag pole with the squadron seal on a flag. Clevis took the flag, hands outstretched and then retracted with the flag and pole close to his chest. Trenchard stepped backwards. Clevis presented the colors to the general who repeated the hands outstretched and retracted procedure. Our squadron's colors were now in the general's possession.

Clevis took a step to the right, two steps back, and a step left. As he did this I took a step forward, taking his place. General Remington presented me the squadron colors, which I took. I returned the colors to Trenchard who withdrew to his original position. I saluted General Remington. "Sir, I assume command." General Remington returned my salute and we three faced the troops at the precise moment his right hand reached his side. The audience applauded.

After a career of public speaking I made a habit of never using notes, only

Flight Lessons 4: Leadership & Command

memorizing my opening and closing lines and keeping a list of topics in mind. I had done so over the years in front of four star generals, the Secretary of Defense, two governors, several senators, and even a visiting head of state. No problem. Facing the squadron – my squadron – the first line came easily but the list of topics evaporated into the upper rafters of the hangar. Nothing. The squadron looked expectantly. Say something important! But the words didn't come and only my closing lines hovered in wait. "Members of the 76th Airlift squadron," I finally continued, "thank you in advance for all the hard work we shall put in together, as a team. General Remington, thank you for the confidence you have placed upon me and this squadron. Colonel Wozniak, we stand ready to accomplish our mission. Squadron mates, let's get to work."

I withdrew to my seat. At first there was a solitary clap. Oh, I guess he's finished. And then the dignitaries joined in. Colonel Wozniak shook my hand. "Short and sweet, Eddie," he said. "Just the right thing."

At the reception, afterwards, I stood awkwardly as the dignitaries filed by, sure to shake my hand and exchange pleasantries, as protocol dictated. But no one lingered and in a few moments, I stood alone. I looked over to a crowd that had gathered around Clevis. There were a mixture of squadron members and dignitaries, all wishing him well with his new career at Southwest Airlines. He was all smiles.

Felix Henderson tapped me on the shoulder. "Nice speech, boss," he said. "It's kind of lonely at these things when you don't know anyone. Let me introduce you to the squadron." I followed Felix as he began my education into the other 148 people who would call me boss. He started his life in the squadron as a line Gulfstream pilot and then instructor pilot. A year ago he became the director of operations, the second in command.

"This here is one of our finest C-20 copilots," he said, waving for a young captain to approach. "Colonel Haskel, this is Captain Rorie Fitzpatrick."

"Good afternoon, sir," she said with a smile. She stood at attention and looked me in the eye as I stole a look at her wings. She was a senior pilot, with at least seven years of experience as a pilot. I knew that all our Gulfstream and Boeing pilots came from other aircraft assignments.

"C-141s?" I guessed.

"Yes, sir," she said. "Charleston Air Force Base."

"Air drop?" I guessed again. I knew that was the mission at Charleston and that most C-141 pilots were proud of the skills required to be an air drop crewmember.

"You got it, sir," she said. She talked for a bit about her progress from C-141 copilot, to aircraft commander, and then to instructor. She was offered a chance to instruct brand new C-141 pilots at Altus Air Force Base in Oklahoma, but she couldn't pass on the chance to fly a Gulfstream in Germany. As she spoke I rehearsed it in my mind. Rorie the redheaded C-20 copilot came from Charleston. Remember!

"How long has she been with the squadron?" I asked after Felix steered us to the next group of pilots.

"Oh, going on two years," Felix said.

"Why is she still a copilot?" I asked.

"Eddie, it takes time around here," he answered. "You got to master the airplane and the mission."

With each introduction, I started to lose my memory of the previous. I struggled to include personal questions, struggled to include the "touchy feely" element I knew I was lacking. But Felix had these skills down to a science. "Here's someone you're gonna like," he said as another captain approached.

"Good afternoon, sir," he said with an easy grin. "I am Captain Tommy Mendéz, your flight safety officer. I hear you are a fellow safety school graduate."

"That I am," I said. "You and I need to talk often, Tommy. Don't ever be bashful." He shot me two thumbs up and a toothy grin. He was of average height with two-thirds a full head of jet-black hair, the line of retreat about a third of the way to a full defeat.

"Well, you made his day," Felix said. "The old boss thought the Air Force safety program was just eyewash for pilots trying to get out of flying."

That was the first negative thing I had ever heard Felix say about Clevis. I knew the rule of "don't badmouth the old boss to the new boss" often gave way after a while, but it surprised me nonetheless. When I heard my "number two" was five years my senior in grade and had been in his position for over a year, I had to wonder why he wasn't given the command. But it became obvious after a day that as a genuinely nice guy, he didn't fit the mold.

The Air Force had recently succumbed to the latest trend in many business schools to classify people into four personality categories, each with a binary classification. An officer could be an introvert or an extrovert, have a sensing personality or one that is more intuitive, could be prone to making decisions based on feelings or by thinking things through, and would prefer to have things settled by judging the merits or perceiving how things should be. Officers, in general, could have any of the sixteen possible combinations but a commander, it was said, could only be cut from one mold. The approved solution was for a commander to be extroverted, intuitive, thinking, and perceiving. My personality test gave me each of these qualities, though I wondered about my ability to fool the psychologist about any extroversion. There was no doubt about Felix. He was extroverted, certainly. But on the other three litmus tests, he failed. He was sensing, feeling, and judging.

Ramstein's cold war mission was to sit and wait for the Russian march to the English Channel and then to unleash all manner of hell from above, most recently from nuclear armed F-16 Fighting Falcons. Once the Soviets decided they were tired of being soviets and we decided we no longer needed the aerial road block, the fighters left and the vast real estate south of the runways was abandoned. The 76th Airlift Squadron took over. The largest ramp belonged to the CT-43 and three C-20s. The C-21s were scattered wherever they could fit.

Leaving our main hangar, we walked between two C-20s toward the squadron. The last taxiway was a lane wide enough for the CT-43, our largest airplane. But much of that was taken by three C-21s parked perpendicular to the taxiway.

"This looks like an accident waiting to happen," I said, pointing to the first C-21 and tracing an imaginary line with my finger to the center of the taxiway. "How much clearance have we got with our bigger jets?"

"Just barely enough," Felix said. "We want to repaint the C-21 parking spots so they are angled in, that should give us another five feet, at least."

"That sounds like a pretty good idea," I said. "Why don't we?"

"Well, we put in the request a year ago," Felix said. "And Civil Engineering just approved it. But they say it will take another eight or ten months for them to get to us. So in the meantime we use wing walkers when we taxi the big birds."

"Oh well," I said. "There is only so much you can control." We approached the squadron as someone from the civil engineering squadron was attaching a new squadron sign, complete with my name as the commander and Trenchard's as the first sergeant. "Seems like their priorities are all wrong."

Felix held the door open and I entered. Susan darted out of her part of our office with a stack of papers. "Colonel Haskel, the group commander asked for you to drop by in an hour. I think he might be looking for our latest effectiveness reports."

"Okay," I said. "Are we late on anything?"

"Always," she said.

"I do my best," Felix said. "Writing isn't my strong point. But a good ER takes a lot of time."

"You aren't so bad," Susan said.

"Okay," I said. "What do I need to worry about, right now?"

"Walk this way," Felix said. "We need to introduce you to the schedule." I followed Felix through the winding hallways to a large room with the same Plexiglas wall found in most flying squadrons. This version had a calendar on top: one month history, the current month, and two months' future. Along the left column were crewmembers broken down by aircraft type and crew position. On the top of the C-20 heap I found my own name with a crew position of "UQ" to one side.

"Unqualified?" I guessed.

"Not for long," Felix said. "We have your first training sortie on the books for tomorrow. We are thinking with your Andrews experience, three rides and a check should do it."

"I'll try not to disappoint," I said. I scanned the pilot crew position column. I wasn't the only UQ but there seemed to be far too many CP versus AC, IP, and EP. "Is this a standard setup where you can pair a copilot with an aircraft commander, instructor pilot, or evaluator pilot?"

"Exactly," Felix said. "I know what you are going to say. We aren't upgrading fast enough. But that's hard to do when you are busy flying trips."

I scanned the previous month and saw a good proportion of the flights were trainers, but maybe that was an unusual month. "Bite your tongue and learn before criticizing," I thought.

Felix looked at his watch and tapped the face. "You gotta run if you want to make it to the other side of the base in time. I'll hold the fort until you get back. In case I miss you before tomorrow, our usual C-20 trainers takeoff at ten and show time is at eight for you trainees."

"Got it," I said. Being a squadron commander trainee seemed to sum up the day so far. As I made my way from the deepest recess of the squadron to the front, I tried to make eye contact with everyone I passed. Any squadron member's first day tends to be overwhelming in many respects. You don't know anyone, nobody knows you, the new surroundings are unfamiliar, you are consumed with trying not to appear nervous, and worried about making a good impression. As a brand-new squadron commander, all those feelings are still there except that everyone knows who you are. The female C-20 copilot I had met in the hangar said hello again. "Hi," I said. I had already forgotten her name. She flew C-141s in a previous life.

During the drive to the north side of the base, I realized I hadn't read any of the effectiveness reports that Susan handed to me an hour before. How much slack do you hand a brand-new commander? Perhaps I would be granted some wait time in Colonel Wozniak's outer office; as busy as I was, he was sure to be busier.

"Go right on in," his secretary said as I walked in. "He's waiting. If those are the late ERs, I'll take them."

I surrendered the reports, still unread, and turned for the group commander's office. He was seated at his desk, opposite a table with six empty chairs.

"You got that squadron mastered yet, Eddie?" Wozniak asked.

"It's a piece of cake," I said. "A trained monkey could do the job. Too bad I've never been trained."

"Monkeys," he said. "That's apropos. You ever heard the saying about a monkey and a typewriter?"

"Sure," I said. "If you give an infinite number of monkeys typewriters for an infinite amount of time, sooner or later you are going to end up with the complete works of William Shakespeare."

"Well you guys don't have an infinite amount of time," he said, handing me a stack of papers. "So that explains the quality of your ER's. I just got here a month ago and it seems the old fighter wing didn't care about what us non-fighters did with our ERs. But we need to change that, and change that fast. Rumor has it we are getting a real non-fighter pilot wing commander next month."

I flipped through the ten new ERs. "These are all signed by Clevis. Not much to be done about that."

"We have twenty blank ERs with his signature," Wozniak said. "You have some writing to do."

"Yes, sir."

I walked into the C-20 training room at the appointed hour and found a young captain studying the flight manual with a Gulfstream III study guide from a civilian training center. He looked up and immediately bolted to attention. "Good morning, sir," he said. "I'm Captain Kyle Knudson."

"Good morning," I said. "I take it you and I are the students for today's training sortie."

"Yes, sir," he said. "Captain Stumm is a little late, I guess. But today is Tuesday and we usually cover the bleed air system on Tuesdays, so I thought I would get a head start on the lesson.

"Good idea," I said. "Maybe you can teach me a few things."

Kyle placed the bleed air system diagram in front of me and started to talk while pointing at the various valves and sensors. His crew cut and wrestler's physique stood in stark contrast to his nimble hand gestures. He spoke confidently and always with a smile. "You sound like an ex-school house instructor," I said. "Altus or March?"

"Altus, sir," he said. That would make him a former C-141 instructor pilot. After thirty minutes our official instructor finally made his entrance.

"Sorry, sir," he said. "I didn't know you were scheduled to fly with me."

"Does that make a difference?" I asked.

"No, sir," he said. "Sorry. We probably ought to get out to the airplane now." He skipped the introduction but the bars on his shoulders made him a captain and his name tag said he was Eric Stumm. His hair was on the edge of being too long for the regulations and his waistline appeared to skirt another regulation as well. I followed him to the aircraft where the flight engineer had completed the preflight and all that was left for us was to hop into the seats. I took the left as Eric sat in the right.

There were no shenanigans during engine start, taxi out, and the initial take-off. It was a pleasant change from the "no holds barred" practice of the 89th Airlift Wing back at Andrews Air Force Base. Eric asked for and we were granted clearance to fly a full procedure turn at Metz-Nancy-Lorraine Airport, just west of Ramstein over the border into France. After I completed the procedure turn and called for the landing gear, I noticed Eric disabled the aircraft ground spoilers.

"Will this be a touch and go?" I asked.

"Yes, sir," he said.

"We just kind-a assume everyone knows what's going on," he said. "Do you need a briefing?"

"Yes," I said. "I haven't flown in over a year and it seems like a good thing to do on every training sortie. Don't you think?" Eric fumbled his way through the briefing and we spent the next hour at Metz flying every maneuver required for my training. Kyle Knudson traded places with me for a touch and go, after which tower informed us we needed to land to sign paperwork.

"Make this a full stop, then," Eric said to tower.

"Paperwork?" I asked. Eric explained that after World War II the French had a massive monetary debt to pay the United States. The French agreed to let U.S. military aircraft access French airports for training in exchange for paying down the debt, but we had to present ourselves to each airport after every one-hundred landings to sign paperwork.

"It's kind of like roulette," Eric added. "We have three hour blocks for these trainers and if you are unlucky enough to get the call, you have to waste thirty minutes or more and that subtracts from your training. But we've already completed your training events, so no problem today."

After we landed I volunteered to run in to sign the paperwork, in hopes I could coax the administrator into doing this by mail or fax in the future. But nobody in the office admitted to speaking English so I signed the form presented and retreated to the airplane. There I found Eric in the left seat gesturing me to take the right. "I think we can get you signed off as an instructor, sir. I just need to see a takeoff, touch and go, and a full stop landing."

"Is that all the training syllabus asks of an instructor?" I asked.

"We really don't have a syllabus anymore," he said. "Ever since MAC went away we have been winging it."

"I wrote a set of training manuals," Kyle said from the jump seat. "Colonel Haney was all for them but he just didn't have the time to approve them."

"Get them to me as soon as you can, Kyle," I said.

Eric flew us back to Ramstein where I coordinated a touch and go followed by a full stop landing. As soon as we began our descent into the radar pattern I started talking, back into my old instructor mode of not too long ago. "This will be a touch and go landing followed by a visual traffic pattern to a full stop. We will land with full flaps and without the ground spoilers. After you set the gear on the runway, I will reset the flaps to 20 degrees and the trim forward. At that point I will call 'power' and you will set takeoff thrust. Once we reach rotation speed I will call rotate and you will. If we have any kind of malfunction worthy of an abort prior to the power call, I will call for an abort and I expect you to do that. After the rotate call, we are committed. Any questions?"

"Ah, no sir," he said. After the touch and go, while on downwind, I pulled the right engine to idle. "Eric, I am simulating a fire on the right engine."

"Let's go to a holding pattern," he said while adding the appropriate amount of left rudder.

"Do you have something else you need to do?" I asked.

"Ah, yes sir," he said. "Fuel cock shut, fire handle pull. Now let's go to a holding pattern."

"Let's say tower says we are trailing a lot of smoke," I said. "The fire light is still on and every indication from that engine is full scale bad."

"Holding pattern," he said.

"Any other votes?" I asked Kyle and the flight engineer.

"If we are on fire and right on top of the runway, I think we should land," Kyle said.

"Me too," I said. "You've done all you can do, let's put the airplane on the ground."

"We don't memorize checklists the way you guys at Andrews do," Eric said.

"I'm not saying don't use the checklist," I said. "I'm saying if you are on fire, you need to have some situational awareness and realize how much time you have before things go critical."

After the flight, Eric handed me a grade sheet that was all praise and recommended me for a night flight followed by an instructor pilot check ride. "Sorry for the confusion about the touch and go briefing and the engine fire checklist," he said. "I agree with you on all that."

I wasn't sure what to say to Eric so I didn't say anything other than the standard, "good flight, thanks." But I wasn't so brief with Felix.

"Why is Stumm an instructor pilot while Knudson is a copilot?" I asked. "It seems we have that backwards."

"Eric isn't the strongest IP we got," Felix admitted. "And maybe Kyle is overdue for an upgrade. You should bring that up at the next quarterly upgrade board."

"When is that?" I asked.

"June," he said.

"Do we have any Gulfstream pilot upgrades going on right now?" I asked.

"No," he said.

"Who is your top Gulfstream copilot?" I asked.

"I guess that would be Kyle," he said.

"Get him trained," I said. "Immediately."

"You mean no more upgrade boards?" he asked.

"No," I said. "We'll talk about more upgrades in June. But by then I want Captain Knudsen to be upgraded already."

"You got it!" he said. "Anything else?"

"Talk to me about having to sign paperwork in the middle of our training flights," I said. Felix gave me the standard, "We've always done it that way" explanation. It was the standard answer in many bureaucracies, made only worse in the Air Force because change often meant challenging the rank structure and sometimes the chain of command.

"You get this changed and you will be a hero," Felix said. "But I haven't the slightest idea where to start."

Susan spent the rest of the day finding the right office at the Metz Airport but once she made it known we had a request, the bureaucrats ceased to *parlez-vous anglais*. The next day we discovered that Rorie Fitzpatrick, the Gulfstream pilot from Charleston, also *parlez-vous français*. She understood the problem immediately and picked up the phone on Susan's desk.

But after an hour Rorie had the look of defeat. "*Donnant, donnant,*" she said. "That's what the clerk said. I think it means 'you don't get nothing for nothing.' My French is rusty, but I can tell paper pusher attitude in any language."

"Thanks for trying," I said. It was, perhaps, another futile effort. Susan smiled at the retreating captain and pointed to the stack of ERs on my desk. The weekly routine, even three days into it, was apparent. Mondays were for the operations group staff meeting, Tuesdays for the squadron staff, Wednesday for the wing staff meeting, and Thursdays and Fridays were to fix all that was broken the first three days. I had the rest of the day to gain some ground before my first wing staff meeting as a commander.

I got up early the next morning to get a start on those ERs, wondering just how bad they could be. The chain of command dictated the pecking order on all effectiveness reports. At the squadron level, every person's ER was written and signed by their direct supervisor. From there, every ER had two more endorsements but at least one had to be the squadron commander's. Having intermediate supervisors write the bulk of the report ensured the views of the person best positioned to make the observations were used, and it gave those supervisors the practice needed to gain the skills as good ER writers. But every ER in my stack appeared to be written by the same person: Felix. Before heading to the wing staff meeting, I caught Felix at the squadron scheduling board.

"I don't write all of them," he said. "But at least half. Clevis was too busy to write any so he had me write them and he signed them without reading. I end up rewriting a lot of what I see, most these kids just don't know how to write."

"From now on let them come to me without your edits," I said. "I'll do my own writing and I want to see the quality of what comes from the troops."

"My life just got easier," he said. "But, Eddie. Be careful what you wish for."

The wing staff meeting was more a farewell and a farewell party planning event than anything else. General Remington sat patiently as each group commander reported all was in readiness for his change of command in less than a month. He reminded everyone that anyone who needed his signature on an effectiveness report needed to have those on his desk no later than two weeks prior to his departure. At the squadron level the only person that would impact would be the squadron commander, and I was too new to be affected. Finally, he made the announcement everyone was waiting for. "It's official, the President approved my replacement. He is a good fit for the new mission, he was born and raised flying C-130s; a true Herc driver." Remington looked for me in the second row. "You're going to like this, Colonel Haskel. He's done a tour at Andrews too."

I felt a shiver that only came to me with dread.

"On the first Monday of next month," Remington continued, "The 86th Air Wing will become the 86th Airlift Wing, and General William Paulson will become your new commander."

The staff didn't react, which could only mean they had never heard of the man or stifled any opinions. I knew him and had more than my share of opinions. All of those were negative. The general signaled the meeting was over and we all rose until he had departed the room. I was lost in thoughts of General William Paulson and predicted hearing "Paul Paulson" several times a day until either he or I had had enough of each other.

"Eddie, did you hear me?"

I looked up to see Colonel Wozniak, Dillon Mayhem, and my fellow operations squadron commanders staring at me. "Sir?"

"Let's meet in my office," he repeated. I fell into line, the baby duck behind the father duck and older siblings. Lieutenant Colonel Dillon May, the Deputy Operations Group Commander, chatted easily with Wozniak as they walked the length of the second floor hallway from the wing to the operations group. Lieutenant Colonel Arthur Johnson, the commander of the 37th Airlift Group, walked just behind. Lieutenant Colonel Maggie Cairns, the commander of the 89th Aeromedical Squadron took two steps for every one of Johnson's, forming a second row. That left me, the baby duck, to bring up the rear. We filed into the office and each took a seat at the side of Wozniak's conference table.

"I've been calling around all morning," Wozniak said. "Ever since I got the news. But nobody seems to know anything about General Paulson. But I guess at least two of you do."

"Don't look at me," Maggie said. "He was just arriving at Andrews when I left."

"Eddie?" Wozniak said.

"I know him," I said. "He doesn't like to be called William, he goes by Paul."

"You can do better than that," Dillon said. "Can't you?"

This was my introduction to my fellow squadron commanders. We met briefly at my change of command but those were just pleasantries. Apparently, Maggie Cairns' tour at Andrews overlapped mine, but I didn't recognize her. Did I want the first words they remembered from me to be a of whiney complainer?

"He's intense," I said.

"Intense?" Wozniak repeated. "Intense is good. Well, we have a month to get our act together. The reason I asked to see you was I got this strange message from the Air Force safety center. They want to know if any operational units are using anything other than the standard Department of Defense approach plates. Well?"

"That's all we normally use," Art Johnson said. The C-130Es of the 37th Airlift Squadron were the only combat airplanes assigned to the wing. "Every now and then we go someplace weird, but usually Maggie comes to our rescue."

"More often than you think," Maggie said. "We keep a complete set of Jeppesen Airways manuals. There are a few places we go routinely without DoD plates."

"Looking at our schedule, we rely on Jepps more than most Air Force squadrons," I said. "I think we have ten sets of Jepps for various parts of the world. I'm not sure what our normal practice is, but I think even when DoD plates are available, Jepps are often a safer option."

"I wouldn't go that far," Maggie said. "The Jepps for Ramstein are harder to read than the DoD plates."

"True," I said. "But if you are going someplace that the U.S. military uses once a year versus a place where a Jepp plate is used daily, the Jepp is more likely to be accurate. You can't catch an error if nobody uses it."

"Any examples?" Wozniak asked.

"I was in Metz yesterday," I said. "The Jepp had several step downs on the NDB whereas the DoD plate had one. If you descend too aggressively using the DoD plate, you could hit something."

"What do you mean, NDB?" he asked.

"Non-directional beacon," I said. "You know, an ADF approach."

"One of those odd civilian things, I guess?" he said.

"I suppose," I said. "But you can't fly into most of Eastern Europe without making an NDB approach."

"Okay," he said, rising. "That's all I got for now. Eddie, stick around."

Once the others left he remained standing and handed me a stack of ERs. "I hate to add to your workload, but the last batch of ERs were rejected by the wing. That makes twenty in total. We need these to get through on the next try or we are going to have to get more blanks signed by your predecessor."

"I'll take care of it, sir," I said.

"How are things, otherwise?"

"Good," I said. "Every now and then I come up with an unsolvable problem and have to learn to let those go."

"Such as?" he asked. I explained the problem with having to stop a trainer at a French airport to sign landing fee paperwork, as well as my efforts to streamline the process. "A fax perhaps?"

"Exactly," I said. "Having to spend 30 to 45 minutes of a 3-hour training sortie doing paperwork is a poor use of time. But the French paper pushers I've been able to reach don't want to change a thing."

Wozniak pulled a rubber-banded collection of business cards from his desk and quickly shuffled through until he found the one he wanted. He picked up the phone and dialed. "Colonel Albert Marcel, please. This is Colonel Stanley Wozniak."

"Albert, this is Stan from Ramstein," he said. "Yes, good to talk with you again. I have something of a favor to ask."

Colonel Wozniak explained the situation just as I had moments before. He listened for a bit. "Thank you, we look forward to it." He cradled the phone.

"I met Albert at a reception for the new chief of staff of the French Air Force," Wozniak explained. "He isn't directly involved with landing fees but he is connected with the government. He'll let us know."

I returned to the squadron and to the scheduling board to take the organization's pulse. We had ten aircraft on the road, five of those due to return before nightfall. The next day was another ten hitter, including a night training sortie for me. Once again, Eric Stumm was the instructor. We also had two Learjet training sorties. The CT-43 was still on the road, not due to return until the next weekend. I studied the board until that familiar Cajun twang cut through the air. "Just the man I wanted to see."

"I was looking for a good C-20 instructor pilot," I said. "What are you doing tomorrow?"

"Sorry, buddy," he said. "The group won't allow you and I in the air at the same time without a waiver. We are somebodies."

"Somebodies?" I said.

"Yeah," he said. "We be important."

"How can you have fourteen C-20 pilots with only two instructors?" I asked.

"In a week we'll have three," he said. "Eric says you are ready for a check."

"That's another thing," I said. "Why don't we have a training syllabus?"

"We had one," he said. "But that was *Back in MAC*."

Indeed, that was true: *Back in MAC*. The Air Force came into being in 1947 against the threat of nuclear war and organized into two distinct combat forces, one for nuclear warfare and the other for wars of a more conventional nature. The Strategic Air Command was the lead dog until about fifteen years later, when the Tactical Air Command started to flex its muscles in Southeast Asia. Through it all, the Military Airlift Command, nee Military Air Transport Service, existed primarily to support the warfighters. One could argue that MAC had its beginnings during the Berlin Airlift. It was somewhat ironic that the fall of the Berlin Wall in 1989 signaled the end for SAC and TAC, and in the end that killed MAC as well. In 1992, all three commands were dissolved. The result was undoubtedly better for the warfighter. But even three years later, the transition was difficult for square pegs in a world of round holes.

Ramstein was a round hole redesigned for combat and the 76th Airlift Squadron was a square peg that worked efficiently because they were able to rely on MAC rules and regulations. But now that MAC was no more, those rules and regulations were no more. The training syllabi were from *Back in MAC*, and no longer existed.

"Do you mind checking out as an instructor pilot right off the bat?" Felix asked. "It would really help out."

Flight Lessons 4: Leadership & Command

"Not at all," I said. "I just need a little instruction on how our training flights are organized, what the training requirements are, the best airports for training, and whatever else you think I can use."

"I'll fix you right up," he said. "I got a training guide around here somewhere." I followed him to his office where he found a thin 3-ring binder on his desk. "Everything you need is right here. Have Susan make you a copy and you will be all set." I thumbed through what appeared to be third-generation photo copies, but the content was very good.

"So what do you think about the Woz?" Felix asked as I closed the notebook. "I attended his first two ops group meetings. He's a different kind of colonel, isn't he?"

"He is," I said. "He might be the youngest colonel I've ever met."

"He isn't even forty yet," Felix said. "He made captain two years early, major and lieutenant colonel three years early, and colonel two years ahead."

"That seems about right," I said. "He doesn't seem to know much about instrument flying but he knows lots of people."

"Who you know, not what you know," Felix said. "That's the way of the Air Force. I think his father-in-law is a two-star."

The next evening I was walking to our C-20 trainer when a blue sedan pulled alongside me. Mayhem was driving with Colonel Wozniak in the right seat. "Hey Eddie," he said as Mayhem slowed to my walking pace. "My French connection came through. They are sending letters to all the French airports we use for training instructing them to accept faxes in lieu of having to come in to sign landing fee invoices. Your scheduler is getting a copy of the order."

"Wow," I said. "That's perfect. Thanks."

"So what's the deal with those C-21s?" he asked. "The taxiway looks too narrow for a Gulfstream, let alone that Boeing of yours."

"It is too narrow to taxi without a wing walker," I said. "We are on request with civil engineering to repaint the Learjet parking lines so they can be angled in. That will make it easier for the Lear pilots when taxiing out and it should give us another ten feet of taxiway."

"So why isn't it done?" Wozniak asked.

"Well, we are on request," I said. "The civil engineers say it will be six or eight months before they get to us."

"We could bend some metal in that time," Mayhem said from the other side of the car. "Not smart, Eddie."

"I'll look into it," Wozniak said. "Have a good flight, Eddie."

I flight planned the training sortie using one of Felix's past sorties and ran the instruction as if Eric was a student aircraft commander. Captain Rorie Fitzpatrick sat in the jump seat as I instructed and never failed to answer a question Eric fumbled. At first she would pause, not wanting to make her squadron mate look bad in front of the new boss. But after a while it was obvious he had no answers to give. It seemed, once again, we had our copilots and instructors mixed up.

With degrees in engineering and economics, my writing style was uncorrupted by college. Various Air Force leadership schools hammered home that everything comes in threes. There should be three main points to every paper. Every paragraph has three sections: an introduction, the main point, and a transition or conclusion. Even every sentence benefits from the trifecta: subject, verb, object. The "dos" were clear. When it came to writing effectiveness reports, the "don'ts" were also clear cut. Don't use acronyms and don't assume the reader has the same background. My cardinal rule was even easier: write so the person's mother would be proud. It was so easy, even an engineer could figure it out.

The weekend of twenty ERs wasn't nearly as difficult as I had feared. Most of the reports had all the necessary information, just poorly presented. "Top marks LR-35 IQC, Lieutenant Cleary's C-21 CP record time upgrade shows he's ready for further advancement." Yuck. "Lieutenant Cleary finished first in his class at the top Learjet pilot school in the United States. He followed that by setting a squadron record for C-21 qualification!" Better.

I put all twenty marked up ERs on Susan's desk first thing Monday morning and headed off to the Ops Group meeting. Colonel Wozniak was flying and Mayhem's meeting took all of five minutes. "ERs!" he said. "Everything is due Wednesday!"

I got back to the squadron, ready to face any retribution for ruining Susan's week. But there was none. She was typing happily and smiled as I headed for my office. "You write so understandably," she said.

"Isn't that the entire purpose?" I asked. As I entered my office there was a knock on the outer office door.

"Sir," the tall captain said. "I'm Lenny Seaton and I'll be giving you your check ride tomorrow."

"Excellent," I said. "Please come in." I sat at the conference table opposite my desk and invited Lenny to sit opposite. "If you could let me know what to expect I'll see what I can do to meet those expectations."

"I was going to ask you the same thing," he said. "I know how to give an instructor pilot upgrade check and I know how to give a requalification check. But I've never given an instructor pilot requalification check to my boss."

"Don't think of me as your boss during the check," I said. "I'm an unqualified pilot trying to meet squadron standards and it is up to you to evaluate how well I do. But I need to know what role you will be playing in the other pilot seat and what I need to do to measure up to those standards."

"I can do that," he said. I knew from his records that Lenny flew tankers in a previous life and turned down a plush assignment to his Sacramento hometown to come to Germany. Felix said he was the best Gulfstream pilot he had ever flown with and his elevation to the squadron's top standardization position was a no brainer. "Sir, you just need to present a 30-minute class on a systems topic of your choice, then a 3-hour flight that teaches me how to fly any combination of precision and non-precision instrument approaches, two-engine and single-engine landings, an engine failure after takeoff, a touch and go landing, and a full stop landing."

"All that in three hours?" I asked, with my best look of faux exasperation.

"I suppose," he started.

"I'm joking, Lenny," I said. "I'll do that."

The next morning I taught Lenny the finer points of the aircraft's ground spoiler system and we flew to Spangdahlem Air Base for much of the instrument work and back to Ramstein for the visual maneuvers. After 3.0 hours we landed and I debriefed my pretend student, ready for him to return the favor.

"I really enjoyed that, sir," he said. "I wasn't expecting that kind of instruction. We don't really do it that way. I heard things were a lot more intense at Andrews. This was actually kind of fun."

It wasn't much of a debrief but it was over. As Lenny left my office, Felix entered. "Congratulations boss, you are now officially a squadron hero."

"It's just a check ride," I said.

"No, not that," he said. "I mean the C-21 taxiway. Civil Engineering just showed up to sandblast the old lines and paint new ones. We've been trying to get that done for a year and it just took you one week!"

"It wasn't me," I said. "It was Wozniak."

"He's been here for a month and nothing got done," Felix said. "We all know it was you with the magic. Nobody is happier than your safety officer."

That would be Captain Tommy Mendéz, the 33 percent bald but 100 percent smiles C-21 Instructor pilot. I spent the rest of the week trying to be visible in the squadron and refreshing my face-to-name recognition skills. Rorie, the French-speaking, redheaded C-20 copilot from Charleston spent most of her time in the scheduling office. She worked for Captain Alan Irish, the short C-21 instructor pilot who was named Irish but looked more Italian. Kyle Knudson, the crewcut wrestler who knows the books, didn't seem to have a squadron job, but was always in the squadron. In a week I seemed to have twenty faces recorded into the appropriate synapses. One hundred and thirty to go.

"Just be careful," *The Lovely Mrs. Haskel* warned during our weekend phone call. "Names like that can hurt feelings."

"I'll ditch the names as soon as I get to know them," I promised. "I've spent most of my career ignoring names and now my job depends on it. It is a skill I should never have overlooked."

"What do you call your boss?" she asked.

"Everyone calls him Woz," I said. "But I think of him as 'The Boy Colonel.' But I haven't thought of that in a while. He's pretty unforgettable."

"It seems you didn't like him from the start," she said. "Just another group commander stepping on the troops trying to become a wing commander."

"Maybe that's true," I said. "You don't get to be seven years below the zone without some huge politicking skills. But he's actually okay."

"I am surprised," she said. "You actually like a politicker?"

"Maybe like is too strong a word," I said. "But he has a knack for getting things done with his connections. He solved a few things for me that I had given up on as too hard. And he did them by calling people he had met at parties. Maybe I can learn something from him."

I got to the squadron early Monday morning, worried that I might have forgotten an ER before the due date. But Susan's calendar confirmed everything made it to the operations group on time. I sat at my desk with the morning's first cup of coffee when a 33 percent bald Learjet pilot knocked on the door. "Guten tag," he said.

"It is that," I said. "How are you today Tommy?"

"I am doing well, sir," he said. "No worries."

"A safety officer is always worried about something," I said. "It is part of your DNA. What worries you the most, Tommy?" Tommy looked almost embarrassed to speak further. I held my tongue and he took two steps into my office. He was committed.

"Well, if you really want to know, we do have one hanging issue in the C-21 world," he said. "But I'm not sure it is solvable."

"Let's find out," I said.

"It has to do with untrained pilots flying our Learjets," he said. "And they are all general officers." Tommy explained that before 1992, MAC rules said the only general officers that could fly any of the Air Force's Learjets had to be in the operational chain of command of that Learjet and they had to be trained first. For our squadron, that limited the potential general officers to our wing commander, the numbered Air Force commander, and the Commander of the Unites States Air Forces, Europe.

"But that was *Back in MAC*," I said. "What do we have now?"

"Well we've managed to keep things in the chain of command," Tommy said. "But none of the three we have flying with us now have ever been to school."

"I can guess their reasoning," I said. "Each of them are accomplished fighter pilots. How hard can it be to master a Learjet?"

"Pretty damned hard," Tommy said. He blushed at letting the "D word" slip. "These Lears can be unforgiving when they get slow. The stall speed shoots way up with any kind of bank angle and when they do stall, they always snap into a roll. I've seen one of our generals wrap the bank angle right to sixty and pull like he was flying a fighter. If the airplane rolls, it will be so fast none of our instructors will be able to recover."

"It sounds like we are relying on luck," I said.

"Exactly," he said.

"Let me see what I can do," I said.

The next morning, I hoped to lay out the unqualified general officer flying issue to Wozniak alone, but my timing was poor. I ducked my head into his office while he and Dillon May were looking out the window.

"Remington's flying the morning run to Bosnia," Wozniak said. "It's good to see the boss fly a Herc. You can't lead from behind, right Eddie?"

"Absolutely," I said. "But if you are going to take a pilot seat, you need to be qualified."

"He's authorized as long as he has an instructor in the other seat," Wozniak said. "Besides, he owns the airplane."

"I know, sir," I said. "I was hoping to ask you about other general officers flying my airplanes without training."

"The floor belongs to you," he said, taking his seat behind his desk while pointing to a chair opposite and to his left. Dillon took the seat to his right and faced me. I laid out the issue much as it was laid out to me the day prior, minus the "Oh I wish I was *Back in MAC*" melancholy. As I spoke, Dillon nodded and shot me a thumbs up from his right side, hidden from Wozniak's view. Neither interrupted and when I finished there was silence. I was hoping for another magical phone call that resolved everything, but it appeared I would get less than that.

"There isn't much we can do, Eddie," he said. "As long as these general officers are in the chain of command and you have an instructor in the other seat, we should be okay."

"Our most senior C-21 instructor pilot is a captain with a grand total of two thousand hours," I said. "That is a lot of pressure to put on such a young pilot. I'm not sure they'll be able to take the airplane from a general officer in time to recover. We're asking too much."

"That's the job," Wozniak said. "If they aren't ready for it, they shouldn't be instructors."

"Okay sir," I said. "I'll keep an eye on it."

Dillon followed me as I withdrew, defeated. As I stepped outside the outer office I felt a tug on my arm. "Don't give up, Eddie," Dillon said. "You are doing God's work here."

James Albright

Flight Lesson: Political Leadership

Any organization with leaders and followers will necessarily be political. A political leader capitalizes on external connections to achieve organizational and personal goals. A leader without political skills operates with a handicap.

Political Leadership Defined

pol•i•tics

- The assumptions or principles relating to or inherent in a sphere, theory, or thing, especially when concerned with power and status in an organization

The Advantages of Political Leadership

A political leader can get things done more quickly and efficiently than a leader who relies on established processes within the bureaucracy. The result can greatly benefit the leader's standing within the organization, as well as the standing of the organization itself and of the leader's subordinates.

Few bureaucracies are inherently efficient and with time can encourage inefficiencies. A well-connected political leader can bring common sense into play at a high level, where lower levels of the organization will favor "how it's done" over "how it should be done."

The Pitfalls of Political Leadership

A political leader is at great risk of falling into "group think" among fellow political leaders. These leaders devise plans and solutions without consulting lower tiers of the organization, where the most relevant data exists. This can blind them to the root causes of problems and the solutions offered by subordinate leaders or followers.

A political leader who is seen as spending more time with higher levels than in the trenches can create resentment from the troops needed to get the job done in the first place.

3: The New Sheriff
May and June, 1995

C-130E and the Ramstein Air Base Tower (Photo: USAF)

I ran over the excuses in my mind as I trailed a slow-moving cargo loader on the perimeter road from the south side of the base. Many of these vehicles had speed limit signs attached to their rear frames, as if apologizing to the cars behind. What does 30 KPH come to in American? Late, that's what. Just two weeks on the job and I was already late for an operations group meeting. As I finally made it to the building and climbed the stairs by twos, I steeled myself for the reaction. But as I entered the office, Wozniak's secretary smiled warmly. "The boss wanted to give everyone a chance to review their kickbacks so he'll be in a little later."

"What's a kickback?" I asked.

"Those are the ERs that got kicked back from the Wing last week," she said. "Everybody except one commander got a ton of kickbacks. You seemed to have figured out the formula, Colonel Haskel." Her smile was my reward and the day's fortunes had suddenly reversed. I walked into Wozniak's office to find my fellow squadron commanders sadly reading from stacks of ERs. I took my place just as we heard our boss enter the outer office.

"Sorry I'm late," he said as he threw his hat onto his desk and himself into his chair. "We need to keep this short, I'm going to have to run down the hall and replay this whole meeting for my own kickbacks. You all have your ERs to work on and they are due, really due, this Wednesday. Oh, Eddie, good job. The wing commander says you write like a fighter pilot."

"I guess that's a compliment," I said.

"It is," Wozniak said. His secretary hovered at the door. "I got to run, see everyone on Wednesday."

We stood as Wozniak left, and I made for the door. "Hey Eddie, wait up," Art Johnson said. "How about coming over to the squadron and giving me a few writing pointers?"

"Sure," I said. "I had the morning blocked off for this meeting, might as well make use of the time." We left Maggie Cairns, still studying her kickbacks. Wozniak's secretary shot me a thumbs up and another smile.

"I guess you figured out how to make the secretaries happy," Art said as we descended from the second floor. He waited until we left the building to continue. "I'm not really worried about the kickbacks," he continued. "I'm wondering about General Paulson. Nobody is willing to talk about him. I've called every base he has a history with and I even found a few who flew with him in the Herc back at Little Rock. I can't get a straight answer from anyone. But you told Woz that General Paulson is intense. That's a word that is hiding something."

"That's true," I said. "I thought it might be best for the new wing commander to introduce himself without me dirtying the dishwater before he gets here. Let me just say that Paulson rules with an iron hand. He doesn't like bad news and once he takes a position he doesn't react well to pushback."

"So far you haven't said anything that makes me hate the guy," Art said. "What else?"

I tried to choose my next words carefully. If what I had already said wasn't enough, I might be speaking too freely with a potential Paulson ally. As we walked I noticed a C-130 Hercules with a collection of maintenance stands on both outboard engines, each missing their cowls. The inboard engines appeared to be intact, but black with soot. "Is this going to consume the rest of your day?" I asked.

"What?" he asked.

Flight Lessons 4: Leadership & Command

"You've got an airplane with two engines opened up and the other two don't look much better," I said. "That can't be good."

He laughed and pointed to two other aircraft that seemed to be in as bad a condition. "You haven't spent much time around 130s, have you?"

"I guess not," I said.

"These are E-models," he said. "These are the oldest C-130s on active duty, most of them are 1963 or 1964 aircraft. When I took over we had an MC rate of just 50 percent."

"MC rate?" I said.

"Mission Capable," he explained. "That's how many airplanes I have on a day-to-day basis that can actually fly and do their jobs. You VIP boys don't have MC rates?"

"I suppose we do," I said. "But if I have even one airplane out of the thirteen that are down, that is bad news. So what's your MC rate today?"

"I got it up to 55 percent!" he said. "That is the highest MC rate for any E-model squadron on active duty."

"How'd you do that?" I asked. "You get more spares? More people? What's the secret?"

"Will power," he said. "You push your people hard enough, and even they will be surprised at what they can accomplish."

"Until you push them to the breaking point," I said.

"That's why we get paid the big bucks," he said. We reached his squadron building and he led me into the first office which was a cavernous affair with C-130 photos from the Vietnam era.

"Is this an E-model?" I asked, pointing to a C-130 dropping a pallet of cargo while flying just inches off a dirt runway, surrounded by what looked like bombs going off.

"You bet," he said. "In fact, that very airplane is the same one you pointed to with the two broken engines." He pulled a stack of papers from his in-box and shook his head. "Damned Crawford." He picked up a phone.

"Kenny, this is Art. Where is Crawford? Pull his flight status and get his ass to the hospital." He covered the mouthpiece and looked at me. "Navigator OUI," he explained. "Who was that?" he asked the now uncovered mouthpiece. "Okay, pull her out of the upgrade program. I guess she was never meant to be an instructor pilot."

In five short minutes Art had dealt with ten problems on the phone, never hesitating, never asking for advice. Every decision was made quickly and forcefully. He cradled the phone. "It never ends, does it?"

"I have my share of problems," I admitted. "But it sounds like you have it worse. I am struggling with upgrades too. Why did you pull that pilot out of the upgrade program?"

"She busted her check ride," he said. "Sometimes you have to cut your losses."

"What did she bust for?" I asked.

"I don't know and I don't care," he said. "It just happened this morning. This was the first I've heard of it."

"Maybe there were extenuating circumstances," I said.

"Eddie, you need to understand something about being a commander," he said. "We are in the Air Force and we have a job to do. I am not here to be anyone's best friend and I am certainly not here to hold hands while my people cross the street. They either cut the mustard or I get rid of them. I don't have the time to waste on children wearing the uniform."

Thankfully Art had forgotten his quest for more information about General Paulson and shook my hand as I excused myself to leave. "Don't be a stranger, Eddie."

As I approached the squadron, Susan rushed out before I got to the door. "Have you heard about Captain Phillips' wife?" she asked.

"Who is Captain Phillips?" I asked.

"He is a C-21 instructor pilot who got married two years ago," Susan said. "Right after he got married his wife started visiting the squadron commander before Colonel Haney. She would sit in his office and cry for hours. He just let her cry herself out."

"I can't imagine that went very well with Clevis," I said. Susan rolled her eyes.

"Colonel Haney kicked her out the first time she tried that," Susan said. "He said if she showed her face in his office again he was going to have her arrested."

"And what does her husband have to say about all this?" I asked.

"Captain Phillips says she's hot blooded and just needs to vent," Susan said. "Do you want me to accompany you?"

"That's a good idea," I said.

We entered the office and the tears started before I uttered a syllable. Susan handed Consuela Phillips a box of tissues and I tried to listen to the cries that were both in English and intelligible. She said her husband had mistresses hidden away all over Europe and spent more time with them than at home. She was a slender and attractive woman with long raven hair, but appeared to be quite a bit older than what I imagined her husband was. As she went on I examined the crew schedule on my desk to see that Captain Shane Phillips did indeed spend more time away than at home, but that wasn't unusual. He spent most of his time in Naples. As her visit went into a second hour, I spotted Felix entering the squadron and avoiding my office. I excused myself.

"Felix," I said. "You got an hour to spare?"

"Not with her," he said. "Anything but that!"

"I'll see you in your office in just a few," I said.

"I have to run," I said as I returned to my office. "Consuela please give me some time to look into this. Shane will be home on Monday. But right now we have to get back to work and you need to go home. Susan, please see Consuela out to her car." Susan stood and Consuela, after a moment, got up as well. I quickly retreated from the battle scene.

On my way to Felix's office I stopped at the scheduling office where Rorie Fitzpatrick was erasing the schedule from two months ago in preparation for the one to come. It was late in the day and she had the office to herself. She heard me enter and stood at attention.

"As you were, Rorie," I said. "Do you have a history of the schedule going back several months?"

"Yes, sir," she said, pulling a large binder from a shelf. It was the standard 8 and a half inches on end but easily 30 inches in width. She turned to a page and I could see the previous month in one view, all 90 crewmembers along one axis and all 31 days on the other. I sat at her desk and read; she returned to her grease pencil board. Of the 40 C-21 pilots, the 10 instructors were very busy. Most of our C-21 pilots spent about half of every month away from home, but the instructors seemed to average around 20 days. Captain Phillips led the pack with between 20 and 25 days every month, and had done so for the past year.

"Why is Captain Phillips on the road so much?" I asked.

"Because he is always volunteering," Rorie said. "We have to force him into flying a trainer now and then, but he lives for overnights."

I studied his schedule again, looking for more clues. In a squadron of 60 pilots, only 5 were women. Rorie was the only female pilot in the C-20, the other 4 flew C-21s. I scanned the last month for a flight with Phillips and one of these; there were none. I went back, month after month, and only found him on one local trainer with a female pilot. I had to go back a year before finding him on an overnight with a female pilot.

"Why do the women in the Learjet seem to avoid flying with Phillips?" I asked.

"I think you might have to ask them," Rorie said, avoiding my eyes.

"You don't have to answer," I said. "But since you fly the C-20 and will never have to fly with him, I would rather ask you. I don't want to make them feel pressured to fly with him if they have reasons not to. This is just between you and me. As a scheduler and as a woman pilot, you have a better view on what is going on here."

Rorie pulled her eyes from the floor and looked into mine. "He's kind of creepy," she said. "He has this way of looking at women as if he is sizing them up. You know. Oh, I guess you probably don't know. He's always looking for the next conquest."

"I see," I said. "Does he have any conquests in Naples?"

"That's what I hear," she said.

"Thank you," I said. "I will not repeat this to anyone."

As I got up to leave she spoke again. "Sir, one more thing. Shane is the senior C-21 pilot. I'm just the assistant scheduler. Captain Irish is in charge of the schedule and he says it is easier just to give Shane the schedule he wants than having to put up with him beating up on the rest of the schedulers."

"I see," I said. "Thanks."

I left her office and headed for Felix's. He was devouring a box lunch and a streak of ketchup continued his ever-present smile to one side. I gestured to the right side of my mouth. He grabbed his paper napkin and erased the red streak. "Fixed?" he asked.

"Fixed," I said. "So talk to me about Shane Phillips."

"You got a handful there," he said, looking over my shoulder to his office door. I reached back and closed it. "He's a strange agent and nobody likes spending time on the road with him, but everyone likes the fact he volunteers for every bad deal trip so they don't have to."

"Why don't they want to spend time with him on the road?" I asked.

"Well I've never been on the road with him, or any of our Learjet pilots," Felix said. "But I've heard things."

"Things?" I said.

"Things," he said. "It isn't my place to tell a man how to lead his life and if he's not a hundred percent on his wedding vows, well that's none of my business. He flies well, he flies all the rotten trips, and all he asks in return is some time in Naples."

"I'm not so sure," I said.

"Well I am," Felix said. "Don't get me wrong, boss. You are the boss and whatever you want to do I'll back you up a hundred percent. But getting in the middle of a pilot's off duty time is asking for trouble."

I sat in thought as he finished the last of his lunch. He crumpled the box into one, neat package and tossed the entire thing into a waste basket. "I got some good news," he said.

"I could use it," I said.

"Kyle passed his aircraft commander check ride today," he said. "With flying colors, in fact. All he needs is an IOE and we have one leaving Friday, returning Sunday. It's yours if you want it."

"What's involved with an IOE?" I asked. I knew an Initial Operating Experience trip varied from base to base and was a long and involved check ride in some squadrons.

"Nothing to it," Felix said. "Let Kyle do all the planning and be ready to pick up any of the pieces when they fall. If you think he can survive on his own, sign his grade book as qualified. But Kyle's been doing this for a while, he should have no problems."

That Friday Kyle was sitting in the left seat of our C-20 as we waited alongside the red carpet painted on the tarmac in front of the base VIP facility, right next to base operations. From the right seat I could see most of the north side ramp and all of the C-130 parking area. I watched as a C-130 prop started to spin, cough, and belch flames from both the front and back of the engine. The airplane was soon surrounded by fire trucks.

"We might be late," I said to Kyle, "but at least we're not on fire."

"Sir, we hear stories about how strict Andrews was on timing," Kyle said. "Is it true you could be fired for a late takeoff?"

"Yes," I said. "But it isn't as simple as that. For departure, 'on time' is defined as being ready when the passenger is. But for landing, you could never be early and the definition of late depended on who was watching."

"Sir, Colonel Haney said the C-20 squadron at Andrews required 5-second block times," he said. "Are we going to start doing that here?"

"No and no," I said. "Some pilots shot for 5-seconds but the official standard was never early and within a minute late. But no, we aren't doing that. Don't be early because you don't want to embarrass the VIP by showing up without anyone to greet them. But I think if you keep to within 5 minutes after the scheduled arrival you should be okay. Isn't any of this written down anywhere?"

"*Back in MAC* it was," he said. "Our rules were anything within minus 5 and plus 15 was on time."

"Let's use minus 0 and plus 5," I said. "But we need to be clear that we aren't doing anything even remotely unsafe to make that happen."

"When you say minus 0 are you saying don't be even a second early?" he asked.

"Let's not get hung up on measuring things to the second," I said. "Our job is to get our important passengers to where they need to be reasonably close to the schedule, but we certainly don't want to pull up to the red carpet without the hosts in place to greet them."

Our VIP showed up 30 minutes late and weather over the Alps made us another 10 minutes late into Rome. After the passengers departed in their motorcade, Kyle tackled the paperwork while the flight engineer busied himself with checking our engine oil levels and putting on various covers. I watched Sergeant Wayne Crosby put on the left engine cover and then he helped me as I struggled with the right. Crosby had no problems with his side and fearlessly stood on the left wing while hooking the straps to the front of the engine. From the right side I managed to do the same, but only with some difficulty.

"I never had a pilot try this," he said. "I can show you how to do the oils next time, if you want, sir."

"I would like that," I said. When I returned to the cabin I found the flight attendant vacuuming while Technical Sergeant Charles Heisman, our radio operator, was alone in his compartment, reading a magazine. I could also see a stack of dishes in the galley that still needed to be washed. It was a like a scene from an early 1960's sitcom: the wife doing housework in heels while the husband sat in an easy chair, smoking a pipe. I tapped Heisman on the shoulder.

"Would you rather vacuum or wash dishes?" I asked.

"She don't want my help, sir," he said.

"That means you are on the vacuum," I said. He looked at me, motionless.

"Do I have to repeat myself?" I asked.

"No, sir," he said.

I walked mid-cabin to Technical Sergeant Kelly Shields. "Sergeant Heisman is volunteering to vacuum and I am volunteering to wash dishes. Put us to work."

She looked at me and froze. I walked past her to the galley and Sergeant Heisman took the vacuum. Her face lit up and soon she was taking the dishes from my hands as soon as I had washed them. She then dried them on the way to their drawers. Kyle approached. "Is the garbage ready yet?" he asked. She gathered the large bag from its bin, threw in the remaining trash, and handed everything to Kyle.

"This has never happened before," she said. "Nobody helps the flight attendant."

"I thought I read a letter from Colonel Haney saying nobody leaves the airplane until everyone is done," I said.

"That lasted for about a week," she said.

"Let's hope we can do better this time," I said.

We reverted to normal officer and enlisted protocols during our ground time in Rome. Kyle and I walked to the normal tourist spots. The flight engineer, radio operator, and flight attendant joined us for dinner, where everyone was very polite and careful not to say anything that might upset their new commander. As uneasy as they appeared to be, I think I was even more uncomfortable for the first dinner. Having grown up spending lots of time on the road with my commanders, I knew that as a commander I could never again be a "crew dog." Everybody was polite and the conversation gravitated to what life was like at Andrews. The 76th Airlift Squadron was considered a second-tier VIP squadron, but nobody occupied the first-tier except the 89th Airlift Wing at Andrews. Technical Sergeant Kelly Shields, like me, had a history with the 89th.

"I made tech at Andrews," she said. "But I don't know how that happened. The flight attendant career field is pretty small and the promotion point system for enlisted crewmembers is stacked against us. I think it was easier at Andrews."

"I seem to remember a lot of tech sergeants and above at Andrews," I said. "Here the only techs are you and Bob, right?"?

"Yes, sir," she agreed. "Sergeant Ferris was in accounting and finance and I was a clerk typist. I think since we both came from large career fields it was easier for us."

"You still compete for promotion in your previous career field?" I asked.

"Yes, sir," she said. "The Air Force doesn't recognize us as having a career field. We are just on temporary duty."

"Sabbatical," Knudson said. "It's like you are taking a break from the real world."

"Exactly," she said. "But as a clerk typist I always thought I wanted to do something with airplanes. This gives me the chance. I'm not really into the

VIPs and all that."

"Like Bob," Crosby said.

"Like Bob," they all agreed.

"Bob Ferris?" I guessed.

"Yes, sir," Kelly said. "He's a great flight attendant and he really works hard to herd all us cats. But he lives for being seen on TV." Everyone laughed.

"There was that time with the first lady," Kelly said. "The crew made it to the red carpet a little faster than he expected and nobody went to open the door." More laughter.

"Why didn't anyone else open the door?" I asked.

"Because Bob knew the arrival would be on the evening news back in Alabama," Kelly said. "That means the world to him, to know that his folks will see him on TV."

I joined in the laughter. There was a level of comaraderie that reminded me of earlier squadrons that seemed absent at Andrews. The pecking order among our flight attendants began with the CT-43, where there were three flight attendants onboard for every trip. Only the top CT-43 flight attendants would graduate to the C-20 where one flight attendant had to do it all. But even with all his experience, Technical Sergeant Ferris chose his trips based on television coverage to make the folks at home proud.

The next morning we were all back to business on the drive back to the airport. "If you are on the road with a copilot," I asked Kyle, "do you trade seats? Does the copilot fly from the left or right?"

"We trade seats," he said. "All our copilots are former instructors in larger aircraft so we allow everyone to fly from the left seat."

"So I guess I should take the next leg so you can supervise me," I said. "Then we can officially bless you as an aircraft commander."

"That would be great, sir," he said. He appeared to be surprised it would be this easy.

Our passengers arrived on time and we headed north, back to Ramstein. The winds were lighter than forecast but I allowed our ground speed to build without correction. Kyle sat happily in the right seat, doing an excellent job as a copilot. "How is our timing?" I asked.

"If we don't get any air traffic delays, we are going to be early," he said.

"Are we going to get any delays on a Sunday afternoon?" I asked.

"Probably not," he said. I gave our inertial navigation system computers a second look and estimated we were now at least five minutes early. Kyle punched away at his INS. I waited. "Why don't we pull it back 10 knots, sir?"

"Good idea," I said. "Talk me through how much speed ten knots is going to lose us in the hour of flight we have left."

Kyle did so and came to the conclusion that 10 knots wasn't enough but was reluctant to pull it back further. "Maybe we can fly a slower descent and check our progress along the way."

"Perfect," I said. The speed adjustments worked and we made it to the red carpet just a minute late. The entire crew pitched in with cleaning the cabin and an hour after landing we were all in our cars headed home. Well, I was headed to visiting officer's quarters. My family was still a month away from joining me.

I was happy to see our Boeing CT-43 on the ramp as I pulled into my parking space in front of the squadron. It was a tired looking airplane overdue a coat of paint but pretty in its own way. Its white top and gray bottom made it look exactly like the aircraft used for navigator training; the only giveaway of its real purpose in life was the "United States of America" above the cabin windows. I bypassed my office and looked into the First Sergeant's office only to find it empty, as it had been for the two weeks the aircraft was away. Deeper into the building I found Chief Master Sergeant Trenchard in the flight engineer's office with four other engineers. The five stood at attention. "Please, be seated," I said.

It was the largest office in the squadron. We had six flight engineers for the C-20 and two for the CT-43. I counted eight desks, one for each engineer. I took a seat behind an empty desk. The walls were due a coat of paint and I spotted a calendar from a German auto parts store with a scantily clad Fräulein straddling what looked like a race car's transmission. The five engineers followed my gaze. "Not really appropriate for an Air Force squadron, is it?" I said.

One of the engineers ripped the calendar from the wall. "Sorry, sir," he said.

I turned to face Trenchard. "Welcome back, chief," I said.

"It's good to be back," Trenchard said. "I've got a list of honey do's as long as my arm when I get home." The other engineers each gave a polite laugh.

"Well, good luck with that," I said. "Can I see you for a minute?"

Trenchard got up and followed me out to the empty hallway. "We need to talk," I said. "When do you plan on being back in the office?"

"I was hoping to take the rest of the week off," he said.

"Do you have leave scheduled?" I asked. He appeared surprised by the question. He was my height, more muscular, and with more gray hair. His face was weathered and punctuated with scars.

"No," he finally said. "But I've been away for two weeks and we have another trip leaving Thursday."

"I need to see you no later than Wednesday," I said. "And put someone else on that trip."

"But that trip is going back to the States," he whined. "I really wanted that trip!"

"Having the first sergeant away three weeks out of four is unacceptable," I said. He stood there, speechless. "You have your orders."

With that, I turned and left. I noticed immediately he had never once uttered the word "sir" but wasn't sure that was worth a rebuke. I had never made an issue of that before. Perhaps as his commander I should have. As a chief master sergeant, he was as senior as he could have possibly been as an enlisted member of the Air Force. He was probably in his late forties or maybe early fifties. He certainly had twice my years in uniform. I was in uncharted territory.

I steered toward the pilot's office with another confrontation on my list of things to do that Monday. I entered to see several familiar faces and two that were new to me. As I entered they all stood at attention. The room was half the size of the engineer's office, though we had ten times as many pilots.

"Be seated everyone," I said. "Please." I offered a hand to the captains that were new to me. "Eddie Haskel," I said, "new guy." They both laughed.

"Captain John Halsey, sir," the first said.

"Captain David Ashworth, sir," the second said.

"John I guess you are on the road again on Thursday," I said.

"Yes, sir," he said.

"Must be rough on the family," I said.

"Well that's part of the job, you know, sir," he said.

"I'm sorry to interrupt your post mission debrief," I said. "But we need to talk for a few minutes. I have to leave in 30 minutes, so can we do that right now?"

"Yes sir," he said. "No problem." He got up and followed as I led the way to my office. He was about my height with an extra thirty pounds and the baby face to go with it. I knew from his record he was a C-5 pilot in a former life and had an exceptional record before and after joining the 76th. As the squadron's only CT-43 instructor and aircraft commander, the aircraft could not move without him.

"When will David be ready to upgrade?" I asked as we made the turn into my office.

"He's ready now," John said. "I was waiting for the June upgrade panel."

"Why wasn't he nominated in the previous panel?" I asked.

"Well, I'm not sure," he said. "I mentioned it to Colonel Haney but he said no."

"But you think he's ready now," I said.

"Yes sir," he said.

"When you get back from the next trip," I said, "start his training. Don't wait for the upgrade panel."

"Yes sir," he said.

"And talk to me about the C-20 copilot situation," I said.

"I really don't know anything about them," he said. "Colonel Haney put me in charge of the pilot section after something happened between he and Captain Stumm. I haven't had a chance to learn about the C-20s or C-21s."

"Well you've been on the road almost continuously," I said. "Take a few days of well-deserved rest and have a good trip on Thursday."

Flight Lessons 4: Leadership & Command

"Thank you sir," he said. He wasted no time leaving my office, perhaps relieved that he had made it out relatively unscathed. Susan stood at the doorway, pointing to the clock on the wall.

I picked up my hat and rushed to my truck. I had just enough time to make it to the group commander's meeting. On my way north I spotted Felix heading south. He gave me two beeps of his MG's horn and a thumbs up. I waved. He would be leaving for a trip of his own on Tuesday.

Colonel Wozniak announced that all of our ERs had been accepted by the wing, thanked us for the extra effort, and announced the next week's focus. "It will be a change of command full of pomp and circumstance," he started. "The ceremony will be officiated by Major General Foster."

"The Seventeenth Air Force Commander," Maggie explained, reading my mind.

"Yes," Wozniak continued. "We need your squadrons fully assembled for a dress rehearsal on Friday and then we do the real thing next Wednesday. Your DO's need to lead your squadrons and you commanders will be in the reviewing stand with the rest of the dignitaries. The 37th will form three flights and everyone else will form single flights."

"We have two flights," Maggie said. "But you want them combined because they are so small?"

"Exactly," Wozniak said. "You too, Eddie."

"Yes, sir," I said.

After the meeting I left the building with Maggie. "Your squadron is organized in flights?" I asked.

"Of course," she said. "The only people in the Air Force that don't use flights are you VIP types, like back at Andrews."

"Andrews reorganized into flights a few years ago," I said. "I suppose I should have picked up on that when I showed up here."

"How is the 76th organized?" she asked.

"We have sections," I said. "We have a section each for the pilots, flight engineers, radio operators, flight attendants, and ground support."

"Like an airline," she said. "That can't be good."

"It isn't." I explained the problem of having a pilot section chief from the smallest crew force having to lead pilots in two other aircraft types. "He's the only AC we have in the CT-43 so he's on the road continuously. Meanwhile we have 15 C-20 pilots and 40 C-21 pilots that work for him. I doubt he knows the first thing about those airplanes."

"It sounds like you got a problem," she said. "I've got a flight for the flight crews and another for the aeromedical crews. It's pretty easy that way."

Back at the squadron Felix was already parked in a seat at the conference table in my office. The squadron manpower chart was spread in front of him. "I see you survived group again," he said. "I got you the manpower chart, just like you asked. But I thought you should hear some rumblings from the trenches first."

"Shoot," I said.

"Well, first off I heard you signed Kyle off and that's good," he said. "But I also heard you made the RO vacuum and the FE wash dishes. The flight attendants are happy and everyone else, well, not so much."

"Do you have a problem with any of that?" I asked.

"Well, no," he said.

"Everyone should certainly tend to their own jobs," I said. "But at the end of a flight, if they are done early and someone else isn't, it's a team effort."

"Sure," he said. "That makes sense. It's just going to take everyone a while to get used to that."

"What else?" I asked.

"Calvin is pretty upset with you for taking him off the stateside trip," he said. "They were going to Colorado Springs and he has family there."

"I know," I said. "But he shouldn't have taken the two-week trip that just got back. As the squadron first sergeant he has specific duties here in the squadron. He can't be an absentee first sergeant."

"I hear you," Felix said. "Again, it's just that this is a change to the way things have always been. The troops just need a chance to adjust to the way you do things."

"Well I got another one for you," I said. "I am wondering why this squadron is still organized with section chiefs and not flight commanders."

"I'm gonna sound like a broken record," Felix said. "But the reason is we've always done it that way. I've always thought it was nuts too. Our C-21 pilots have to freelance because they either work for a C-20 pilot or a CT-43 pilot, depending who is flavor of the month. Everyone was assuming Eric was going to get his section chief job back. But it is pretty apparent you don't care for Captain Stumm."

"I want a flight commander system," I said. "Put all the C-21 crews under your best C-21 pilot. Do the same for the C-20s, every crew position under the best pilot. Even if that ends up being Captain Stumm. The same goes for the CT-43s. I'm not sure about the flight attendants."

"They already have two sections," he said. "Most of the CT-43 flight attendants only fly that bird. Our most senior flight attendants are on the C-20 and they only fly the CT-43 as needed."

"That should continue to work," I said. "I want everyone to know exactly who they report to."

"Okay," he said. "This is going to be quite the upheaval."

"What about office space," I asked. "Can we reorganize the offices so everyone lives in the correct flight?"

"I'll figure that out," Felix said. "We have some extra real estate around here."

"Keep this to yourself," I said. "We'll announce this at next week's squadron staff meeting. We'll invite the new flight commanders too."

I returned to my office where a captain I didn't recognize was waiting. "Captain Phillips," he said. "Reporting as ordered."

"Come on in and have a seat," I said. He took a seat at the end of my conference table and I took the seat opposite. He appeared to be the oldest C-21 pilot in our squadron, judging by the lines under his eyes and what appeared to be pale skin peeking through wisps of hair combed from one side to the next of his scalp. "You come from 130s, right?"

"Yes sir," he said.

"How many years have you been at the 76th?" I asked.

"I guess it has been five," he said.

"And when are you up for major?" I asked.

"I'm primary next year," he said.

"How do you feel your chances are?" I asked.

"Pretty good," he said. "I was an instructor in the C-130 and I'm an instructor in the C-21. That has to count for something."

"I'm not so sure," I said. "You don't have a master's degree and you still haven't completed the required professional military education courses. But we can talk about that another time. I want to know why you rack up the most away time of any crewmember in the squadron. What does the wife say about that?"

"She knows that's part of the job," he said. "We have an understanding."

"That's not what she told me," I said. I studied his eyes, which never wavered. I was anticipating some kind of reaction, but there was none.

"That's kind of personal," he said. "I'll make sure she doesn't bother you anymore, sir."

"Maybe you should spend more time with her than your squadron mates," I said. "Give that a try."

"I will, sir," he said.

Captain Phillips left my office and I stared out the window, wondering what else I could have done. I first met *The Lovely Mrs. Haskel* when we were in high school, before either of us had even considered our lives to come would involve a pilot's nomadic lifestyle. I had to be away, sometimes for months at a time, but on average I spent more time at home than away. Being a marriage counselor was not part of my commander's training.

The next morning I was disappointed to see that the first sergeant's office was still empty. I stood for a moment, thinking of my options. "He's in the flight engineer's office," Susan called from across the hall.

"Thanks," I said. The flight engineer's office was in the opposite side of the squadron, wedged between what looked to be the start of a nice weight room and the flight attendant's kitchen. Each of the desks were littered with manuals, magazines, and what appeared to be auto parts. Open cabinets continued the theme, but the spare parts appeared to be from aircraft. I recognized a fuel control unit from my past.

"Good morning," I heard from behind me. It was Trenchard, who headed for his desk and sat down.

I picked up the fuel control unit. "Boeing 707?" I guessed.

"C-135B," he answered. "It's from Miss Piggy."

Flight Lessons 4: Leadership & Command

I knew that was what they called the aircraft that was replaced by the CT-43. "That thing's been gone for five years now, right?" He nodded. I looked around the office. "I am guessing most of this stuff is from those days. All of our maintenance is by civilian contract now, why do you keep all this stuff?"

"I guess I like having them around," he said.

"Get rid of them," I said.

"What?" he said. And then, "Why?"

"You aren't authorized to use any of these parts on our aircraft," I said. "You aren't authorized to perform this level of maintenance on any of our aircraft. And this office is a pigsty. Do you need any other reasons?"

"None of the other commanders had a problem with this," he said.

"Did any of the other commanders allow this level of insubordination?" I asked. He stared daggers at me, but kept silent. "How long have you been in this squadron?"

"Nine years," he said. "Sir."

"I guess you like it here," I said.

"It's a good squadron," he said. "The COLA isn't too bad either."

He had a point. An Air Force enlisted member, even a chief master sergeant, wasn't paid very well compared to a civilian doing similar work. The Cost Of Living Allowance for an assignment in Germany gave our enlisted members a significant boost in pay.

"The Air Force rarely lets its chiefs homestead for nine years," I said.

"Finding someone with my background isn't easy," he said. "I guess I'm needed most here."

"Perhaps," I said. "We need a good first sergeant, but we need a first sergeant who spends more time in the squadron and less time on the road."

"Yes, sir," he said.

"We have to organize a formation of troops for next week's change of command," I said. "Report to Colonel Henderson and offer him whatever help he needs."

"Yes, sir," he said.

"Pomp and circumstance" barely did the ceremony justice as a description. The wing was assembled in the base's largest hangar with a formation of troops that had to number a thousand, including about sixty from the 76th. A large band flanked us in the reviewing stand and the cleanest available C-130 graced us on the other side. The Commander of the 17th Air Force, Major General Samuel Foster, stood at the podium to thank Brigadier General Lesley Remington for his stewardship of the 86th Air Wing and to welcome Brigadier General William Paulson as the new commander of the 86th Airlift Wing.

General Paulson looked exactly as I remembered from three years ago back at Andrews. As the 89th Operations Group Commander he was a recognized "fast burner" who seemed too young to be a colonel. I first saw him hiding in the bushes with a pair of binoculars, spying on his crews flying our nation's top leaders. He publicly chastised me for wearing sun glasses that day when the Chairman of the Joint Chiefs arrived at my airplane. Colonel Paulson had become, in my list of pet names for senior officers, "the colonel in the bushes." Now he was a general officer and would once again determine my fate as an Air Force officer.

He spoke easily from the podium, with no case of nerves for what had to be his largest audience ever. He was three or four inches short of the desired 6-foot model height for an Air Force commander, but his thin frame made him appear taller than he really was. His black hair had a slight hint of gray, providing a subtle contrast to his black skin and telegraphing his wisdom gained through the years that would have otherwise been missed in his young face.

As he threw out his first cliché, "Ramstein is the spear's pointy end," I flashed back to my years of listening to him speak. None of the memories were good. "Combat airlift is our priority," he said at one point. Looking at the assembled troops and the dignitaries in my peripheral vision, I could tell they were buying it; eating it up, cliché after worn cliché. He had them where he wanted them. I positioned the watch on my wrist so I could check it more often without being too obvious. I wanted this to end.

"Paul Paulson will always give a hundred percent to the mission," he said finally. "And Paul Paulson expects you to do the same." He took a step back from the podium and the dignitaries applauded. I could see smiles from the ranks of the C-130 squadron, they realized that they were now the "spear's pointy end."

"Isn't it the 'pointy end of the spear'?" Maggie asked as we descended from our elevated reviewing stand.

"It is," I said. "But Paul Paulson never met a cliché he couldn't mangle."

"And where does that come from?" she asked. "His bio says William R. Paulson. Do people just naturally call him Paul?"

The reception that followed was packed with local German dignitaries and military personnel with uniforms I didn't recognize. Once the higher end of the rank structure had paid their respects, we in the squadron commander tier started to file through the reception line.

"Good afternoon, general," Maggie said when her turn came. "I am the commander of the aeromedical squadron and I was at Andrews a few years ago too."

"I remember you," he said. "And I am going to depend on you, Margaret, to keep those C-9s flying."

"I will, sir," she said. He shifted his gaze to me and his smile disappeared.

"Colonel Haskel," he said before I could utter a syllable. "Imagine my surprise to see your name in the Ramstein command structure."

"I can imagine, sir," I said.

"Well you are no longer a safety officer," he said.

"I've always thought that we are all safety officers," I said. "Especially those of us who are commanders."

"Well tell me what your focus is," he said. "Do I have to worry about you?"

"Sir my focus is on my people," I said. "I don't think you should have to worry about me at all."

"People, that's right," he said. His smile returned, confusing me at first, but then I realized his glance had already shifted to the next person in line.

"What was all that about?" Maggie asked after we were out of the general's earshot.

"I don't know," I said, adding, "Margaret."

"Don't you ever call me that," she said. She shot me a glance to underscore her words, and headed for the hangar floor and to her squadron. I headed in the same direction, but adjusted my course towards the tallest officer in sight.

"Nice bit of marching, Felix," I said.

"It's a good thing all we had to do was move forward a few feet," he said. "I haven't done anything like that since I was a cadet. Let's head over to the party. I hear they have a boatload of shrimp cocktails there."

"You go ahead," I said. "I want to get a head start on a few things. Have you come up with room reassignments for the big reorganization?"

"Sure did," he said. "They are on your desk."

I returned to my office and stayed late into the night. Felix's reorganization plan was very good but he added a few suggestions with question marks. One had a double question mark. "Captain Phillips – C-21 flight commander??" I hadn't considered that. He was senior, he was an instructor, and keeping him closer to home might be the thing to patch a broken marriage. But he was also considered "creepy" by some, was not a good role model, and giving him more time at home might be the wrong solution to a question that didn't have an easy answer.

Military pilots often joke that while away from the family they are, "Class 2 Bachelors" and therefore given free license to misbehave. Over the years I had witnessed a lot of that and knew the divorce rate in every squadron was not only tolerated, but assumed to be a part of the environment. The life of a military pilot was prone to cause these things, but *The Lovely Mrs. Haskel* and I had escaped those troubles. We met in high school, before the Air Force, and survived more than a few extended separations. In fact, our current time away would be the longest, but it would end once our two kids finished the school year in Virginia. My weekend would be taken by inspecting and signing for a rental house in a nearby village. But I would be thinking about other marriages too. Where was the line between commander and arbiter of personal relationships? Was there a line?

Colonel Wozniak had a different look about him on Monday. His smile was subdued and he cradled a notepad filled with scribbles. Instead of speaking freely about a long list of topics, he read carefully from his scribbles. "General Paulson had a quick introductory meeting with his group commanders last week and he shotgunned a long list of things to do," Wozniak said. "His list wasn't in any particular order and some of it applied to multiple groups. So I might have some of this wrong. But here's what I got for us."

"First, we need to produce a list of people metrics. He mentioned promotion rates, separation rates, and OUIs. I gather that means 'operating' under the influence, as opposed to 'driving' under the influence. Second, he wants flying metrics. He listed MC rates and OTTO. We all know what MC stands for, but what's an OTTO?"

"Not a clue," Maggie said.

"Never heard of it," Art said. Mayhem and I simply shook our heads.

"I guess we're going to find out," Wozniak said. "Finally, Art, he said he has news about combat airlift. He didn't have time to explain any of this, but on Wednesday we need to be armed with what we know."

On my drive back I played variations of the letters in OTTO in my head and came up empty. Colonel Paulson was cliché driven back at Andrews; perhaps he had learned the value of confusing his troops with undecipherable acronyms at general officer school. I knew the best way to defend against a Paulson attack was to anticipate it and come up with something to unbalance it. I came up with the strategy after learning Colonel John Boyd's OODA Loop: Observe, Orient, Decide, Act. It was a technique designed for ground combat but seemed to keep me one step ahead of Colonel Paulson. But what about General Paulson? Was I letting my history with the man cloud my judgment? Returning to my office I found a friend from years past chatting with Susan.

"Colonel Haskel it's good to see you when you aren't a prisoner," he said. Susan shot me a raised eyebrow. Major Mark Honable rose to shake my hand. He was wearing combat fatigues and had added a maintenance officer's badge underneath his navigator's wings.

"We were at POW school together," I explained. "Mark is an expert at survival, but not so good at avoiding capture." I gestured him into my office, took a seat at my conference table, and gestured for him to do the same. "It is good to see you. I heard you have the most demanding job on base."

"You know it is every navigator's dream to get a commander's job," he said.

"When I got one of the largest maintenance squadrons in Europe I thought I hit the jackpot. But the more I learn about the C-130, the more I realize some dreams can be nightmares."

"Art tells me you have the highest MC rate of any E-model unit on active duty," I said. "You can be justifiably proud of that."

"Thanks," he said. "I'm just not sure how long we can keep that up. We are undermanned, we don't have enough spares, and rumor has it we are trading in air drop for combat landings."

"You have to admit the idea of using air drop in Bosnia is pretty stupid," I said. "How often does a pallet dropped from 12,000 feet actually make it to the good guys?"

"Everyone knows that," he said. "But if we land and takeoff in the combat zone, that doubles the chance of something breaking."

I sat quietly as Mark gave me a recent history of the European theater combat airlift mission, and how the current conflict in Bosnia meant the tempo of their C-130 operations had increased every month for a year. Air combat, for the C-130 fleet, could mean anything from dropping a pallet with a parachute from 12,000 feet, to actually landing where the shooting is. But on top of all he had to worry about, Mark had been told his enlisted member effectiveness reports were unacceptable.

"Ineffective effectiveness reports," I said. "There is a lot of that going around this base."

"Art says you have it figured out," he said. "I was hoping you would teach an old friend the secret."

"There is no secret," I said. "You just need to write them like you are trying to make the person's mom proud. And then you need to read them aloud until it sounds good. If you can't make it just flow off your tongue you need to rewrite it. I'll have Susan get you some examples with the names blacked out."

I asked Susan and within a minute I could hear her printer busy churning as she worked on the redacted reports. Mark seemed pleased with this. "Can I return the favor in any way?" he asked.

"Maybe," I said. "I have been struggling with a few military issues. As you probably remember, military isn't one of my strong points."

Flight Lessons 4: Leadership & Command

"I have to admit I was surprised to hear you got a flying squadron," he said.

"Me too," I said. "But here I am leading a squadron of unmilitary airplanes with a few unmilitary pilots trying to be military. So my first issue is squadron organization. We were not organized by the Air Force 'flight' system in most of my squadrons but all that changed a few years ago when it became mandatory. We even reorganized at Andrews. But this squadron still uses section chiefs."

"That's not good," he said. "My squadron was already reorganized when I showed up, two years ago. You better fix that before the next inspector general visit."

"I'm doing that tomorrow," I said. "I thought the section chief system would probably work best in a maintenance squadron. But if you guys can make the flight commander system work, we should be able to. I just need to figure out how to best sell the troops on the idea."

"Sell?" he said. "Eddie we are in the Air Force. The regulation says we are organized by flights. End of story."

"I suppose," I said. "Second question, do you have any incidents of extramarital affairs among your troops?"

"Not that I ever hear of," he said. "I rely on my first sergeant to keep the troops in line when it comes to discipline."

Susan brought in a stack of enlisted ERs. I moved my eyes to Mark and she changed her heading from me to him. I got up, hinting that I was needed elsewhere.

"Well I got to go," Mark said. "Thanks for these and good luck with the reorg."

I showed up the next morning to my office where Felix had already organized our staff and erected a large easel with a series of charts covered by a blank page, just as we had rehearsed. Everyone rose as I entered. "Please be seated," I said.

"First off let me say that I am very impressed with the job everyone is doing," I started. "Looking at today's schedule we have airplanes in Siberia, Turkey,

Israel, Senegal, France, England, and even one in the United States. And we are doing all that with an incredibly young crew force. So, congratulations and thank you. But there are a few issues we need to address. I don't like the fact we don't have a clear chain of command and that our decision makers are usually disconnected from the decisions being made. Captain Halsey does a great job as the chief pilot, but he doesn't have the background in the C-20 or C-21 to make informed decisions, especially when he is always on the road. Sergeant Heisman does a good job keeping the radio operators current and qualified, but he doesn't have a reporting relationship with any C-20 pilot except me. By the time an RO issue comes to me, it might be too late. I could say the same thing about Sergeant Ferris, who has three times the issue because he has three times as many flight attendants as Heisman has radio operators."

I could read a sense of dread in their faces. The new boss was about to change years of established protocol. Our longest serving member came to the squadron nine years ago and in all that time there was a chief pilot, engineer, radio operator, and flight attendant. Nine years of history was about to change.

"Starting today, we are going to have a clearer chain of command," I said. "Felix, how about showing us how all this is going to work."

Felix uncovered the first chart and the staff fell silent. He revealed that we would have four flights: one for each aircraft type and a ground support flight. The senior CT-43 flight engineer would report to the CT-43 flight commander. The senior C-20 flight engineer and radio operators would report to the C-20 flight commander. Our flight attendants were already divided into two sections, now one would report to the CT-43 flight commander and the other to the C-20 flight commander.

His next chart revealed the main building floor plan and the moves that would be needed. Everyone carefully eyed the layout and Felix was flooded with questions about timing and the need to move furniture. Through it all, Chief Master Sergeant Trenchard just sat and quietly fumed. After the meeting I looked at him and gestured to his office. He got up and waited for me to lead the way. We entered his office and I closed the door behind us. "Speak your mind," I said.

"You can obviously do this," he said. "I know we are the only squadron on base that wasn't using flight commanders. But I can't have my flight engineers working for the pilots. They work for me."

"They don't work for you as a flight engineer," I said. "A flight engineer is a crew position and a flight engineer works for a pilot. They are also enlisted and noncommissioned officers in the United States Air Force. In that capacity, they look up to you as their first sergeant. You have two capacities here and if you can't live up to both of those responsibilities, you need to find another assignment."

"Okay," he said. I looked into his eyes. "Sir," he added.

"One last thing," I said. "I want the auto parts store in the engineers' office cleared out today. They go to the dump, or they can go to the garage at your house. I don't care where you put them, but they are not to be anywhere in the squadron. Is that understood?"

"Yes, sir," he said.

I returned to my office where most of the staff had already adjourned. Captain Alan Irish was just leaving and stopped as I entered. "Sir, thank you very much," he said. "I am very excited with this new position and I won't let you down."

"I know you won't," I said. "You have a big challenge in front of you. Just remember to take care of your people and they will take care of you."

"I will, sir," he said.

I fell into the chair behind my desk as Felix took the nearest seat opposite it. "That went much better than I thought," he said.

"No rioting in the streets?" I asked.

"I saw you already took care of our biggest problem," he said. "Trenchard can't be too happy."

"He isn't," I said. "Let me know if he's plotting anything."

"Not if," Felix said. "When. He's an institution around here and not many lieutenant colonels can challenge a chief master sergeant and get away with it."

"Anybody else?" I asked.

"No," he said. "And that surprised me. But I think even the radio operators and flight attendants like the idea of reporting to someone flying the same airplane. I think the biggest surprise was that you gave Eric Stumm the C-20 flight commander's job."

"Other than you and me, he's the only instructor pilot," I said. "We need to fix that. But maybe he'll grow into the position."

"We can only hope," Felix said. He sat back and looked at the hand drawn organization charts and building layout still pinned to the easels. He had the look of a proud father. We could start to hear the sounds of furniture being moved. "I better get back there and herd some cats," he said, getting up.

"Before you go, a question," I said. He stopped. "Ever heard of the term OTTO"?

"No," he answered.

"Okay," I said. "Ask Susan to come in, please."

I spent the rest of the day compiling our squadron metrics with Susan. She had most of the information I needed, but most of it was disheartening. In the previous year we didn't have any divorces but we did have two OUIs. Of 60 officers, 20 had been eligible for new assignments. Of those, 7 had the option to separate from the Air Force and all but one did just that. Every first lieutenant eligible for promotion to captain made it, every captain eligible for promotion to major did not.

The new floor plan gave the largest office to the C-21 flight, where they had already hung up a large poster with a drawing of a Learjet and the words, "C-21 Country." The former tenants of that room were now relegated to two desks, one each in the C-20 and CT-43 offices. The flight engineers had lost ground in the battle of real estate.

The weekly wing staff meeting took place in the main wing headquarters conference room where the wing commander sat at the head of the table, flanked by seven group commanders and the vice commander, all colonels. Behind each group commander sat their subordinate squadron commanders, each of these either lieutenant colonels or majors. The operations group commander had the primary spot at the table and his squadron commanders the closest spot to the apex of the room. General Paulson sat at that apex and listened intently as each group commander reported their introductory metrics.

Flight Lessons 4: Leadership & Command

In every case the group commander reported that things were good, though the metrics in question tended to lag Air Force standards. "But we're working on it," seemed to be a common theme. General Paulson listened quietly and thanked each group commander as they finished. Finally, it was his turn.

"I am very impressed with the people of this wing and want you to let your people know that," he started. "You let them know that Paul Paulson said that. Paul Paulson's number one priority is people! And that should be your number one priority as well."

I could see Maggie had written "1. People!" on her notepad and I had to stifle an urge to give her a Mel Brooks inspired "Harumph!"

"Paul Paulson has a plan to bring good things to Ramstein," the general continued. "We need a way to distinguish ourselves. When we do that, we make it possible for our people to get promoted, to get good assignments, and to elevate the reputation of Ramstein. A good reputation attracts good people and good people build good reputations. Can you see where I am going with this?"

The staff murmured and a few of the group commanders said, "absolutely!"

"Harumph!" I said, quietly.

"So here is part one of Paul Paulson's plan for Ramstein," he said while raising a hand to quiet the staff. "I called General Harold Reece at the Air Staff. When you've been around as long as Paul Paulson, you know people. I told General Reece that Ramstein is ready, willing, and able to double our contribution to the combat airlift into Sarajevo. It's a tragedy what's going on in Bosnia and we are going to do our part to support the effort. Our air drop program has been vital to keeping the good guys supplied and we ought to be very proud of our contribution to this point. But the army has secured the airport and most of the area around it. That's our opening to start air land operations." The room erupted into multiple conversations. The non-operators were asking about "air land" versus "air drop." The operators knew instinctively that the danger level had shot through the roof. Dropping a pallet from 12,000 feet is dangerous; while you are above the bullets, you are still over enemy territory. But landing in the battle zone, amongst the bullets, is an entirely different matter.

"Combat airlift, that's the mission. That's our number one priority. Isn't that right, Woz?"

"Yes, sir," Wozniak said. "That's a great idea."

"It is that," Paulson agreed. "We do good for the people of Bosnia, for the Air Force mission, and for Ramstein. Our people get promoted and get good assignments. Our reputation is elevated and that does what?"

"Attracts great people," a few of the colonels at the table said.

"That's right!" Paulson said. "But that's not all. This wing has two other very important missions. You may be wondering how such a young-looking general gets command of the most important base in all of Europe." The staff laughed on cue. "Well it's because Paul Paulson has experience in all three missions." He looked over to Maggie. "Colonel Cairns, you probably didn't know that I've flown the C-9 before, did you?"

I looked over to Maggie, who by this point had added "1. Combat Airlift!" to her notepad.

"No sir, I didn't," she said. "But you are invited to fly with us anytime."

"I'll do that," he said. "But not only that, Paul Paulson was once the group commander at the 89th at Andrews, right Colonel Haskel?"

"Yes, sir," I said.

"That's right," he said. "And how did we SAM FOX pilots define an on time takeoff?"

He was staring right at me but I wasn't expecting the question. "On time" was critical at Andrews, but the takeoff portion wasn't something that took a lot of effort. "An on time takeoff at Andrews is determined by being ready when the VIP shows up at the aircraft."

Now it was General Paulson's turn to look unprepared. "What?" he said. "No, what is the timing criteria, you know, in minutes?"

We didn't have that at Andrews, but clearly Paulson didn't know that. "The standard criteria is minus 5 or plus 15 minutes," I said.

"That's right," he said. "So that is our number one priority. Do I make myself clear?"

"Yes, sir!" everyone responded. With that he got up and we all stood at attention. As he filed out Maggie turned to Art and Wozniak. I grabbed the notepad from her seat and made an addition:

Flight Lessons 4: Leadership & Command

1. People!
1. Combat Airlift!
1. OTTO!

By Friday the squadron furniture relocation program was complete and the next week's schedule sat on my desk, ready for my signature except for a yellow tab with an arrow pointed to a three-day C-21 trip to Naples. Captain Kendra Munroe was assigned as the aircraft commander with a new copilot. It appeared to be in order but the arrow said otherwise.

Felix walked in. "Ah, the weekly schedule. Do you mind me being gone for five days?"

"No, you should go," I said. "You said you've always wanted to go to Israel. Here's your chance. What's with this Naples flight?"

"I just wanted to warn you of possible pushback," he said. "When you elevated Alan Irish to be the C-21 flight commander that left Rorie Fitzpatrick in charge of the schedule. She knows that Shawn Phillips wants to go to Naples whenever possible but she put Kendra there instead. Now Shawn is saying we shouldn't have C-20 pilots scheduling C-21 trips and that she is playing favorites because she favors females over males. He was yelling at her in front of the lieutenants and his language wasn't, shall we say, 'officerly.' Rorie didn't budge, but you can tell she wasn't happy. I had to pull him away. He's complaining to Alan now. He says that as the senior C-21 pilot he should have the final say on the C-21 schedule."

"What do you think?" I asked.

"I think that's a bunch of BS," he said. "Naples is a favorite spot for the Lears and I think Alan always gave in because Shawn can be intimidating. Shawn says he's doing everyone a favor by always flying trips. But the real workload for an instructor is flying local trainers. Shawn almost never flies a trainer because he is always on a trip."

I signed the schedule. "If he wants to complain, send him my way. You tell Rorie she has our support."

"Sounds good," he said.

Susan stepped into the doorway. "Colonel Johnson on the line for you," she said.

Felix got up and waved. "See you for beer call."

I picked up the phone. "Art, are you having an OTTO day?"

"Well that's why I called," he said. "I'm looking all over for that minus 5 or plus 15 you told the general and I can't find it. Wasn't that *Back in MAC*?"

"It was," I admitted. "I don't think we have a set limit in this wing, at least not one that is written down."

"I guess we do now!" he said, laughing. "Damn you!" Another laugh.

"While I have you on the phone, a question," I said. "How do you deal with one of your pilots who is abusing the trip schedule to conduct an extramarital affair? He isn't letting his personal life impact his professional life, so aren't my hands tied?"

"I don't get 'touchy feely' with my people," he said. "If you are sure about it, you tell him to stop. If you suspect it but don't have evidence, you put road blocks in front of the bastard."

"But isn't this none of my business?" I asked.

"He's an officer and this is conduct unbecoming an officer," he said. "That makes it your business."

"That is the sanest thing I've heard all week," I said. "Thanks."

I cradled the phone and walked to the C-21 office. It was getting late and most of the pilots were collecting in the lounge for our Friday beer call. I heard two voices in the office and thought I was going to be lucky. I found Alan Irish seated at his desk with Shawn Phillips standing. A young lieutenant sat at another desk. All three rose.

"Please give us the room," I said to the lieutenant. The young pilot left, and closed the door.

"Alan," I said, "I would like you to remove Captain Phillips from all future trips and restrict him to flying only local trainers until further notice."

"Yes, sir," Alan said.

I turned to Shawn. "All I want to hear about you is that you are doing a fantastic job as an instructor pilot. If I ever hear about you abusing other officers in this squadron you will not be flying at all. If, after a month of spending every night in your own home, things improve both domestically and professionally, I will consider allowing you on trips again. Can you do that for me?"

"Yes, sir," he said. His eyes were moist and he was trembling. I left the room.

An hour later Felix handed me a stein of beer in the squadron lounge. "Word is going around the squadron about Shawn," he said.

"And?"

"I think it's fifty-fifty," he said. "Everyone who deals personally with Shawn is doing cartwheels. It is amazing how many enemies he has. But for everyone else, well, this is a side of you they've never seen."

"Win some, lose some, I guess," I said.

"Another thing you should know," he said. "Chief Trenchard has been saying he's seen eight commanders before you and will see eight commanders after you. But after you leave he's going to get the engineers back into their old office and things will be back as they were before."

"I see," I said. "I'll handle this."

I finished my beer and found Trenchard in his office, the first sergeant's office. I entered and closed the door. "I need you to find another assignment," I said. "Stateside."

"I'm not going to do that, sir," he said. "I like it here and the squadron needs me."

"No man is indispensable and a flying squadron this size doesn't warrant a chief master sergeant," I said. "I'm going to give you all of next week to find an assignment, and if you don't do that, I will find one for you."

He sat, speechless. I left and drove home to a small village just west of the base. My family was arriving in a day.

James Albright

Flight Lesson: Authoritarian Leadership

An authoritarian leader relies on the official powers vested in his or her position to exercise control. Other leaders can move seamlessly between authoritarian and more democratic styles, as the situation dictates.

Authoritarian Leadership Defined

au•thor•i•ty

- The power or right to give orders, make decisions, and enforce obedience
- A person or organization having power or control in a particular, typically political or administrative sphere
- The power to influence others, especially because of one's commanding manner or one's recognized knowledge or prestige

The Advantages of Authoritarian Leadership

An authoritarian can get things done quickly and efficiently and realize short term objectives with less effort than a leader who first attempts to convince followers to achieve the desired goals, even if those goals are contrary to what the followers perceive as desirable.

There are times when an authoritarian approach is the only available option, particularly when time or mission objectives are the overriding concern. It can also be necessary when an organization is beset with inertia and needs to be "jolted" into action.

The Pitfalls of Authoritarian Leadership

An authoritarian risks alienating followers and will rarely achieve a maximum effort from those being ordered to do something they perceive as suboptimal. Even if the authoritarian's goals are perceived as good, without follower "buy in" the achieved result is rarely as high as it could have been with greater participation from all levels of the organization.

While an authoritarian approach can achieve the desired goals in the short term, long term objectives can suffer as followers may tend to leave the organization or even sabotage the effort itself. Because subordinates may fear bringing unpleasant news to the boss, the leader can be blind to these problems.

4: Blind Spots
July and August, 1995

CT-43A 73-1149 at Palma de Mallorca, March 1994 (Photo: The Werner Fischdick Collection)

I was hoping I would have settled into some kind of routine after four months, but that wasn't the case. Between my self-imposed chaos – the squadron reorganization – and the chaos that would naturally follow General Paulson, there was no routine at all. I was confident that Felix had a handle on our operations but there was only so much he could do without the right mix of people. In a squadron of 13 aircraft, the three C-20 Gulfstreams and nine C-21 Learjets were not humming along in perfect health but at least they didn't need intensive care. I wasn't so sure about our one and only Boeing CT-43.

"It's okay, sir," Captain John Halsey said. "All I need is a few weeks off from the trip schedule to get Captains Nance and Ashworth upgraded to aircraft commander, and we'll be all good again."

"Ashworth seems pretty sharp," I said. "I don't recall ever meeting Nance."

"Rich Nance is one of those guys who shows up an hour before each flight and leaves the first chance he gets when the airplane returns," Halsey said. "He's an excellent pilot but he doesn't do anything outside of the cockpit willingly."

"Good thing he's an Air Force captain then," I said. Halsey laughed, nervously. "Who do you upgrade first?"

"Rich, no doubt about it," he said. "He's been here a year longer than Dave."

"What about hiring an already qualified CT-43 aircraft commander?" I asked.

"There is only one other CT-43 base, in Panama," he said. "They aren't in much better shape than we are."

I spotted Susan at the door, pointing at her watch. "I'll let you go, John," I said. "I know you have a trip to get ready for and I have someplace to be."

He stood and walked out, turning left into the squadron. I grabbed my hat and turned right. "It's not at the hospital," Susan yelled from the door as I reached my truck. "They moved it to the O'Club."

"Thanks," I said. Somehow, she knew I would forget. I knew I was headed for the change of command ceremony for the 86th Medical Squadron and thought it would only be logical to do that at the hospital, where the squadron resides. But I suppose you can't very well do such a thing in a hospital. Holding the event in the Officer's Club would make it easier to show my face at the reception. With my family finally in Germany I was trying to spend more time at home. But it was a losing battle.

The 86th Medical Squadron, home to most of the doctors, nurses, and just about everyone else who had provider-to-patient contact, was what General Paulson would call the spear's pointy end for the hospital. I was surprised to see both the outgoing and incoming commanders were majors. The outgoing doctor appeared to be in his forties, weather beaten, and happy to be leaving. The incoming doctor looked to be in shock. Major Linda Roslin was on the south side of petite and could barely be seen over the podium. The crowd laughed politely as the public address system creaked in protest when she lowered the microphone about a foot and a half. She read from a single notecard and in just a few minutes we stood to applaud. I looked at my watch and headed for the door; it would be a new record.

"Eddie, stick around," I heard from Colonel Wozniak. "You are starting to get an antisocial reputation, that's never a good thing."

"Yes, sir," I said. A part of my brain did an inventory of all the things that needed to be done but another part squelched the list before it made its way to my mouth. I caught Colonel Wozniak's eyes track over my left shoulder.

"Woz I need a moment," I heard General Paulson say just before we made eye contact. "Good to see you Colonel Haskel, how is life in VIP land?"

"We are doing okay airplane wise," I said. "But we are still playing catch-up on manning."

"Well that's your expertise, as I recall," he said. He gave Colonel Wozniak a nod and the two turned, leaving me alongside a table of cheeses and German brotchen. I surveyed the landscape, considering my next move.

"I don't often see you at these things," I heard from opposite the bread table. It was Mark Honable with a plate filled with bratwurst.

"Wo ist die bratwurst, Herr Honable?" I said.

"I think you mean 'der bratwurst' and I'll lead you to it," he said. "I was planning on dropping by so you've saved me a trip. I'll talk while you eat."

"I was hoping you would write my promotion recommendation," he said as soon as we arrived at one of the most beautifully arranged tables of food I had ever seen. "I know the regulation says it has to come from the general, but he's going to want my group commander to draft a suggestion and my group commander is going to delegate that to me."

"Nürnberger wurst?," I asked, with a mouthful of my first choice from the table.

"I think so," he said. "It looks pretty juicy."

"Sehr gut," I said. "How's the competition?"

"That's the thing," he said. "Until today there was none. The wing only has three majors primary for lieutenant colonel this year and I was the only one with a command title. But as of today, there are two."

"So you are competing against another squadron commander, and this one's a doctor," I said.

"And a female," he said.

"I guess you are hosed," I said. "When's the board?"

"In six months," he said. "The promotion recommendation is due two months from today."

"Okay," I said. "I'm happy to help. I just need a copy of your personnel records. You mentioned three majors who are primary. Who is the third?"

Mark looked at me, his mouth forming to speak his first thought but then shifting to a new one. "Are you joking?" he asked.

"No," I said.

"He's one of yours," he said.

"I don't have any majors," I said. "I would have noticed a thing like that."

"I'm just telling you what AFMPC told me," he said.

"Okay," I said. "Get me those records and I'll go hunting for a missing major."

If the Air Force Military Personnel Center thought I had a major on my roster, I wasn't paying as much attention as I should have. Most Air Force officers get used to calling the AFMPC on a regular basis, they knew they'd be moving every few years and being proactive helped steer the process in their favor. All of my assignments after the second one were "by name" requests. The gaining unit was allowed to select me without AFMPC's involvement and I hadn't called AFMPC in years. But now I was in a squadron where AFMPC was in charge. We were told at squadron commander's school that getting to know our AFMPC representative was critical. In three months, I hadn't bothered to call him even once. As soon as I got back to the squadron I took care of that.

"Yes, sir, you have two majors scheduled to report for duty next week," the AFMPC major said. Unlike the 89th Airlift Wing near Washington, D. C., the 86th Airlift Wing did not warrant any special status and getting an assignment was a matter of volunteering and satisfying a secret formula known very simply as, "the needs of the Air Force."

The needs of the Air Force meant we got two older majors, one from a staff position with two tours as a C-130 pilot, and another from a C-5 squadron with an unknown pedigree. Both completed Learjet 35 training on the same day and were expected to report Monday morning at 0730 sharp. Other than the fact they were "older" majors, it was all good news.

"I still need two more," I said. "And if you could find me a CT-43 instructor pilot that would be great."

"Not much I can do about that, sir," he said. "But once these two majors show up you are only undermanned by two field grade officers. That's not bad."

I felt like arguing but there was nothing a major could do about inept manpower regulations. My Boeing 747 squadron had 20 officers and was allowed 6 field grade officers – majors or lieutenant colonels. The balance would be company grade officers – lieutenants and captains. That gave us a ratio of 30 percent. The 76th Airlift Squadron had 60 officers and was allowed the same 6 field grade officers, just 10 percent. But we only had two and were about to double that to 4. "That's not bad," I agreed.

"We do have good news, sir," he continued. "We are going to approve your request to extend Chief Trenchard for another three-year assignment. It's going to be some kind of record, twelve years on station for a senior non-commissioned officer."

"I never made that request," I said.

"I have it right in front of me on my computer," the major said. "Chief Trenchard called last week and said you asked him to stay another three years because of your enlisted manpower situation."

"He may have called, but those were not my orders," I said. "I want him out of this squadron as soon as possible. He was a C-141 mechanic many years ago and he's been a chief master sergeant for three years now. Where does the Air Force need him right now?"

"Well, we do have a chief's slot at Anchorage that has been open for a year now," he said.

"How soon can we cut the orders?" I asked.

"I can have that done in a day," he said. "But the quickest we can start his move is thirty days. I'll need something in writing with your signature."

"I'll fax you a letter right now," I said.

I typed out a simple letter, signed my name, and fed the fax machine behind Susan's desk. The Air Force satellite phone system balked and my anger about a lying chief master sergeant was redirected to the electrons between the fax machines in Germany and Texas. As the machines synced themselves on the second try my mood lifted. A smile came to my face as I imagined Trenchard's reaction when he found out he was being sent to Alaska.

I returned to my desk and tried a few more stateside numbers but most of my contacts were at lunch, reminding me I should be at dinner. *The Lovely Mrs. Haskel* was embracing our new German home with full force and had already enrolled herself and the kids in a local tennis club. They would have eaten already and my dinner would be sitting in the microwave. It was time to go home.

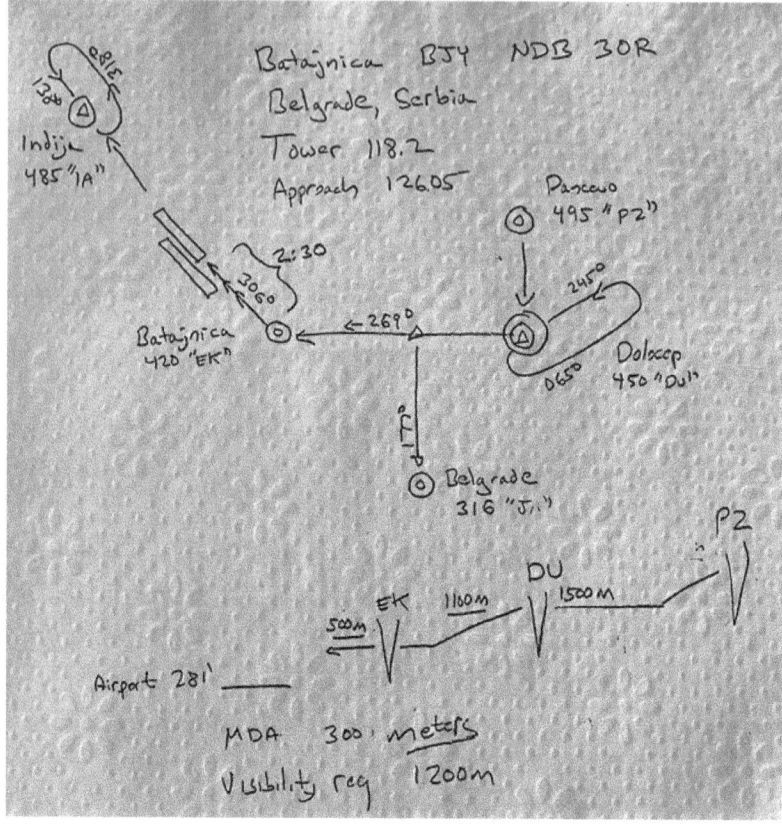

The Instrument Approach Napkin

On Monday I found the center of my desk was taken by two stacks of paper. Having banished in-boxes from every desk I had ever occupied as an Air Force officer I told anyone who asked that if I need to handle something, put it in the center of the desk and I would handle it. I recognized now that one of the stacks was the leftovers from Friday. On top of the new stack was a trip report from a C-20 that had returned from Serbia over the weekend. It caught my eye because it was more than the customary single page and it had stapled to it a napkin with an NDB approach drawn on it. Captain Lenny Seaton's report was terse but complete.

TRIP WAS ETAR – EGUN – LSGG – ETAR

DURING OVERNIGHT AT EGUN, LSGG CHANGED TO LYBT

NO JEPPS, DOD, OR RAF PLATES AVAILABLE

CALLED US EMBASSY SERBIA, GOT NUMBER FOR AIRPORT

Flight Lessons 4: Leadership & Command

AIRPORT MANAGER SAID ONLY APPROACH IS NDB TO RUNWAY 30R

SAID ONLY APPROACH PLATE IS OLD SOVIET AIR FORCE ONE HANGING ON WALL

HE READ APPROACH TO US, WE COPIED ONTO ONLY THING WE HAD AT THE TIME, A NAPKIN (ATTACHED)

APPROACH CONTROL RADAR WAS OUT, 2ND NDB OUT, GOT A VECTOR BETWEEN 1ST AND 3RD NDBS BUT NOT SURE HOW THEY COULD DO THAT WITHOUT RADAR

WEATHER A FEW HUNDRED FEET ABOVE MINIMUMS

WE SHOULD COMPARE NAPKIN TO TERRAIN CHART BEFORE GOING BACK

I stared at the napkin for signs that this might be a joke. Many of our destinations were former Russian Air Force bases given up as the Union of Soviet Socialist Republics (USSR) became the Union of Fewer and Fewer Republics (UFFR). The crew's original trip – Ramstein (ETAR) to Mildenhall Air Base U.K. (EGUN) to Geneva, Switzerland (LSGG) and back – would have been a fun week. Getting the change to Batujnica, Serbia (LYBT) would have thrown many crews for a loop. But somehow thinking that flying an approach off a napkin was okay was unlike Captain Seaton. It would have been a firing offense in many squadrons.

The tide of paperwork rose and fell as I completed one stack only to have it taken and replaced by another. The ebb and flow only got interrupted when I noticed Susan standing at the door, not knocking or saying anything. I never knew how long she had kept her pose when she seemed to magically appear. She could have just gotten there or it could have been an hour since my last glance upward. "More?" I asked.

"No sir," she said. "Major Hammer is reporting in."

"Send him in," I said. She retreated out of the office and gestured to the door. The major walked in to the center of the office, opposite my desk and saluted. "Major Michael Hammer reporting for duty, sir."

I returned the salute. "Mike, have a seat," I said, pointing to my conference table. He picked the middle seat on one side and I took the opposite. He was a large man by all measures. He stood about six foot five, probably weighed in at the limit for that height, and wore a broad smile that never seemed to dim as he spoke or listened. "Do you need a shoe horn to fit into the Lear?"

"No sir," he said, laughing. "I'm a tight fit but once I'm in there she's a good flying jet."

"Tell me about yourself," I said. "Start with Day One in pilot training and take me through to Learjets."

Hammer spoke easily and comfortably about his days flying the T-37 and T-38 trainers, and his progression from copilot to instructor pilot in the C-5 Galaxy. "The biggest jet the Air Force has," he said.

"Second biggest," I said, pointing to the Boeing 747 photo on the wall behind him.

"Second biggest," he agreed. He had pinned on his major oak leaves a few years ago and still had two years before meeting his next promotion board. It was a fairly standard resume, except for a school he had attended a year earlier: the Air Force Instrument Instructor School.

"AFIIS," I said. "I'm very happy to have an AFIIS grad in the squadron."

"And now you have two," he said. "I saw that on your bio."

"It was ten years ago for me," I admitted. "I still think it was one of the best pilot courses I've been to, but I think I am a bit rusty." I retreated to my desk and fumbled through the oldest stack, returning with Lenny Seaton's napkin. "What would you say about someone flying down to minimums using this?"

Hammer studied the napkin and his smile momentarily extinguished before reigniting. "I'd say that would be some kind of stupid, sir. First off, it's an NDB approach, something the Air Force hasn't taught in years. Second, it has more than one NDB and that ratchets up the skill required to fly it. And last, who knows who wrote this and according to what standard?"

"I would guess most Air Force pilots have never flown an NDB and wouldn't know how," I said. "I think it is a lost skill and good riddance. They are unreliable and can drive you into a mountain. But they are still out there. I was never formally trained until I got into this VIP flying thing. There are just too many of these approaches where we fly. But why is having a second, third, or fourth NDB that much worse?"

"For all the reasons you mentioned," he said. "Let's say the first NDB is okay but the second one is along a powerline or other electrical interference. Now you get to the first NDB and the second one sends you off course. Now you will never be able to see the third NDB if you have one, or the runway if you don't."

"Good point," I said. "What about what you said about the standard?"

"All of our Department of Defense approaches are written according to TERPS," he said. "On a Jeppesen approach plate you are going to see that annotated. On the international side of things you'll see PANS OPS. Either way, you know the host nation has written the procedure according to internationally agreed upon rules."

And of course that was true too. Air Force pilots were given a broad understanding of TERPS, the "United States Standard for Terminal Instrument Procedures." Military procedures as well as U.S. civilian procedures had to be designed in accordance with TERPS. But it wasn't until going to AFIIS that I heard of PANS OPS, the "Procedures for Air Navigation Services / Aircraft Operations," the international equivalent.

"This squadron operates in parts of the world where an NDB approach is the only option," I said. "Most our pilots have never seen one until we teach them how to fly them."

"Then we need to make sure our training includes TERPS and PANS OPS," he said.

"I agree," I said. "I need you to check out as quickly as possible, get the lay of the land, and then I would like you to find your way into the training shop. We need to capitalize on your expertise as an instrument pilot."

"I can do that, sir," he said. I got up and he followed me out the door. where we found Felix Henderson standing, as if on cue.

"New guy?" he asked.

"Not just a new guy," I said. "A new guy who knows more about instrument flight than you and I combined. Get him checked out and put him to work."

Felix and Mike departed, both smiling, making me smile. Susan stood and handed me another folder. "Group staff meeting in fifteen minutes, sir." My smile evaporated.

The group staff meeting was almost always a purely C-130 discussion, starting with the latest taskings and ending with the maintenance squadron's failure to provide enough airplanes. "We've got sixteen airplanes," Art Johnson said whenever he wanted to telegraph his helplessness. "Why we can't put more than eight in the air is beyond me."

"General Paulson wants a 65 percent mission capable rate," Wozniak said. "Are we going to get that?"

"The maintenance squadron commander says we will," Art said. "I'm pushing as hard as I can."

"The maintenance group has their hands full," Wozniak said. "As operators we are pretty much at the mercy of the maintainers. But let's do the best we can." He thumbed through his notes. "Eddie, the General wants to know why your schedule goes dead at 0100. An important visitor made it late to one of your C-21's in England and was told they couldn't depart after midnight because it got them here after 0100. Was this a noise issue?"

"Yes sir," I said. "As the regulation is written, no takeoffs or landings are permitted between 0100 and 0600. If the wing approves, we can make that apply only to Stage II or noisier airplanes."

"What's a Stage II airplane?" he asked.

"International rules, including German national rules, are written to classify noise levels in stages," I said. "The C-130 and C-9 are Stage I aircraft, the noisiest category. The C-20 is a Stage II aircraft, considerably quieter but still too noisy for most German airports at night. The C-21 is Stage III, the quietest category. I don't think any German civilian airports restrict Stage III aircraft."

Wozniak wrote as I spoke. "Okay," he said. "Let me talk to Paulson about this." He looked up from his notes. "Anything else?" I looked over to my fellow squadron commanders and joined the collective negative nod. "Okay," he continued. "See everyone at the wing staff meeting on Wednesday."

As I got to the door Wozniak called out. "Eddie, you have the only major up for promotion this year. We need a look at a promotion recommendation. You know the game."

Flight Lessons 4: Leadership & Command

"I do sir," I said. "As soon as that major checks in this week I'll get to work on it."

It was a game, to be sure. The wing commander had to personally write all promotion recommendations but didn't know all of the officers in his or her command personally. So a "draft" would be completed by the respective group commander. But in the case of majors, the group commanders were unlikely to know the officer any better than the wing commander. So the next tier of command had the chore. As I left the headquarters I remembered that I actually had two recommendations to write. I bypassed my truck and walked across the ramp to what a hand painted sign assured me was "Home to the Best C-130 Maintainers in the Air Force."

As I made my way through the maintenance squadron I started to realize the sea of personnel parted as I approached. In my squadron of 150 personnel, more than a third were officers. In Mark Honable's squadron of 200 personnel, only 2 were officers. Having a lieutenant colonel wander the halls seemed to be a big deal. I found Mark at his desk, writing on a yellow steno pad.

"Hey Eddie," he said as I entered. "You caught me doing ERs. I think I spend more time on effectiveness reports than anything else."

"I was going to ask you about that," I said, sitting opposite his desk. "I've read every word in your records file twice and am pretty impressed with how much you've done since the day we met. But I need something more about the job you are doing now if we are going to get you promoted."

"There's not much to say that isn't in the records," he said. "I guess I am hosed, just like you said."

"I was joking, Mark. You have a lot of responsibility here and we are going to get you promoted. We just have to tell a good story in your promotion recommendation. But I need to know more about your squadron."

"What can I do to help?" he asked.

"Your last two effectiveness reports seem to say you are just doing paperwork here," I said. "The squadron seems to run itself while you sit on the periphery dealing with hiring, firing, the occasional alcohol incident, and other personnel issues. They hardly mention maintenance."

"Well that's kind of my job," he said. "I have five very good senior master sergeants who know how to fix airplanes and I let them take care of that part of the business. I don't know the first thing about fixing a toaster. What can I do about an airplane?"

"Let me walk the shop floor with one of your senior master sergeants," I said. "Maybe if I get a better idea of what they are doing I can do a better job writing about what you are doing."

"Fair enough," he said, standing. I followed him through his squadron out to a large hangar with four C-130s in various stages of health. Judging by the missing engines and other airplane parts laid out on benches, we appeared to be in an intensive care ward. But it was unlike any hospital I had ever seen. The floor was littered with trash, random tools, and at least four types of fluid. I started to wonder about what four fluids are usually found in and around airplanes when we approached a husky sergeant holding a clipboard in one hand and an unlit cigar in the other. He spotted Mark and pushed the cigar into a pocket.

"Good to see you on the floor today, major," he said. He glanced my way and stood at attention. "Colonel," he said with a nod.

"Hi," I said.

"Sergeant Freeman, this is Colonel Haskel from the VIP squadron," he said. "I promised him a tour of our main hangar floor so he can get an idea of how maintenance is done the Air Force way."

"All my maintenance is done by civilian contractors," I said. "Maybe I can learn a thing or two from you."

"My pleasure, colonel," he said. Mark smiled and retraced his path out of the hangar. Senior Master Sergeant Freeman led me through the hangar and gave me a history lesson of each of the four ancient birds, their current prognosis, and his forecast on the immediate future. "I got three shifts going and we expect to have two of these done by midnight tonight."

"Maybe you'll get a chance to catch up on some house cleaning," I said.

"Maybe so," he said. "But as soon as we get an airplane done there are two more just outside waiting to get in. House cleaning is a luxury around here."

"You guys have the highest E-model MC rate in the Air Force," I said. "You must be doing something right."

"We do all right," he said, pointing to a puddle of hydraulic fluid and then to an alternate route to the next airplane. "But we can't go on like this."

Flight Lessons 4: Leadership & Command

"What's Major Honable like as a commander?" I asked. "We've known each other since we were lieutenants."

"The major is tops in my book, sir. He stays out of our way and lets us do our jobs. He's a real hands-off kind of officer. Wish more of you commanders were just like him. Sir."

"Most commanders aren't like that?" I asked.

"They are not," he said. "Due respect, sir. But most you pilots like to meddle in things you don't know a thing about and that just slows down us guys who do the real work. You see, Major Honable was a navigator. He knows how to let the people who do the work, do the work."

"I think the world of him," I said. "I heard you got the MC rate up to 60 percent, that's fantastic. I also heard the wing is asking for another 5 percent. Can you guys do a 65 percent MC rate?"

"Hell no," he said. "Sir we could barely hold our own against the Air Force average for E-models. We are undermanned by ten percent. We turn over faster than they do in the U.S. which means we have fewer fully qualified techs. I'm surprised as hell we got it up to 60 percent. Sixty-five? No way."

Senior Master Sergeant Freeman introduced me to another senior master sergeant and we repeated the tour in the next hangar with the same stories. I declined a third tour and opted instead to have another sit down with Mark.

"So how are things?" I asked.

"Things are okay," he said. "Everyone is working hard and we'll get the job done."

"I have to tell you, Mark, that your hangars are filthy. There are loose tools lying around, fluids of all kinds, wires, spare parts. You guys need to clean up now and then."

"No time," he said. "We're too busy to clean."

"You guys going to get to 65 percent?" I asked.

"Yeah," he said. "We'll figure some way to do that. It's not like we have any choice."

"You always have a choice," I said.

"You might, Eddie, but I don't," he said. "I'm in the military part of the Air Force. You might have heard about the military."

"Only rumors," I said.

The next day I was in my morning paperwork trance when I heard a knock at the door. "You want to fly or are you really happy glued to that desk?" Felix held a copy of the weekly flight schedule with several red lines through the coming weekend. "We got a nice juicy trip to Madrid, out Friday night, back Sunday night. It will give you a chance to spend time with Master Sergeant Queen before you make him the new first sergeant."

It was tempting. My marching orders to the troops were that I would fly as needed, but I preferred the weekends so I could attend to the business of running the squadron during the week. Felix, on the other hand, was cleared to fly as much as possible, but never when I was on the road. I did need some time with Sergeant Queen. Once Trenchard left, Queen would be the senior enlisted member of the squadron. But I was willing to pass Queen over to avoid another homesteading sergeant who ran his own fiefdom.

"Okay," I said. "I guess I could use some time away from all this glamor."

"You ready for some scuttlebutt?" he asked.

"Always," I said.

"Chief Trenchard is holding court whenever he gets a chance," he said. "He's listing the ways you are going to ruin the squadron and how you are going to regret sending him to Alaska."

"I suppose that's to be expected," I said. "Let him fume. He'll be gone in a week."

"But there's good news too," Felix said. "The C-20 engineers have been avoiding him and spending their office time in the C-20 flight room. The CT-43 engineers are stuck with him, but you can tell they are counting the days before Trenchard is gone."

"So the flight commander system is working then?" I asked.

"Too soon to tell, boss. But things are looking up. Especially in C-21 Country."

"The young kids are pretty resilient," I said.

"That's another thing," he said. "Major Marc Stück reported in to the C-21 flight commander."

"Major Stück reported in to Captain Irish?" I asked.

"He sure did. You know when we put his name on the board people were calling him Major Stuck."

"Easy mistake," I said. "Those umlauts can throw most Americans. The 'ooh' sound takes some getting used to."

"Maybe stateside but not here," he said. "You can't live in Germany for more than a week without being corrected. So, anyway, I made them stop."

"Good call," I said. "He is a major, after all. We should try to pronounce his name correctly."

"That's the thing, Eddie. Major Stück pronounces his own name 'stuck' and seemed a little hurt when I called him Stück."

"Wow, so I guess he's Major Stuck after all," I said. "So go find Stück or Stuck and educate him on how reporting in for duty works. I want to meet him."

"Already done," Felix said. "He'll be in later today."

Later had to wait for the weekly wing staff meeting. I took my normal seat behind and to the right of Colonel Wozniak, taking up the right flank to my two fellow operations group squadron commanders. After the customary reports from each group commander, General Paulson asked for one final slide.

OTTO

	lates / sorties
C-130s	12 / 15
C-9s	3 / 6
C-20s	3 / 14
C-21s	6 / 32
CT-43s	0 / 2

"Get used to this one because you are going to see a lot of it," he said. "Big things are coming and we have to pull together as a team. Do you know what 'OTTO' means?"

"On time take offs," a few offered.

"Yes," he said. "OTTOs are the most important metric we have at this wing. OTTOs are the best way to gauge if we are succeeding as a team. It isn't just the pilot. Everyone on this base has a hand at making these numbers better than what they are. And these numbers right here are terrible." He shifted his eyes to his left and looked everyone in the eye, in turn. The room fell silent as he made eye contact with all thirty or forty of us. When his eyes completed the sweep they fell on mine, then Maggie's, then Art's. They stayed on Art.

"Colonel Johnson," he finally said, ending the silence. "We might as well list the number of times your airplanes were on time instead of late. How did you manage to have 12 lates out of 15 in just one week?"

"No excuses sir," he said. "We are going to do better."

"That's right," Paulson said. "We are going to do better. Any questions? Then let's get to work."

I returned to the squadron where I could see a plump major sitting in my outer office, holding a C-21 flight manual and looking blankly at Susan as she typed. As I entered he stood but remained silent. Susan got up and instead of introducing the major, walked to the side door. "Coffee, Colonel Haskel?"

"Yes, please," I said. It appeared she was at odds with the new major's name too. I knew it was rude, but I wanted to hear it for myself. "Who are you?" I asked.

"Ah, I'm Major Stuck, sir," he said.

"I see," I said. "Come on in, let's talk." He followed me in. "Take a seat."

"Which one?" he asked.

"Whichever one you like," I said.

"Which would you like me to take?" he asked. I stared at him, wordlessly. He took the closest seat.

"Tell me about yourself," I said. "Tell me about pilot training, Learjet school, and everything in between."

"There's not much to tell," he said.

"Humor me," I said.

He spoke nervously but managed to relate the last fifteen years of his life in about the same detail as I read in his personnel file. He learned to fly the T-37 and T-38 in Oklahoma, went to C-130 copilot school in Arkansas where he remained for his first tour. He eventually made it to the left seat just before getting sent to another C-130 squadron in Georgia. After five years he was sent to Australia as a C-130 liaison officer and was promoted to major. After four years down under he volunteered for and was selected to fly the C-21 in Germany.

"You've never been an instructor," I said. "Why is that?"

"Well, sir, I just got busy with other things," he said. "The needs of the Air Force meant I had to go to a staff job in Australia."

"That must have been fun," I said.

"It was," he said.

"Did you learn a lot?" I asked.

"Learn?" he said. "What do you mean?"

"Never mind," I said. "I hope you figured out that you are only our fourth field grader. We very much need you to step up to the plate and take on a leadership role. Can you do that for me?"

"Ah, I think so sir," he said. "But I really need to concentrate on getting checked out first." He held up his flight manual. "But once I get checked out I will do whatever you need me to do, sir."

I dismissed him and picked up his personnel record. He wasn't what I wanted in a major, but he seemed to be what I had expected. I thumbed through his records until I found what I wanted. He started his Air Force career in 1980, just a year after me. He was trapped in the same year group as Mark Honable and was a year junior in age, two or more years junior in rank. I dropped his records on Susan's desk.

"You're going to need those," she said. "General Paulson wants his promotion recommendation in three weeks and Colonel Wozniak wants it in two." I retrieved his records and put them with Mark Honable's. I had some writing to do.

It wasn't my first trip to Madrid but it was my first with more than a few hours on the ground. The crew was unfailingly polite as they waited for me to order my first beer before they ordered any beer at all. After my second beer the alcohol shyness evaporated. It was a good time to introduce the concept of the post flight critique.

"So let's talk about today's flight," I said. "Everyone gets a chance to critique themselves and to comment on what others have to say. I'll go first. I was a little late on starting my descent so we got rushed during the transition through 10,000 feet. But things seemed to be in control by the time we started the approach. So I'll have to keep an eye on that in the future."

Nobody had a comment about my critique and everyone seemed to manage a self-critique that generated some discussion. The flight engineer had the most interesting critique. "I don't really understand what's going on with the engine oil, sir. One day it's fine, one day it's several pints low. No rhyme or reason."

Sergeant Crosby was an avionics specialist by initial training but had cross-trained into airframe structures to become a crew chief. He didn't have a lot of experience with engines. "These engines tend to burn more oil on trainers than on longer flights at altitude," I said. "Can that explain it?"

"I don't know, sir," he said. "The Gulfstream mechanics take care of it at home so I never service the engines after a trainer. But I can tell you that short flight, long flight doesn't seem to matter. We flew just an hour to Spain and burned a pint of oil on the left engine and nothing on the right. I flew to the states last week on the same bird and burned about the same. But when we came back we burned three a side."

I promised to look into the case of the unpredictable oil consumption and we ended our first night's dinner and critique. The next day we decided that we all wanted to visit the Museo del Aire, or perhaps I decided that we all wanted to visit it. Having flown with the two pilot, one engineer, one radio operator, and one flight attendant crew for a while, I knew crews tended to break into officer and enlisted components. But everyone appeared to be interested in the city's museum of flight, especially the radio operator.

"Do you recognize this plane, sir?" Master Sergeant Steve Queen asked.

Flight Lessons 4: Leadership & Command

"The sign says it is a Vilanova Acedo," I answered. "Never heard of it."

"That's because it is really a Blériot," he said.

"French?" I guessed.

"Yes, sir," he said. Steve spoke at length of the airplane's history and seemed to know more about aviation history than I ever did.

"Are the other radio operators into airplane history too?" I asked.

"Not really," he said. "But now that we share an office with the pilots and engineers I think they are starting to."

"How is that working out?" I asked.

"It upset everyone immediately," he said. "But now that we got everyone moved around I think they are starting to understand the advantages. I'm starting to get to know the pilots better and I think the radio operators are doing better with the sterile cockpit rule."

"Was that a problem before?" I asked.

"It was," he said. "And it sort of still is. But I think getting to hear the pilots talk about these things in the office makes us understand better what you pilots go through."

"Aren't you upset that you now report to a captain flight commander instead of a lieutenant colonel squadron commander?" I asked.

"That will hurt on my effectiveness report, I have to admit," he said. "But it makes the squadron operate better so it is worth the price."

"I would like you to be my first sergeant," I said. "It sounds like you have what it takes. You want the job?"

"That would be great, sir," he said. "I won't let you down."

"I know you won't," I said.

We got back Sunday night and were met by our civilian maintenance team, three technicians from Gulfstream Aerospace, based in Savannah, Georgia. The passengers didn't ask for any meals to or from Madrid and our cabin clean up went quickly. In just fifteen minutes everyone was done with the aircraft and I presented the airplane's logbook to Mr. Bobby Chambers, the lead mechanic.

"Would you mind if Sergeant Crosby and I watched you check the engine oils?" I asked.

"Not at all, sir," he said. "But you will have to wait. We only check them exactly 30 minutes after engine shutdown."

"Why is that?" I asked.

"Because the oil has to drain from the top of the engine!" Sergeant Crosby said. "That makes total sense!"

"You got it," Chambers said. "It can impact the final reading by as much as three pints."

After we got the readings, Sergeant Crosby returned to the squadron and I followed Chambers into our hangar, where another Gulfstream sat on jacks. "Are we doing a tire change?" I asked.

"New sneakers on the inboards," he said. "We try to stagger the changes so you never find yourself on four tires needing a change at the same time."

I wandered under the wing and from the nose to the tail. I divided my scan between my eye level to avoid walking into anything, and the spotless white floor. "Do your guys ever spill anything on this beautiful floor?" I asked.

"Sometimes," he said. "But when that happens we stop everything and everyone until it is mopped up."

"Why 'everything and everyone'?" I asked.

"Because it doesn't help anything or anyone if somebody slips and falls," he said. "I can't stand a messy shop. I won't put up with it."

Major Honable's promotion recommendation was easier to write than I had feared. It would have been better if I could have included some kind of innovation that he brought to his squadron to improve production, efficiency, or safety. But he insisted all of that was done by his sergeants. But he had managed to increase the mission capable rate a few percentage points in his first year and then another five percent in the last few months. It was now the highest for any E-model in the active duty Air Force. That was good for a sentence.

Major Stück's promotion recommendation, on the other hand, sat on my desk, mocking me. I took almost as much pride in my writing skills as my flying skills, but still it sat. Untouched. I needed more time.

Flight Lessons 4: Leadership & Command

I knew our Monday Operations Group meeting would be consumed with OTTO and I memorized the nine reasons my late takeoff rate was unchanged from the previous week. Unchanged, another word for unimproved. Colonel Wozniak began the meeting by reminding me that I only had a week to go on Stück's recommendation; I promised to have it on time. That done, the rest of the meeting was consumed with OTTO.

"Nice job, Maggie and Eddie," he said as he read from his notes. I looked down to my own notes just to be sure: nine lates.

"We're getting better. Art, your guys got better too, but better than really bad isn't much to brag about."

"No, sir, it isn't," Art agreed.

"Six lates out of ten sorties is better but you got to get it to under 50 percent in the next two days, Art," he said.

"We're trying, sir," he said. "The maintenance squadron just put two of their top mechanics into the hospital. They were undermanned before, now they are really undermanned."

"Was anyone seriously hurt?" Wozniak asked.

"Yes sir," Art said. "A mechanic slipped on a patch of engine oil and tripped into another mechanic. The first mechanic broke his wrist and the second got shoved into a landing gear door. It looks like he's going to lose an eye."

Wozniak flipped through the pages of his notebook, looking for any unchecked items. "Eddie," he said, checking another item. "The general approved a change to the base noise regulations. Effective immediately, the C-21 is allowed to land at all hours of the night. If we don't get any complaints in the next 90 days, he'll consider allowing takeoffs too."

"Great," I said. "I'm not sure we need the takeoff approval, but allowing landings will help our workload, overnights, and scheduling."

We left the meeting and spread to the wind, but not before Maggie caught up with me on my way to the parking lot. "Why the look after being congratulated for improving your OTTO?" she asked.

"That's the thing," I said. "We didn't improve at all. We had nine lates last week, and nine lates this week."

"I saw the printout," she said. "It shows you cut your rate in half."

"But I didn't," I said.

"Well Mayhem is in charge of the report," she said. "I guess those fighter pilots aren't so good at math."

I spent the rest of the day watching our civilian C-21 maintenance teams doing post flight checks on four airplanes. Each mechanic was dressed in white coveralls and followed printed checklists for each task. The difference between our civilians and Honable's military mechanics was stark. It was an unfair comparison, of course. The C-130s were older than most of my pilots. Our C-21s were almost new and simply built. Unlike our Gulfstreams, just about everything on the Learjet could be done without a ladder. I was peering into an access door of a C-21's left engine nacelle when I heard my name.

"Colonel Haskel, we knew you couldn't resist joining C-21 Country!" Captain Irish said. "But we would rather have you as a pilot than a mechanic."

I accepted the rag he offered and cleaned the oil off my hands. I waved at the real Learjet mechanic who waved back. "Thanks for the offer, Alan. I'll think about it. How are things in C-21 Country?"

"We are doing pretty well," he said. "We have two new copilots, two upgrading to aircraft commander, and pretty soon one to instructor. So our training department is busy."

"How are those copilots doing?" I asked.

"Major Hammer is great!" he said. "He learns quickly and I've never seen someone attack our lesson book so hard. He's only been here a week, has already flown twice, and I bet he's going to set the land speed record for checkout."

"What about the other one?" I asked.

"Oh, him," he said. "Well, lieutenant major is the flip side of the coin. He hasn't even started on the lesson book. His ground training is really going slowly."

"You said lieutenant major," I interrupted. "We're talking about Major Stück, right?"

Alan's face turned beet red. "I'm sorry, sir. I shouldn't be calling him that. It's just that he is really timid for a major and reminds everyone of a brand new second lieutenant. The guys started calling him that a few days ago.

Colonel Henderson told us to stop and we are trying to. But it's hard to kill a name like that."

"No need to apologize," I said. "Let me know if his training gets worse."

"Yes, sir," he said. We entered the squadron and Captain Irish seemed to be grateful when I wished him a *guten tag* and turned into my office.

I sat at my desk and looked at the two personnel records and two promotion recommendations. One for a major failing while commanding a very large squadron and the other for failing at being a copilot. I respected the former and was growing to loathe the latter. I opened my notebook to a fresh sheet of paper and started to write.

James Albright

Flight Lesson: Delegating Leadership

A delegating leader relies on the abilities and shared goals of subordinates in the organization to achieve understood objectives. While often considered a leadership ideal, it requires ideal conditions and subordinates to achieve.

Delegating Leadership Defined

del•e•gate

- entrust (a task or responsibility) to another person, typically one who is less senior than oneself

- send or authorize (someone) to do something as a representative

The Advantages of Delegating Leadership

A delegating leader empowers followers to operate autonomously and can encourage them to do things as they think best in the long run. The leader's workload can be significantly reduced and administrative burdens can be significantly eased.

Delegating leadership works best where the mission is unchanging, and the followers are fully capable and willing to accomplish the task with minimal supervision.

The Pitfalls of Delegating Leadership

A delegating leader risks failing to meet organizational goals if those goals are not perfectly understood or supported.

A delegating leader relies on the abilities and intentions of subordinates and if those abilities fail to measure up, the leader may not have the feedback needed in time to make changes. Subordinate leaders may not be willing to make the same commitments to realize organizational goals, since they do not have as much at stake.

A delegating leader can easily lose touch with subordinates and fail to understand a quick changing situation has made earlier assumptions invalid.

5: Go Along to Get Along
September and October, 1995

C-9A in Pisa, Italy (Photo: Piergiuliano Chesi)

"This might work out," I said to Lenny after checking in with Ramstein Tower. We held our position as the C-9 aeromedical airplane took the runway in front of us. The conflict only dawned on me as I saw them approach the runway the same time we did, both vying for the same on time takeoff.

"Maybe we should stagger our takeoff times with the rest of the wing," Lenny said. "Why make life hard when it can be easy?"

"I will do that," I said. "That's a common-sense solution." It shouldn't have been a problem, but the C-9 was a little late and so were we. The schedule said 0800 but we didn't make it to the runway until 0810. In another five minutes, we would be officially late.

"There she goes," Lenny said as the C-9 started to accelerate. "Sandra Jennings is in the left seat and this is her fini flight. Her next flight will be with American Airlines. We were dating, but we knew that would come to an end after she leaves."

The "fini" flight is an Air Force ritual, reserved for a pilot's last flight in a squadron. Seems we lose more pilots to the airlines than to other Air Force squadrons. I let Lenny's personal life story drop while getting ready for my right seat duties on our way to a secret runway on the island of Cyprus. We were flying down empty to pick up film canisters from a U-2 spy plane scheduled to land minutes after us. We would then fly the film to London for processing. The film of recent Bosnian troop movements was vital to NATO's next steps in the burgeoning war that had officially already ended. Of course none of that mattered to us. We had built in an hour of buffer in the timing and taking off at 0800 minus five, plus fifteen only mattered to the OTTO-nuts at the wing.

"Aborting!" I heard on the radio. I looked down the runway and saw a cloud of black smoke from the C-9's thrust reversers. "We blew a tire," a female voice announced. "We can clear the runway but somebody needs to do a sweep."

"Roger that," the tower said. "Runway operations on the way."

"Good thing we don't have any pax, sir," Lenny said.

"I suppose," I said. I looked at the clock at my right knee and realized OTTO would have another victim today. The C-9 trainer would be a cancelled trip due to maintenance but not an OTTO casualty. Our C-20 operational mission would be classified as a late takeoff, even without passengers and even if our timing with the film canisters was perfect.

The runway sweepers found three tire fragments and at 0823 we were headed for Crete. "The U-2 is target outbound," Master Sergeant Steven Queen said from the radio operator's station. "They should be ten minutes early so our timing is excellent."

"Remind me again about the logistics," I said. The flight engineer unstrapped and gave up his seat to Sergeant Queen, who stowed the seat and knelt behind the throttle quadrant while holding a map of the secret air base's runway.

"We are to pull off on this taxiway," he said while pointing to a patch of asphalt south of the runway at its eastern end. "We wait, with engines running. The U-2 lands and shuts down. They say it will take a few minutes to get the film and a truck will drive it directly to us."

"With our engines running we need to take some precautions," I said.

"I already told them that everyone on their team needs to de-FOD prior to approaching our airplane," he said.

"Nice," I said. "This isn't your first rodeo, eh, Steve."

"No sir," he said.

The Foreign Object Damage program, simply known as FOD, was nothing more than a poster found around most flight lines in the Air Force. Other than pilots, few crewmembers gave it a second thought. I had thought a radio operator would have needed a reminder. But it appeared Master Sergeant Queen wasn't just any radio operator.

While we took off 23 minutes late under the OTTO program, we landed 37 minutes earlier than the operation required. The U-2 landed 10 minutes earlier so we ended up 10 minutes early on our way to London. My radio duties eased considerably as we left Swiss airspace giving me time to replay the events of the morning in my head. "Why is Sandra separating?" I asked Lenny. "Has she always been a future airline pilot in the making?"

"Anything but!" Lenny said. "Her dad and her granddad were both career Army. She always wanted to fly but the Army couldn't guarantee her a fixed-wing, so she went Air Force instead. As long as I've known her she wanted to be a career Air Force officer."

"So why . . . ?" I started to say, but then stopped. Perhaps it was none of my business.

"That's something I wish everyone in the wing could hear," he said. "I'm not sure I should be talking about her behind her back like this."

"I understand," I said. He gave the cockpit another sweep with his eyes and then looked blankly forward. He wanted to talk, it was just a matter of finding the right trigger. "It's a shame she's leaving the Air Force," I continued. "But that's water under the bridge and I am sure she'll have a great career with American. I wonder what we can do to make things better for the pilots who haven't gotten to that point yet. If something chases you out, Lenny, what could I have done to change things?"

"Oh, no sir," he said. "I'm perfectly happy flying this airplane, for this squadron, here at Ramstein. I wasn't so sure a year ago, but now that, well. You know, HTSS."

"I don't know what that is," I said.

"Well, we had a lot of it a year ago," he said with a sideways grin. "Haney Traumatic Stress Syndrome. We didn't have to deal with him a lot in the C-20, but you never knew what was going to upset him so you learned to avoid the squadron if you knew he was in town."

"I knew Colonel Haney at Andrews," I said. "I am getting to know Colonel Cairns here. The two are nothing alike."

"That's true," he said. "But they have a different set of problems in the Aeromedical Squadron. Sandra was pretty gung ho a year ago when she upgraded to aircraft commander. She was always talking about upgrading to instructor, getting promoted to major, and maybe someday becoming a squadron commander. She's done all the right things, and she's a great pilot. I thought she would have been a good Air Force recruiting model."

"So what went wrong?" I asked. Vienna Center asked us to contact Munich and I busied myself with my radio chores. In a few minutes we were cleared to a new altitude and new course and I thought my question was left behind in Austria. But it was clear Lenny was rehearsing an answer.

"I think she lost to the good ol' boys in the squadron," he said. "The top three instructor pilots there run the show and the squadron commander doesn't want to upset the status quo. When it came time to upgrade the next instructor, Sandra was next in line and got passed over."

"Maybe she wasn't as good as someone junior to her," I said. "That has to sting when someone junior gets the nod, but we don't do everything based on seniority. As I recall, you were upgraded ahead of your peers."

"That's true," he said. "But the guy they upgraded busted his initial check ride and doesn't lift a finger around the squadron. Sandra has never busted a check ride, ever. She's the squadron safety officer. But the squadron commander refused to nominate her for safety school or any advanced officer schools. Sandra wasn't going to get promoted the way things were going."

"Does she get along with Colonel Cairns?" I asked.

"Not really," he said. "She never talked about her when Cairns was the director of operations. Sandra upgraded to aircraft commander about a year before Cairns became the squadron commander. Sandra's records went to the last quarterly upgrade panel and everyone thought she was a shoo-in. When she didn't make it she thought maybe a career in flight safety would be another way to go. But Cairns said there were no available safety school slots. A month later we sent Tommy Mendéz and the month after that the C-130 squadron got a slot too. That's when Sandra put in her papers."

"Do you see that kind of favoritism in our squadron?" I asked.

"I did," he said. "But things seem to be changing for the better."

"If you see anything worth mentioning, please tell me," I said.

"I will, sir," he said with a grin.

Flight Lessons 4: Leadership & Command

"You want my opinion?" Felix asked.

"Always," I said.

"You are going to make the most folks happiest with Eric Stumm," he said. "He's been around for a while, he's got more C-20 IP time than anyone in the squadron, and it frees up the flight commander position for others to move up. You are always talking about developing leaders, Eddie. Besides, if there was a vote, Eric would win hands down."

"It's not a vote," I said.

"I know," he said. "You have the only vote that counts. I'm just saying picking Eric gets the job done, shows people there is upward mobility, and improves morale."

"The position is ADO," I said. "As the Director of Operations, you should have the most to say about who is the Assistant Director of Operations. I just want to make sure it is someone who can credibly do your job in your absence. This young officer is going to represent you and me and we need to make sure he can wear that role responsibly. I don't see Captain Stumm commanding anyone's respect."

"Fair point," he said. "Who, then?"

"What about Major Hammer?" I asked.

"He's not an IP," Felix said. "He's only been an aircraft commander for a week. The ink is hardly dry on his upgrade orders."

"An ADO is an officer and leader first," I said. "He'll be an IP soon enough."

"This is going to upset the squadron instructor community," he said. "But Mike Hammer can be a hammer, no doubt about it. I think this might work."

"What about these other upgrades?" I asked. "How did we come up with this list?"

"I sat down with the instructors from each aircraft type," he said. "It was a consensus. Then you added a name and removed two others."

"You fought with me on one of those," I said. "I agreed to 'unremove' him."

"That you did," he said. "All things considered we got ourselves a good list."

"Do you think we overlooked anyone just because they aren't a part of the 'in crowd' or are we playing favorites with anyone because they are?" I asked.

"I think you overthink things, Eddie," he said. "We got a good upgrade list here. I'm half surprised you didn't put Mike Hammer on this list."

"I thought about it," I said. "How's our other major working out?"

"Major Stück is stuck in copilot upgrade hell," Felix said. "He's slow rolling the program. He refuses to fly more than once a week because he needs a week to prepare for the next lesson. Every instructor he flies with says he's impossible to teach and after trying to motivate him a few times I'm starting to think they're right."

"How many rides has he had?" I asked.

"Next ride will be number sixteen," he said. "That's double the average and he's still not ready."

"Tell him I'm considering sending him over to the command post and having flight records pull his wings," I said.

"Seriously?" Felix asked.

"I haven't done it yet," I admitted. "But I'll do it in two weeks if I don't hear that he has passed a C-21 copilot check."

"You got it," Felix said.

That night, *The Lovely Mrs. Haskel* regaled me about our son's new best friend in school, a young lad by the name of Ian Stück. "They have so much in common and his mother is a doll. And, did I mention this? His father is a pilot!"

"I know," I said. "He's an unqualified pilot, but we're working on changing that."

Later that night I spent an hour in front of a blank promotion recommendation form and Major Stück's record folder alongside my laptop. I had managed to cull together eight lines of what would have earned me a "Piffle of the Week" award at the Pentagon. The lines were exaggerations bordering on falsifications of course, designed to make Mrs. Stück proud of her boy but could not be defended in a court of law. And still line number nine sat empty, mocking my lack of eloquence.

"What's wrong," *The Lovely Mrs. Haskel* asked after chasing the children to bed.

Flight Lessons 4: Leadership & Command

"Writer's block," I said.

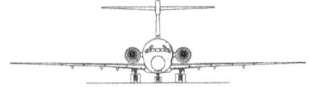

"You've got me scheduled for two hours," I said to Susan. "Nothing around here is worth two hours."

"The quarterly upgrade panel always takes at least two hours," she said. "And if you don't get moving, you are going to be late."

I turned to face the door only to see Captain Fitzpatrick with her scheduling book. "Can you take a call for me, sir?" she asked. "Believe it or not, it's the White House." She pointed at a blinking light on the phone on Susan's desk. I picked up the phone and punched the button.

"Lieutenant Colonel Haskel," I said.

"Are you the squadron commander of the CT-43 we've got going from Senegal to Monrovia this morning?"

"Please identify yourself before I answer," I said.

"This is Major General Johnstone of the White House Military Office, that's who this is!" he said. "Now explain to me why your goddamn pilot is refusing to move on a White House mission!"

"Standby just a minute, general," I said. I pulled the phone from my ear to squelch his angry reaction. Rorie held out an intelligence report, dated that morning. It revealed that rebels had taken control of the airport and were boarding aircraft, killing all foreign passengers. The bottom of the message had Rorie's handwritten note that said, "Ashworth informed pax they cannot go, offered to fly on to next destination instead."

"General, have you seen the morning DIA intel brief on Liberia, date time group of today and 0314?" I asked.

"It's two in the morning here colonel," he said. "I just got a call from the Secretary of Commerce! Of course, I haven't seen that. Now I am still waiting for an explanation!"

"I'll read you the report, sir," I said. "It will clear everything up."

After I finished reading there was an "Oh," and a pause. "I see," he finally said. "Tell your pilot 'good job' and keep up the good work." The phone went dead.

I handed the message back to Rorie. "Tell David that the top Air Force general at the White House says good job and keep up the good work. Tell him that I knew he had what it takes to do the right thing."

Susan smiled and pointed to the clock. "You're late again," she said.

As I walked out the front door, Major Stück was walking in. He saluted without saying anything. "Major Stuck," I said, careful to use his preferred pronunciation. "I am almost done with your promotion recommendation but I don't have a thing about the last few months. I need you to write one line about your time in Germany so far."

"But I've just been in training, sir," he said.

"That's a problem of your own making," I said. "I need one line by close of business today. Did Colonel Henderson talk to you about your check out deadline?"

"Yes, sir," he said.

"So you've got the rest of today to give me a single sentence," I said. "And you've got the rest of this week to finish your training and next week to pass a check ride. If you don't, I predict your flying days will be at an end. Do you understand?"

"Yes, sir," he said, saluting. I returned the salute, and headed for the parking lot.

Driving north to the main base, I forced myself to stop thinking about Herr Stück, his son's favorite playmate, and *The Lovely Mrs. Haskel's* disappointment when she find outs I was plotting the cleverest ways of orchestrating his promotion pass over. My neurons needed to focus on pilot upgrades. The quarterly upgrade panel would be an opportunity for each squadron to sell those pilots worthy of the time and jet fuel to elevate from copilot to aircraft commander, and from aircraft commander to instructor pilot. The operations group would have the final blessing, but how could they possibly disagree with the squadron's commander? How indeed.

"It's come to our attention you've had two extra – ordinary upgrades, Eddie," Wozniak said as he started the meeting. "I don't mean extraordinary, I mean extra – ordinary, outside the ordinary process. Can you explain how Captains Knudson and Ashworth have gone from copilots to aircraft commanders without the formal blessing of this board?"

The "board" consisted of Colonel Wozniak, his lieutenant colonel assistant, and the three lieutenant colonel squadron commanders. In the back row of the conference room sat most of the operations group's evaluators, all of whom were captains and majors. It was highly unusual for the colonel to dress down a lieutenant colonel in front of so many lower grade officers. But there I was.

"It was a manning issue, sir," I said. "Both pilots have extensive instructor pilot experience in larger aircraft and, in my view, their upgrades were long overdue."

Wozniak cast me a doubtful eye until Dillon May raised a hand just enough to catch Wozniak's attention. "Eddie mentioned this to me and I have to agree the upgrades were needed. We've made upgrade decisions like this in the past and I also agree these were both highly qualified candidates and the upgrades were fully justified."

"Okay then," Wozniak said. "Let's see if we can be more complete today so we won't have to do these extra – ordinary measures in the future."

In the next two hours, we got all of our planned upgrades approved and the only remaining controversy was a lack of upgrade candidates in the aeromedical squadron. "We had it all planned out," Maggie Cairns complained, "but our best laid plans were shot to hell when we had three pilots put in their papers at the same time."

"You got three more who just signed in," Wozniak said. "So at least you are even."

"I lost two instructors and an aircraft commander," she said. "I'm replacing those with three copilots. Not much of a trade, if you ask me."

"Things are going to get worse," Dillon May interrupted. "Your latest batch of effectiveness reports just got kicked back. If you don't write good ERs, your people don't get promoted. If your people don't get promoted, the rest of your people aren't going to stick around."

"Noted," she said. It was a touch of sarcasm I had never seen from her before, but perhaps justified. May, who had come to my rescue, seemed equally ready to allow her to drown.

"Speaking of reports," Wozniak said, "Eddie you still owe us one for the upcoming lieutenant colonel's board."

"Tomorrow morning for sure," I said.

"Okay we're done here then," Wozniak said. We all rose until he left the room and the majors and captains remained in place until it appeared we lieutenant colonels were no longer standing at attention. I left my seat and headed directly for Mayhem, until I felt a tug at my sleeve.

"Care to spend some time with a fellow beleaguered squadron commander?" Maggie asked.

"Absolutely," I said. "But I need to have a word with Mayhem first."

I freed myself from her clutches and caught up with Dillon May before he found the exit. "Thanks for the assist, wingman," I said.

"Anytime, Eddie," he said. "You and Woz weren't here at the last upgrade panel when Clevis refused to upgrade any of his pilots. It was the first time in anyone's memory that had ever happened. We told him he was courting trouble, but he wouldn't budge. You did good with your audibles."

"Audibles?" I asked.

"You aren't much of a football fan, are you?" he asked.

"No," I admitted.

"Football, the best training there is for a squadron commander," he said. "Once you've learned a good head fake, you can do anything."

He turned to leave and I turned to face Maggie. "Word on the street is you are offering redacted copies of your top ten ERs," she said. "I need an emergency dose, stat."

"You aeromedical types are always on the critical list," I said. "I'll have them for you whenever you can drop by."

"An hour from now?" she asked.

"Sure," I said. "Between you and me, I think my pilot retention problem could be worse than yours. I don't know if I can blame anyone for jumping ship. Their chances for promotion are slim, the quality of the next assignment is doubtful, and the airlines will double their salaries. I almost feel I am doing them a disservice by trying to talk them out of it."

"I don't know if there is anything we can do, Eddie," she said. "I try to run a democracy with as few constraints as possible. If I have to make a military decision I usually figure out how to put it up for a vote. That way they at least know they had a say in the matter. There is only so much we can do."

"Why do you think your last three left you?" I asked.

"The airlines," she said.

Flight Lessons 4: Leadership & Command

"Nobody even considered the Air Force as a career?" I asked.

She thought for a bit while wagging her head in the negative. But then she reversed herself. "We did have one who could have been a lifer, but she was impatient. I kept telling her good things would come but she had to wait. I can't upgrade everyone as soon as they want. I can't send everyone to the high demand schools because there are only so many slots. She just got hired by American."

"I want to send a few guys to squadron officer's school," I said. "What are my odds?"

"Ain't going to happen," she said. "Those slots are reserved for the warfighters. Plus the group commander and wing commander are both part of the 130 mafia. What chance have we got?"

I returned to my office where Susan was wearing a frown that only meant disappointment and "now what do we do?" I marched in front of her desk and she handed me a yellow steno pad with a single sentence written in the block case of a terrorist's letter bomb, as if from a writer familiar enough with the English language but unpracticed in its written execution.

WORKING HARD TO MASTER THE C-21 LEARJET.

"Add it to my draft," I said. "Just as written."

"You're kidding," she said. "Please tell me you're kidding."

"Nope," I said. I retreated to my desk and typed out a memo on squadron letterhead, addressed to General Paulson. "I do not believe Major Stück should be promoted. It is my opinion that the needs of the Air Force would be best served by promoting any other candidate."

Susan came in with the finished promotion recommendation and placed it on the center of my desk. I placed my memo to its left and Honable's recommendation to the right. I stared at the three for a few minutes.

"You look as unhappy as I've ever seen you," I heard. I looked up to see Felix with a suitcase in one hand and clipboard in the other. "I'm off on a trip and thought I would give you some good news."

"I could use it," I said.

"Stück finished his training this morning," he said. "We put him up for his check on Friday."

"Good," I said. "Please read this and tell me what you think."

Felix took Stück's promotion recommendation and my memo and studied both. He remained expressionless until the last line of the promotion recommendation. His eyes lit up after reading the memo. "Eddie, you can't do this."

"I know," I said. "But I think it's the right thing to do."

"It isn't up to a squadron commander to torpedo one of his own," Felix said. "You are supposed to give him your best possible recommendation and leave the hatchet job up to the wing commander."

"I know," I said again. "But Paulson doesn't know Stück. Even with that last line in there, if Paulson recommends promotion Stück will get promoted and a more deserving officer will get passed over. I can't let that happen."

"I've heard your spiel on integrity enough times to know I can't talk you out of this," he said. "But you need to consider the damage this is going to do to your reputation with the wing, and that in the end is going to hurt the squadron."

"I hadn't considered that," I said. "I'm glad I asked you."

"That's why I'm here," he said. "But now I need to leave."

I studied Mark Honable's recommendation anew. It was a strong recommendation and might be worthy of a promotion even without Paulson's backing. But the odds were long. The wing commander had three majors eligible for promotion to lieutenant colonel but could add "definitely promote" to only one of the recommendations. Promotion boards rarely went against a wing commander's "definitely promote" and those with the "DP" were promoted at over a 99 percent rate. All other officers would get a "P" which meant "this officer should compete with all others for promotion" or a "DNP" which meant "Do not promote this officer, even if there is a vacancy." The promotion rate to lieutenant colonels with a "P" was less than a third. No officer with a DNP had ever been promoted. Mark needed that DP.

The next morning, I studied the previous week's OTTO report, knowing I would be called upon to explain one or more of the late takeoffs at the wing staff meeting. I needed to stop by Colonel Wozniak's office first to turn in Stück's promotion recommendation, with or without my memo. But my thoughts were on OTTO during a breakfast of cold cereal and strong coffee. We had a good week with only two late departures, both in the C-21. The first, from last week, was easily explainable. The most recent, from yesterday, was not. The morning trainer was delayed because the student copilot wanted to rebrief the takeoff procedure a third time. The major copilot pulled rank and refused the captain instructor's pleas to take off on time for the sake of OTTO. My decision was made. I stopped at Wozniak's secretary's desk and borrowed a stapler. I attached my memo on top of Stück's recommendation and headed for Lieutenant Colonel May's office.

"Dillon," I said, "here's Stück's promotion recommendation."

"Edward," he said, "why can't you call me by my call sign like everyone else does. I don't really like my given name."

"Okay," I said. "Mayhem, here's Stück's recommendation. This is going to cause some flak."

"Flak I can take," he said. "Thanks, Eddie. See you in a few."

I reversed course and found Mark Honable in his seat for the wing commander's staff meeting. "Here you go," I said. "I hope it does the trick." Mark read the nine lines. His frown turned to a smile around line three.

"Eddie I can't thank you enough," he said. "This is great."

"The game isn't over," I said. "Your group commander has to go to bat for you. You have a good record but it may not be good enough to get you promoted without a DP."

"That's probably right," Mark said. "But you've given me a good shot at it. My group commander is going to like this."

He reread the nine lines and I looked opposite the large conference table and noticed the operations group was missing one person. I patted Mark on the shoulder and took the long way around the table, shaking a few hands along the way.

"We need to talk after the meeting," Wozniak said from his seat at the table.

"Yes, sir," I said while taking my seat from behind and to his right. My fellow squadron commanders gave me a worried look while Mayhem shot me a thumbs up. Everyone around me stood at attention and I followed suit, seeing General Paulson enter. He had a broad smile and walked around his desk to shake hands with several of his group commanders, starting with

Colonel Wozniak.

"Guten tag," he said to the group, to which he received a "guten tag" from just about everyone seated. The usual slides took up the first forty minutes of the meeting, a steady flow of predictable data that could only portend the crescendo to come.

OTTO	
C-130s	4 / 10
C-9s	2 / 7
C-20s	0 / 11
C-21s	2 / 27
CT-43s	0 / 2
	lates / sorties

The all-important slide came up and the wing staff gasped at its beauty. "That's what it all comes to!" Paulson said to some polite applause. "If this wing puts its mind to doing something, that something gets done! When Paul Paulson set out this goal, I knew there were doubters. But look what we can do when we put our minds to it!" More applause.

"Woz, good job," he continued. "But don't anyone here think this was just the result of a pilot pressing some buttons at the right time. There was a mechanic turning a wrench. There was a pay clerk cutting a check. There was a driver delivering a part. This was a team effort. So applause is good. But you all deserve the applause." He stood and clapped, aiming his praise at each corner of the room. He sat down and the applause ebbed once he raised a hand. "But we aren't done yet. I see some zeroes up there but we aren't going to stop pressing until every line has a zero. So let's examine one late per aircraft and see what we can do to make things even better."

He started with the C-130 and picked a delay from Thursday, a case where the daily air land mission was delayed by three hours because the aircraft's flaps wouldn't extend after engine start. I knew from our earlier ops group meeting the spare aircraft came in late the night before with shrapnel damage to its rudder after receiving small arms fire in Sarajevo. It was the perfect excuse, if there ever was one.

"No excuses sir," Art Johnson said when asked. "The spare was broken too but we should have gotten both aircraft mission capable overnight in time for the launch. We'll fix that."

"Good," Paulson said. "All these solutions are within our grasp. We just need to grasp them!" He clenched both hands for emphasis and there were nods around the table.

He also picked a delay from Thursday for the C-9 example. I glanced over to Maggie's notepad and saw both delays listed. The first line read, "pilot overslept." The second said, "flight nurse overslept."

"No excuses sir," she said. "We've identified a weak link in our scheduling system and will assign a person to verify the schedule with every crewmember the night before every flight, even the trainers."

"That's a start," Paulson said. "All it takes is for one bad actor to forget to set his alarm clock and the battle is lost. If it happens once, shame on the crewmember. If it happens twice, shame on us for letting it happen."

"Yes sir," she said. I could feel her trembling as she spoke.

"Now, on to Colonel Haskel," he said. "Last Thursday C-21 oh, oh, nine six was more than an hour late. Can you explain why the pilots delayed takeoff for more than an hour?"

"They thought it wise to not takeoff without their passengers," I said. The room erupted in laughter. Paulson's expression remained blank for about a second and then he too joined in with the laughter.

"Fair point," he said. He looked over to the Mission Support Group commander. "Heidi, let's get the word out to all our users that if the passengers aren't on time, they aren't going."

"Can do, sir," the colonel said.

General Paulson rose without a word and everyone stood at attention. As he left he looked at Wozniak and said, "come with me." Wozniak followed. As the rest of the staff left, many gave me a look that telegraphed they wanted to cast eyes on the squadron commander that would soon be gone.

I sat in Wozniak's office alone for about 30 minutes until Mayhem walked in and took a seat opposite mine. "That was pretty funny, Eddie," he said.

"In a sane world that would have gotten the message through that the entire OTTO concept is nuts. But we aren't in a sane world, are we?"

"No," I said. "I guess not."

"Don't worry about it," he said. "I think everyone except the most important one believes in you."

"Paulson?" I asked.

He looked at the door and then to me. "Woz," he said in a whisper. "If you anger Paulson, you are going to anger Woz." We heard Wozniak enter the outer office and in a flash he was behind his desk.

"You have a good talking to with Eddie, Mayhem?" he asked.

"Yes, sir," he said. "Eddie is suitably apologetic."

"Eddie, Eddie, Eddie," Wozniak said, shaking his head with each mention of my name. "What are we going to do with you? I originally wanted to talk to you about the memo you attached to Stück's promotion recommendation but now I've decided to let that go through. What I am wondering about now is the first thing you ever said to me about General Paulson. You said he was intense."

"Yes, sir," I said.

"Do you care to revise and amend those remarks?" he asked.

"How do you mean?" I asked in what may have been a too obvious stall for time. Was he looking for additional ammunition to hand my scalp to the general or was he looking out for his own defense?

"Well the general wants only the very best for this wing," he said. "We all share in this and we support him, of course. But all of us were taken by surprise by his, well, by his intensity, as you put it. But perhaps you could have done a better job of preparing us for what hit us."

"I've obviously had run-ins with him in the past," I said. "As the chief of safety at Andrews I often found myself working against his wishes. But he always seemed to flourish in a political environment and I was hoping that his focus would have shifted as a general officer."

"Has it?" Wozniak asked.

"I'm afraid not," I said.

"And what is his focus?" Wozniak asked.

Flight Lessons 4: Leadership & Command

"I don't know," I said. "He says he wants the wing to excel so that all its people can excel, but he has chosen a strange metric to demonstrate that. Whenever I've dealt with him in the past I a used a technique in prisoner of war school."

"You feel like you're a POW here?" Mayhem asked.

"No," I said. "I feel that my squadron is being held captive by a series of circumstances, all piling on top of each other. Before he showed up we had too much work without enough people, poor promotions, poor assignments, and not enough opportunity to advance within the wing. I think General Paulson thinks OTTO will change all that, but all it has really done is increase the work load. So we've gone from trying to do the best we can to trying to survive the onslaught using a POW's passive resistance."

"What do you mean by that?" Wozniak asked.

"When you are a POW you are powerless against your captors," I answered. "All you can do is do as they say, but in a way that makes it more difficult for them to the point where they figure you aren't worth the effort to harass and eventually they leave you alone."

"Who is doing the resisting?" Wozniak asked.

"And who is being resisted?" Mayhem added.

"I think that as subordinate commanders we need to carry out our orders," I said. "But we have to let the person doing the ordering know that the orders are going to break the wing before they achieve the end goal. So I think it is us, the commanders between the top commander and the troops that are doing the resisting."

"And that pits us against our boss," Wozniak said. "That is hardly the way the military is supposed to work. And your resistance in public is blatant insubordination."

"I didn't mean to embarrass the general," I said. "It was a case of my internal squelch failing. But I needed to illustrate the absurdity of OTTO when your operational mission is carrying passengers from Point A to Point B. An on-time takeoff for our business means being ready to go when the passenger is ready. Not before. I'll do a better job of checking my sarcasm in the future."

"See that you do," Colonel Wozniak said. "Dismissed."

I got up to leave, oblivious to my surroundings. I knew I had failed in my role as a commander but didn't know why I had allowed the failure in the first place. My "quip," to be charitable, may have been an effective technique in a verbal spar with a peer. But Wozniak was right, it was blatantly insubordinate. I made it to the parking lot, still unaware of the world around me to the point I was surprised by the hand that tugged at my shoulder.

"Don't be too hard on yourself," Mayhem said. "I was just as lost as Woz was until you mentioned passive resistance. That's exactly what this madhouse needs. The general is going to break us if he doesn't back down. You're doing the right thing; you just need to figure out a more subtle approach."

In one of my earlier squadrons we used to say that it was okay to screw up, as long as someone else screwed up in a more spectacular way soon thereafter. Lieutenant Colonel Maggie Cairn's screw up wasn't more spectacular but the circumstances may have had a more powerful impact. In the 7 days that followed, her squadron managed an impressive 6 late takeoffs out of 7 total sorties.

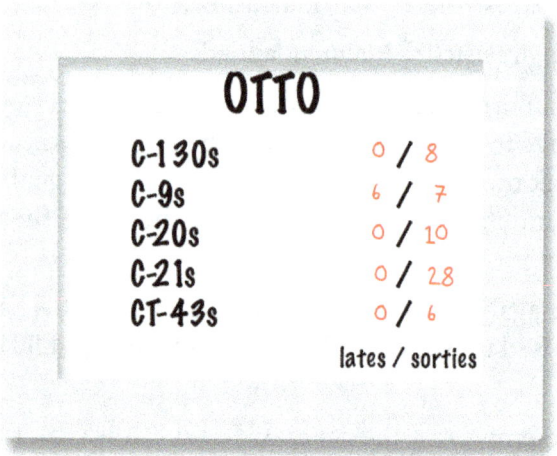

The rest of the wing managed to achieve Paulson's goal of zero late takeoffs. The staff braced itself for the onslaught to come. But Paulson looked at the slide, then to Wozniak, and then to Maggie. "Colonel Cairns, I need to speak to you after this."

A chill swept the room and the quiver in her meek, "Yes, sir," exposed a level of fear seldom heard in such a venue. If I could have qualified my emotions at the time I would say it was sympathy for a comrade. But that came to an end with Paulson's next words. "Colonel Haskel, I need to speak to you first."

Once the meeting was over, Maggie and I traded our side-by-side seats in the conference room for another pair in the general's outer office. She sat quietly, staring at her notepad with the circumstances behind each of the six late takeoffs. Most of them were within minutes of being on time. "That's not too bad," I said. "At least not in a sane world."

"Well this is only half of the problem," she said, pointing to the list of six. "By the time we got to yesterday we were batting zero for six. I was desperate to get at least one on time takeoff. It was a trainer to upgrade Captain Spicer to aircraft commander but he overslept. So I ordered them to takeoff without him. Now I have an IG complaint citing me for fraud, waste, and abuse."

"Spicer filed an IG complaint?" I asked.

"No, it was an enlisted member of the crew," she said. "They won't tell me who."

"It just seems so unfair," she said. "You were always the one spitting in the face of authority and always getting away with it. I always follow the rules. I give my people more latitude than I've seen any commander give and this is the way they thank me? Does that seem fair?"

General Paulson's secretary emerged from his office and spoke as if sending me to the gallows. "Colonel Haskel, the general will see you now."

I marched into the office, wondering if a salute was called for. He spoke before I had a chance to raise my right hand. "Do you know who the only person in the chain of command with the authority to issue a 'do not promote' is, Colonel?"

"The wing commander," I said.

"That's right," he said. "I know you think you are smarter than me and I suspect you probably think I secretly agree with you." I remained at attention. "But apparently you are the one with the case of stupid because you didn't think twice about writing 'do not promote' on your cover sheet. Have I got that right, Colonel?"

"I recommend you do not promote Major Stück, sir," I said. "That much is true."

"Is that your call to make?" he asked.

"No sir," I said. "It is my duty to recommend . . ."

"It is your duty to salute smartly and follow the letter of the regulation," he said. "Your recommendation is noted. Have your secretary give my secretary a copy of this on disk. Dismissed."

This time I saluted. He returned the salute and I withdrew. As I left the office the look on Maggie's eyes shook me back to reality. I hadn't realized that Paulson had been yelling.

Flight Lessons 4: Experience

Flight Lesson: Leadership by Consensus

A leader who seeks consensus above all else relies on the good intentions and shared goals of subordinates in the organization to achieve understood objectives.

Leadership by Consensus Defined

con•sen•sus

-   General agreement

The Advantages of Leadership by Consensus

A leader who achieves consensus before acting empowers followers to believe they have a stake in the operation; they can be then motivated to work hard to achieve those goals. The leader's workload can be significantly reduced and administrative burdens can be significantly eased as the team "buys in" on all decisions.

Leadership by consensus works best when tasks are routine, the expertise of the group is uniform, and tasks are unchanging.

The Pitfalls of Leadership by Consensus

Leaders who rely on consensus often fail in rapidly changing situations or at tasks that require difficult decisions or go beyond the group's collective experience. When a consensus leader is placed in a group of strong willed subordinates, the leader often becomes the led.

6: Team Ramstein
November, 1995

C-21A 840096 (Photo: Paul Nelhams)

My favorite part of every day began at 0700. By 0700 I was on my third cup of coffee, had completed my leisurely 20-minute drive to the base, and had settled behind my desk with a stack of things to do. Susan would rank order the stack by what she thought was important and I would alternate between trusting her judgment or doing a brand new rack and stack of my own. Since the morning trainers never took off before 0800, the only exceptions to this Monday through Friday routine was when I was flying or when one of our VIP's needed to launch obscenely early. But in the last few weeks a new exception made its presence known every Monday.

"We got a late C-21 in the works," Felix said over the phone.

"Details, please," I said.

"They were scheduled to depart for Zagreb five minutes ago," he said. "If they don't make it off the ground in ten minutes they are officially late. And get this, they aren't flying any passengers. They are waiting for a load of blood from the hospital."

"Isn't this a weekly run?" I asked.

"Yeah," he said. "You want them to launch anyway? I got the pilots on the radio."

"No," I said. "That would be silly."

"This is the third time in two months we've been late because of a late blood shipment.," he said. "Maybe we should launch just to teach them a lesson."

"Have them wait," I said. "I'll visit the hospital squadron commander. Maybe we can work something out."

Almost two hours later I drove to the Operations Group headquarters for our weekly meeting but got stopped at the edge of the taxiway as a C-130 limped into its parking spot. The nose was peppered with bullet holes and the windshield in front of the pilot was completely obliterated by the spider-web patterns created by a very large bullet attempting and failing to penetrate bulletproof glass. Two teams of medics sprung from an awaiting van with litters as soon as the aircraft came to a halt. I completely forgot about my promise to fix the C-21 blood shipment issue as the hospital squadron's "go team" took care of what appeared to be two injured crewmembers.

The traffic guard allowed me to continue and I drove past the wounded airplane, thinking I recognized the pilot. Colonel Wozniak's car crossed my path going the other way, tempting me to reverse course in light of what would be a delayed meeting. But I didn't. I entered his office where Maggie and Mayhem stood at the window, watching the C-130 from the second story perch.

"It's Art," Maggie said. "They took some triple-A leaving Bosnia this morning. The navigator and a loadmaster were hit."

"So much for the airport being secured," I said. "Is Art okay?"

"That's him looking at the nose of the airplane," Mayhem said.

After 30 minutes of speculation, Colonel Wozniak returned to his office and filled us in. "Art is okay," he said. "He was in the left seat when they got hit, about two miles after takeoff and just over 1,000 feet above the terrain. The bullet-proof glass and Kevlar around the cockpit stopped all the bullets, but one of those pushed the Kevlar hard enough to get the navigator in the leg. The doc says it broke a blood vessel but it should heal on its own in a few weeks. The loadmaster got the same treatment to his abdomen. They are both doing fine."

"Is this going to stop Sarajevo operations?" I asked.

Flight Lessons 4: Leadership & Command

"Not a chance," Wozniak said. "The Kevlar worked. This is all a part of combat airlift."

"It's why we get paid the big bucks," Mayhem said.

The shattered windscreen made its way from Art's wounded bird to the wing staff meeting on Wednesday, where the "oohs and ahs" were only interrupted when Lieutenant Colonel Art Johnson entered the room. There was a single clap followed by another and soon everyone in the room was applauding him. The applause ended abruptly as General Paulson entered. Paulson made his way to Art and gave him a hearty handshake and a pat on the back.

General Paulson asked Art to give a blow-by-blow account of the flight, which took about 20 minutes. Paulson pontificated on what could only be called the C-130 version of "The Right Stuff" and that left only a few minutes for the regular slides. Paulson shot through the list until the last item on the agenda: OTTO.

OTTO

C-130s	5 / 8
C-9s	2 / 7
C-20s	0 / 9
C-21s	1 / 22
CT-43s	0 / 2
	lates / sorties

It wasn't a good week for most of the wing and I prepared myself for Paulson to glare down at Art, Maggie, and me, demanding an explanation from each of us for a late takeoff of his choosing. I had practiced a diplomatic answer for the late blood shipment, a way to cushion the blow against the hospital group commander, who was seated at the table at the end opposite Paulson. I planned to say the C-21 was waiting for cargo and leave it at that. If Paulson asked for more details, I would have no choice but to lay the blame on the hospital. I stole a glance at Colonel Wayne Hubbard, the Hospital Group Commander. He was a pudgy doctor wearing thick glasses, a receding hairline, and a worried look that one day he would have to speak in front of the wing staff. He would fumble about for an answer and then look behind to Major Linda Roslin, the hospital squadron commander, and demand an explanation. Although she was also a medical doctor, I could imagine her withering under Paulson's glare. But I needn't have worried.

"It's been a busy week," Paulson said, looking at the slide. "Paul Paulson realizes you are all working hard, but there is more work to do." He looked at the Operations Group row. "You got that?"

"Yes, sir," we said as one. Paulson got up and everyone came to attention. As he left I could hear Maggie's sigh of relief. Or maybe it was my own, but I was too busy making a beeline for the Hospital Group to be sure. Major Roslin was collecting a sheaf of papers from underneath her seat as I approached.

"Linda, we need to talk," I said. "I'm Eddie Haskel from the Learjet squadron."

"I know who you are, sir," she said. "We spend a lot of time in the meetings seeing you three get beat up, after all."

"Well I got lucky today," I said. "And so did you."

"Me?" she asked, freezing every limb and turning white. I pointed to the slide on the wall which still projected the week's OTTO and my squadron's "1 / 22" opposite the "C-21."

"If it weren't for the C-130 hit this week, Paulson would have asked each operations group squadron commander to explain one of the lates," I said. "I would have had no choice but to cite your squadron as the cause of this delay. This is the third or fourth time a shipment of blood didn't make it to the airplane on time."

"I don't know how to fix this, sir," she said. Her weary eyes told me she just wanted to get back to the hospital to get back to work.

"How about a tour of your squadron?" I asked. "Maybe I can learn something that will make it easier for us both."

We walked from the wing headquarters to the hospital. She explained that as a medical doctor, she divided her time between her staff responsibilities and seeing patients. I was familiar with the hospital but had never envisioned the inner workings of an Air Force squadron encapsulated within its walls. Her office was on the third floor and barely contained a desk, a file cabinet, and a grease pencil scheduling board. Her phone rang and she spoke quietly.

"I need to take care of something," she said. "I promise you I'll be back in ten minutes."

"Sure," I said. Looking at the board, I could see her doctors were doing 50-hour weeks on 10-hour shifts. She was doing the same 50-hours with an additional 10-hours for "admin." The nurses and technicians seemed to be equally taxed. The workload, as far as I could tell, was evenly distributed.

"Doctor Roslin?" I heard from the door. "Oh sorry, I was looking for Major Roslin."

"She said she'll be back in ten minutes," I said. "I won't be taking much more of her time."

"I was just dropping off some lab reports," the captain said. "I'll leave them on her desk." She was a nurse, I guessed, perhaps a few years older than Roslin. Where a pilot wears wings, Air Force doctors have a badge with a serpent climbing a staff. It's all Greek mythology, of course. A nurse has the same badge with the lantern of Florence Nightingale behind it.

"I'm from the operations group," I said. "I was just chatting with her about the workload around here."

"Crazy Ramstein," the nurse said. "We all wonder why we signed up for this."

"Yeah, me too," I said. "What's it like? Working for Major Roslin, I mean."

"She's the best," she said. "She pulls the same shifts, works just as hard, and never pulls rank. I just hope she doesn't go insane with all that she has to do."

"Crazy Ramstein," I said. Roslin appeared at the door, the two exchanged what needed to be exchanged, and then returned to her desk.

"I'm sorry the blood was late," she said. "But I don't have time to think. It's all I can do just to keep up with patients."

"You are doing God's work here," I said. "I won't take much more of your time, but maybe if you show me where the blood comes from, we can come up with something." She nodded meekly at the added imposition but got up and led the way to the nearest elevator.

"The hospital keeps a staff on-call twenty-four-seven," she said as we descended to the first floor and entered the blood clinic. "But not everyone is qualified to handle blood. It is perishable and the lab here is stretched pretty thin just to keep two shifts going. The first person normally shows up at seven, except on days we have your blood shipment when they bring one person in at six."

"Why six?" I asked. "Or better yet, why does the blood need to be off the ground by seven?"

"I don't know," she said. "The other hospitals set the time they need it and I'm not about to question their requests. The lieutenant in charge of the blood lab is a competent officer and a team player. We are all team players in this squadron. Isn't that the way it is supposed to work?"

"Sure," I said. "But we are all part of a larger team too. How about if we just schedule the weekly shipment one hour later?" I asked. "If the people on the receiving end are okay with that, we can take the pressure off your schedule and my pilots."

"Can we do that?" she asked.

"With the stroke of a pen," I said. "Give me the names and numbers of the people depending on the blood and maybe we can make this entire problem go away."

"Good news, bad news, sir," Captain Irish said as I returned to the squadron.

"Dealer's choice," I said.

"The good news is the Zagreb Hospital doesn't care when they get the blood," he said. "They just need it on Monday. So we agreed to slip the delivery one hour."

"Great!" I said.

"Bad news is that we took major flak from yesterday's two-star trip," he said. "We scheduled a non-instructor just as we planned and the general was pissed he couldn't fly the jet. Colonel Wozniak wants a call, ASAP."

"Don't worry about it," I said. "It was my decision, I'll deal with it." I threw myself at my desk chair and looked at the phone. When I first saw the hot button marked "86 OG/CC" I thought it was funny. It was the line to the Kremlin, the line to NORAD, the Bat Phone in Commissioner Gordon's office. I punched the button.

"I heard you denied Major General Vance the left seat of a C-21 yesterday," Colonel Wozniak said with all the irritation that was possible to shove through a phone line. "I apologized on your behalf and assured him that wouldn't happen again."

"He's never been trained," I said. "We agreed to grandfather the USAFE commander, the numbered Air Force commander, and the wing commander. Everyone else needs to go to school first."

"He's a decorated fighter pilot, for God's sake!" Wozniak said. "We agreed that if the general officer is in the chain of command and if you have an instructor in the right seat, we are good to go."

"That's not what I remember," I said. "But if that's the way it is, we'll pair him with an instructor in the future."

"Good, General Vance is on the board again next week," he said. There was a pause, almost as if he was expecting more pushback. "One more thing. Are you familiar with the tradition of the 'Airlifter's Ball,' Eddie?"

"No, sir," I said.

"Well get familiar," he said. "The wing is working awfully hard and we could use an opportunity to blow off some steam. You have the only hangar on base that isn't filled with broken airplanes. I want you to host an Airlifter's Ball at the end of the month. Make it a good one."

"Yes, sir," I said.

As pecking orders go, the path to delegation in a flying squadron always goes through the second in command. Felix did not disappoint. "I have just the man for the job," he said. "Tommy has been bugging me for something to do. This will teach him to be careful what he wishes for."

"Mendéz?" I asked. "This is a pretty big job."

"He'll handle it," Felix said. "I can guarantee it."

"How is it that he has any free time at all?" I asked. "He just got back from safety school plus he's an instructor pilot, right?"

"C-21 Country is running like a Swiss watch, Eddie," Felix said. "Ever since we gave them the biggest office in the squadron and took them away from the big airplane flight commanders, they have things running real smooth. They have more instructors and aircraft commanders than ever before, and, with one exception, the copilots are doing great too."

"Stück?" I asked.

"Stuck," Felix said. "Herr Stück may be finally qualified, but he's still Major

Stuck to the rest of the squadron."

My standing orders to the schedulers was to use me once a week on a trainer, but only on days free of other meetings. During those trainers, I would only steal enough stick time to keep legally proficient. I would volunteer for the worst weekend trips without hesitation. But they should avoid using me during the week if it involved an overnight. I had long ago vowed that if I ever became a squadron commander, I wouldn't be one that stole all the best trips and hogged all the flying time. So far, I was living up to my promises.

For this weekend we had three legs, with Friday night in Bucharest and Saturday night in Prague. I gave both legs to Captain Knudson and flew us home, Sunday night. The weather was poor intermittent-terrible and a problem with the instrument landing system meant I had to fly a PAR, or precision approach radar. The controller issued gentle turn and pitch instructions and, in theory, I would precisely fly those until we found ourselves with a runway in front of us.

"Going further left of course," the controller said as we descended through a thousand feet. "Turn right heading one, one, zero."

"Small bank corrections, sir," Captain Knudson said from the right seat. It was humiliating. The controller and the captain were telling me how to fly. But he had a good point: five degrees of bank, not ten.

"Correcting to course, on glide path," the controller said. Calm down, I thought to myself. Keep the pitch right where it is.

"Turn left zero, nine, five," the controller said. Two degrees of bank, not five, I reminded myself. "On course, on glide path," the controller said. "Over the landing threshold," he added.

"Runway in sight," Knudson said. I landed.

"Nice approach," Knudson said as I exited the runway.

"Not really," I said. "But your instruction was spot on."

"You might be a little rusty, sir," he said. "You should fly more often."

I sat in my office the next morning, reliving the approach. Was I a pilot or a commander? Why couldn't I be both? Susan's stack beckoned me from the bout of self-pity and I immersed myself in paperwork until there was a knock at the door.

"You have a meeting to go to," Felix said. I looked at the clock, it was 0830.

"Thanks," I said.

"You notice something different about this Monday?" he asked.

"No," I said.

"The blood shipment was on time," he said. "Showed up at precisely 0730 and they made it off the ground at precisely 0800. How about that!"

"Indeed!" I said. Thoughts of bank angles and PAR controllers evaporated and I showed up at the group staff meeting reenergized. Wozniak was also in good spirits until his normal list of topics was exhausted.

"What do you think about flying a C-20 into Sarajevo," he asked.

"Not much," I said. "We don't have any armor, any detection equipment, and none of us have been trained in air combat tactics."

"That ain't the half of it," Art Johnson interrupted. He delivered a beautiful soliloquy on the foolhardiness of sending anything but a combat airplane into Sarajevo under the current threat situation and appeared to be getting angry at the thought.

"I defer to the expert," I said. "Bad idea."

"No argument from me," Wozniak said. "But members of Congress want to visit and the only one to do that so far lost his lunch all over the flight engineer last week."

"It took us all of the next day to clean the cockpit," Art said. "Funny what a ten-degree descent into a nest of surface-to-air missiles can do to a congressman."

"I believe that Congressman was pretty upset about the way he was treated," Wozniak said. "Imagine his disgust at such non-VIP conditions! Well, Eddie, the question is going to come up so you might as well get smart on the subject."

Every Air Force intelligence officer I've ever met has the same aura of dire consequence about him. Every statement is meant to alarm. Every photo is meant to sensationalize. They have critical information that is of the highest national importance. And if we listened carefully, maybe we could learn something important.

Major S. Kowalski was no different. I had arranged the meeting with the two members of the squadron with the best combat airlift training, both from flying low level missions in big airplanes. Felix Henderson's experience was in a C-130 and Kyle Knudson's in a C-141. We sat behind a table as Kowalski fumbled with a projector remote.

SA-6 "Gainful" surface-to-air missile (Department of Defense photo)

"Sir, we have the highest-level confirmation of the presence of this bad boy right off the eastern edge of the Sarajevo airport," he said. "The SA-6, code name 'Gainful' is not the biggest SAM out there, but it is big enough to ruin your day. It can reach you up to 7,000 feet and has a range of 20 kilometers. It is radar guided and has a likelihood of kill score of point seven."

"How does it do low to the horizon?" Knudson asked.

"Good question, captain," the major said. "It doesn't do so well since it has a low power radar. But the system is mobile, so we can't count on it staying on the eastern side of the runway. Your best bet is to stay high, and if you must go low, do so very quickly."

"Going low is kind of a requirement when you land," Felix said.

"You guys are landing in Sarajevo?" Major Kowalski asked.

"And taking off too," I said. "I hope."

"What kind of airplane did you say, sir?" He asked.

"C-20," I said.

"You know," Knudson added. "The blue and white pretty ones with the winglets."

"The VIP birds?" he asked.

"Yeah," Knudson answered.

The major looked at me and shook his head. "Due respect, sir," he said. "That's nuts."

I spent the next day translating "that's nuts" into a classified eighteen-page report, complete with SAM threat envelopes and geographic threat areas. I only came up for air for our weekly squadron staff meeting where the flight commanders revealed plans to capitalize on our recent blood run scheduling victories.

"We found six regular passengers who were not only willing but fully supportive of shifting their departure times," Rory Fitzpatrick said. "In fact, a few of them said they had wanted to do that but figured we couldn't change anything, since we've always done it this way."

She went on to reveal a plan to withhold training schedules until the day prior to allow instructors to tailor their flights to capitalize on weather and projected runway closures. "That's ingenious," I said.

"We put together a planning team to take things even farther," she said. "We can make allowances for the needs of crewmembers on any particular day. If we can avoid making a pilot or flight engineer have to jump through hoops for day care, as an example, we can better ensure they'll make it for the flight on time."

"What about maintenance?" I asked.

"Sir?" she said.

"If you shift your takeoff times unpredictably you are asking for trouble," I said. "Now you have each crewmember and the mechanics having to remember what the time for the next day will be. If you have a predictable takeoff time, you remove doubt."

"We hadn't considered that, sir," she said.

"I like the idea of adjusting for known variables outside our control," I said. "That is just brilliant. Why spool everyone up for the normal 0800 launch when you know the runway won't be free of snow until 0900? But let's not adjust flight schedules for day care."

"Yes, sir," she said. "I guess the team got carried away with this."

"The team did good," I said. "Keep it up, please."

We were blessed with good weather for Major General Vance's flight to and from Naples, Italy. He listened carefully to the instructor pilot's cues and flew the airplane conservatively, as if afraid he might break something. When he returned to his office he called to say Captain Irish had done a great job. "He's a fine young man," the general said before hanging up. "I look forward to more flights with your squadron."

I reported as much to Wozniak who wasn't as pleased as I predicted. "See, Eddie," he said. "There was nothing to worry about. We lost a lot of style points over this. And it was all about nothing."

That was Friday. By Monday I knew my squadron had a good week and I also knew the other squadrons were doing well. We didn't want to talk about it, in fear of jinxing the effort. But as we closed the books on Tuesday, everyone in the operations group knew we had done it. General Paulson kept his poker face during the Wednesday staff meeting, even to the seconds just before the big reveal.

OTTO

C-130s	0 / 9
C-9s	0 / 5
C-20s	0 / 9
C-21s	0 / 25
CT-43s	0 / 2
	lates / sorties

I think there may have been a gasp. But the silence lasted no more than a second. The applause took over immediately.

"That's how it's done!" Paulson said. "I want everyone to stand up and shake the hand of the person next to you, and the person next to them. This was a team effort. This shows what Team Ramstein can do!"

I saw pure joy in many of the faces that came by to shake our hands in the

Flight Lessons 4: Leadership & Command

Operations Group, but I think each of us squadron commanders knew this week's victory would be followed by future defeats. We had been lucky this week; the schedule was light. Most of the C-130 combat flights were grounded by bad weather in Bosnia and that gave them time to fix what was broken. But it was nice to chalk up a win for the first time.

At the end of the meeting, Paulson looked over to our corner. "Woz, I need to see you and Colonel Haskel." He got up, we stood at attention, and I followed Colonel Wozniak who followed General Paulson. The two spoke quietly as I brought up the rear. In his office, I recognized my classified report on his desk. The general gestured for us to sit as he sat.

"Good report, Colonel," he said. "It is clear, unequivocal, and does more to illustrate why it is we need combat airlift for this war than anything written so far. But not every commander in the Air Force understands combat airlift the way we do. The Chief and I had a long talk about your report yesterday." He thumbed through the report as I ran through the possible commanders who could be called, "The Chief." There was the Chief of Staff of the Air Force (CSAF), the Commander of the Joint Chiefs of Staff (CJCS), and the Commander in Chief of the United States Air Forces in Europe (CINCUSAFE).

"Ben and I go way back," he continued. Ah, General Benjamin Tyson, CINCUSAFE. "Ben is a big picture guy, just like me. I gave him our concerns and he agrees with us. But he needs to factor in all sides of the argument. So he wants to hear it from you, Colonel Haskel, and you alone. So you go see him tomorrow at 0900. Do this alone and make us proud."

"Yes, general," I said.

"Dismissed," he said.

As we walked out of the wing headquarters side of the building I followed Wozniak to his office, assuming he would have more to say to me. "Well," he said as we got to his office. "You know what to do. Let me know how it goes."

I returned to the squadron thinking about SAM threat envelopes, electronic counter measures, and fuel tank fire suppression systems. They were all topics outside my area of expertise and something CINCUSAFE was sure to be well versed about. I thought about convening my team of combat airlift experts to help prep me for the meeting, but General Paulson was clear about doing this "alone." I handed the classified document folder to Susan and finally noticed the three officers waiting for my return.

"Wow," I said, "what a crowd. Colonel Henderson, Major Roslin, and Captain Mendéz. Shall we do this alphabetically, by rank, or should we honor our guest first?"

"Tommy and I are here to talk about the Airlifter's Ball," Felix said. "We can circle round back here in thirty minutes. In fact, since this isn't the whole team, it'll give us time to collect the rest of the 'Airlifter's Ball Working Group.' We got your table covered with Tommy's plans, if you don't mind."

"Not at all," I said. "See you in thirty."

I escorted Major Roslin to the table opposite my desk and gestured for her to sit. "Thank you, sir," she said. "Congratulations on the perfect OTTO week. I just got my signed promotion recommendation and was hoping you would read it, and maybe offer some career counseling."

The irony hit me instantly. Looking at her promotion recommendation meant I will have seen all three. By regulation, they were to be written by the wing commander personally and viewed only by him, the promotion board, and the individual officer. I wrote two and was about to view the third. She handed the single sheet complete with her name, the nine lines of text, General Paulson's signature, and the box marked "P" for "promote."

"Who wrote this?" I asked.

"I did," she said. "The group commander asked me to, he handed it in as I wrote it, and it looks like the wing commander signed it as I wrote it. I know that's not the way it is supposed to work."

"I'm afraid to say that is the way it works for most of us," I said. "I'm sure you know about the odds of a 'DP' versus a 'P' on the top line."

"Yes, sir," she said. "Statistically I'm down to 33 percent. I'm pretty worried about this, as you can tell. My group commander says I'm almost a shoo-in because I have a command billet. That's not that common for a major, is it?"

"It isn't," I said. "I also think the fact you are a medical doctor should count for a lot, but I don't know that it does. If this was a pilot's recommendation, I would say you are doomed. The content isn't written with the necessary style to get the promotion board's attention." She diverted her eyes downward. "But you aren't a pilot and that's a good thing. We need good doctors and that has to count for something."

"The Air Force is run by pilots," she said. "Won't they protect their own?"

"Pilots?" I asked. "No, we eat our own!" She laughed. "In my opinion you should have got the 'DP' and that would have got you promoted. The fact you didn't get the 'DP' means we can't predict this. But I wouldn't get your hopes up. Do you have a Plan B?"

"Plan B?" she asked. "There's always the second board."

"Your chances of promotion on the second board are very small," I said. "Don't count out promotion just yet, you might be promoted. But if I were you, I would start to consider civilian options."

"But that would mean I failed as an officer," she said.

"No it doesn't," I said. "Did Uncle Sam pay for med school?"

"Yes," she said.

"Have you finished your commitment?" I asked.

"Yes," she said.

"Well then, you should be proud of what you have accomplished," I said. "You have made a difference for your fellow men and women in uniform. If you get promoted, life is going to get tougher with bigger and more exciting challenges as a lieutenant colonel. But guess what? If you don't get promoted, life is going to get tougher with bigger and more exciting challenges as a civilian."

She smiled and offered her hand, which I shook. "That's the first honest thing anyone has said to me about promotion," she said. "If I get promoted, I owe you a beer. If I don't get promoted, I still owe you a beer."

After she left I sat at my desk and wondered about the decisions I had made unofficially on behalf of Mark Honable, my friend of nearly fifteen years, and officially on behalf of Marc Stück, the failing copilot under my command. The former is a fine officer who deserves promotion simply based on an outstanding service record, in spite of more recent failures due to an inability to lead. The latter is a lazy officer with no real accomplishments and a failing record in every cockpit he had ever touched. And now we had Linda Roslin. She appeared to be a well-liked doctor doing her best but failing to keep up because she couldn't elevate herself above being a team player in a team that needed leadership. Somehow I had gotten to know them better than the man making the only promotion decision that mattered, but my knowledge was of no use in the end.

I stood up to shake off the dread and noticed for the first time the overhead drawing of all three of our aircraft types flanking our largest hangar. It was to be a tribute to the squadron masquerading as an entry way for all who attended the Airlifter's Ball. I looked up to see Felix, Tommy, and a collection of others watching my gaze.

"I like it," I said. "We get to show off to the rest of the wing while hosting their party."

"Exactly," Felix said. "And that isn't all."

"We put together a team of people from each aircraft type and crew specialty in the squadron," Tommy said. "Sergeant Shields came up with a great idea." Tommy stepped to one side and Sergeant Shields came forward.

"Sir, we heard that most of these Airlifter's Balls use the cheapest catered food they can find," she said. "We can do so much better. We can cook everything from scratch and make it a meal to remember."

"Kelly that's great," I said. "But how many people are we talking about?"

"Three to four hundred," Tommy said.

"But we can do this," Sergeant Shields said. "It will just take a couple of days of prep. We want to do this, sir."

"We want this to be a first-class event," Tommy said.

"What's the biggest challenge going to be?" I asked.

"We have David handling that one, sir," Tommy said.

From behind the crowd, Captain Ashworth came forward. "It's going to be parking, sir."

"I hadn't thought of that," I said. "How do we fix it?"

"I've identified a contact in each squadron and with the base motor pool," he said. "We'll have bus service between each squadron and our hangar. Our flight engineers are putting together a designated driver service in case things get out of hand, alcohol-wise."

"We're serving alcohol?" I asked.

"By order of the group," Felix said. "I had the same thought, but Colonel Wozniak said you can't have an Airlifter's Ball without beer."

"You ever been to an Airlifter's Ball?" I asked.

"Never," Felix said. "In fact, I can't find anyone in our squadron who has.

Flight Lessons 4: Leadership & Command

The combat airlift squadron hosted one two years ago but we weren't invited. I spoke with Art Johnson. He said it was a great time."

"I've never been to one either, but I think we have ourselves a winner here," I said. "Okay, let's do this," I said. "Nice job, everyone."

It looked like a good plan, but something seemed to be missing. I wasn't a true "airlifter" in the strictest sense of the word and had no experience whatsoever with the concept of an airlifter's ball. But Tommy's team was diverse and we certainly had many pilots who could truly call themselves airlifters. Perhaps I was overthinking things, again.

As the commander of the United States Air Forces Europe, USAFE, General Benjamin Tyson wasn't a combatant commander. That is, he reported to the Air Force Chief of Staff and not to the Secretary of Defense. This meant he was more political than military. If his aim was to put non-combat aircraft into combat, the push was coming from the Congress. I sat in his outer office, reading the report I had written only a week ago that necessitated my presence.

General Tyson was a war hero of sorts, with half an air-to-air combat victory in the closing days of Vietnam, meaning he and another airplane shared in the actual shooting. He had a mix of command and staff jobs, all carried out with some level of distinction. But he had the misfortune of commanding the Air Force War College during the 1990 Gulf War, and missed out on an even higher level of distinction. Most of his experience was spent preparing for war and not actually fighting a war.

For a lieutenant colonel with one command assignment I had already had a full indoctrination into the four-star general mystique. I had flown with a number of them and spent many hours in the Pentagon either briefing or sitting in meetings with them, the highest level of military officers. Despite all that, I was surprised to be asked to visit General Tyson in his office. Lieutenant Colonels are a dime a dozen at a base with a headquarters staff.

"The general will see you now," his secretary reported.

"I read your report," he said after I entered and saluted. "You write very well, no doubt about that. But I need to hear your points face-to-face, colonel. I digest things better on that level."

"Yes, sir," I said. "We have confirmation of at least an SA-6 threat combined with rogue elements with small arms. Only half of the airport is under NATO control and the area along the approach path of both ends of the runway is under bad guy control. Our C-130s are armed with Kevlar, electronic counter measures, and chaff. The airplane is designed for high angle approaches and their crews are trained in air combat. None of that is true for my airplanes or crews."

"There is a surface to air threat, no doubt about it," he said. "But it is a low altitude threat. I know the risks, but I think those risks are manageable. But you need to consider this isn't the only threat out there. There are bigger threats and we need to be ready for them. How can we hope to face the bigger threats if we can't handle something like this?"

I didn't have an answer, so I didn't offer one. Of course, it was pure sophistry; his statements were true but had nothing to do with the question at hand. But it was, of course, a tool general officers were fond of using. The general sat back, behind his desk, and started to rock in his chair. I waited.

"Tell you what, Colonel," he said. "Why don't we put you on the next C-130 into Sarajevo so you can judge the risk for yourself?

"That would be great, General."

"It's settled then," he said. "You see for yourself before we make any decisions."

Flight Lesson: Teamwork Leadership

A teamwork leader relies on his or her skill in motivating a group of skilled followers to pool efforts and produce more as a collective than possible as individuals.

Teamwork Leadership Defined

tēm•werk

- The combined action of a group of people, especially when effective and efficient.

The Advantages of Teamwork Leadership

A teamwork leader empowers followers to contribute and use peer pressure from the group to prevent individuals from failing to help. The group's workload can be significantly reduced and the tasks at hand can be completed more quickly.

Teamwork leadership works best where the mission is clearly understood, individual team members get along, and the challenges are within the group's capability.

The Pitfalls of Teamwork Leadership

A teamwork leader risks ceding the leadership reins and group direction can be commandeered by a stronger informal leader. When the workload is high or the challenges require extraordinary efforts, the group can adopt an "it's impossible" mindset or the idea that producing the bare minimum will have to do.

7: Transformation

December, 1995

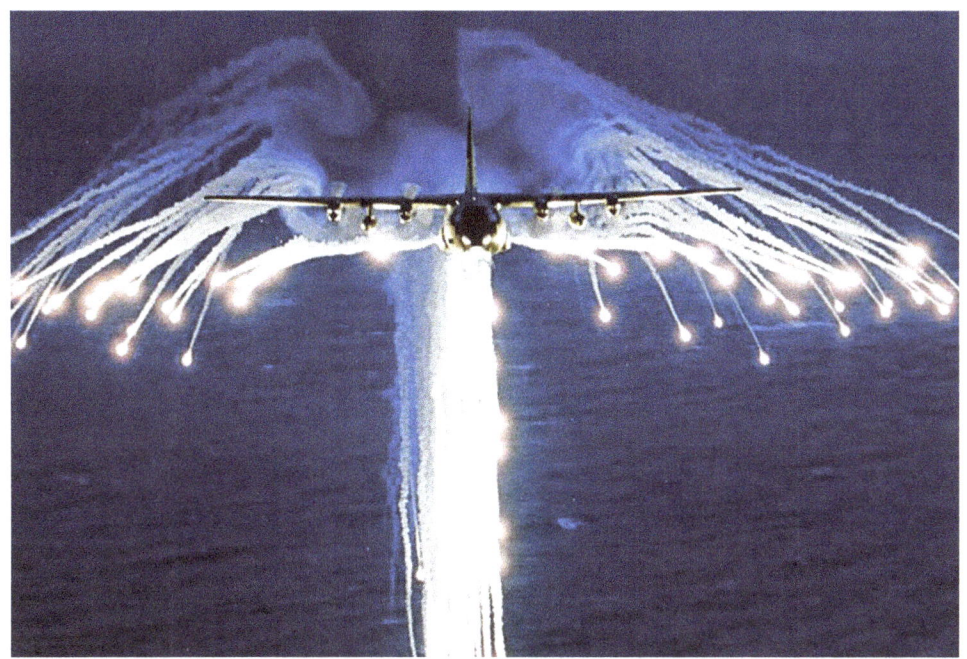

C-130 Angel Flares (Photo: Tidus Tia)

The airplane wasn't what I had expected on several counts. As soon as I entered the side door I realized I was in a combat aircraft. The interior walls appeared to be originally bare, covered only with pipes and electrical conduits. Kevlar blankets were stuffed behind these to line the walls, fastened with tape and baling wire. The predominant color was gray, accented only by the yellow and red of various cranks and pulleys. It reminded me more of a battleship bridge than an airplane cockpit. But the second sensation was size; it was cavernous compared to my bullet-nosed Gulfstream. The pilots greeted me cordially and invited me to sit in the jump seat to the left of the flight engineer and just behind the pilot. The engineer and I sat on raised seats that gave us an elevated view of the pilots below. I felt, for the first time in many years, that I was a part of military aviation.

"You're going to need these," the engineer said, handing me a headset with thick ear cups. I donned the headset in time to hear the pilot say, "turn one." The aircraft shuddered and a row of round dials came to life. It was at first like an un-tuned race car with half its pistons at odds with the other half. The C-130, of course, has four turbine engines. Each engine is a jet with a propeller attached up front. As the engine came to speed the noise turned more rhythmic, but the vibrations persisted. "Turn two," the pilot said. With each engine the noise amplified and the vibrations eased. "Turn three," gave rise to a harmonic that resonated in the back of my skull. This was a headache in the making, I thought. "Turn four." As the fourth engine came to speed, the dissonant harmonics ended but the noise continued.

The engine start and taxi out were slow motion repeats of what I grew up with, but each step brought back memories of the choreography required of a large crew. Halfway down the runway I was wondering how much more runway was needed. But the nose rotated with several thousand feet remaining and I looked down at my watch and said, aloud, "on time takeoff."

"Yes, sir," the pilot said. "We're getting better at OTTO." I realized my chatter over the hot intercom wasn't what the crew needed during a critical phase of flight and pushed the microphone away from my mouth.

We climbed at 190 knots indicated airspeed and once level at 19,000 feet seemed to settle in around that speed, plus or minus 20 knots. The pilot turned in his seat to face me. "Sir, we are going to head south to the western edge of the Adriatic before turning east. AWACS will identify us and then we'll do our pre-combat checks. Sergeant Towser will get you your flak vest and can answer any questions you might have. The 'co' and I will be pretty busy at that point."

"Don't worry about me, captain," I said. "I am just here to sit and learn." The engineer handed me the vest which was heavier than what I expected; it almost constrained my breathing. I looked around and noticed everyone in the flight crew was also wearing a flak vest. The navigator, seated to the right and furthest aft, was also wearing a helmet.

I could see the western shores of Italy slip below us and recognized Ancona, a city once famous for being Caesar's destination after crossing the Rubicon, but now known mostly for its seaport and airport. The wing dipped left and the nose dropped for our descent over the Adriatic.

"Pre-combat checklist," the pilot said over the interphone.

"Fuel vents," the engineer said.

"Roger," he answered. "Left wing first." I could see him extend his right leg and the airplane yawed to the right.

"Sir," the engineer tapped me on the shoulder. "We're putting the left wing into the wind to flush out any fuel in the vents. If we get hit with a missile or triple-A, we want those vents to be empty."

"Pilot, loadmaster. No more fuel spray left," I heard from the interphone.

"Roger," the pilot answered. "Right wing next." The pilot reversed his feet and the aircraft yawed to the left. I thought about the procedure and the fuel vents. Our Gulfstreams also had fuel vents in the wings. But any fuel trapped in them was miniscule compared to our total fuel.

"Sergeant Towser, what about the fuel in the fuel tanks themselves?" I asked the engineer. "Aren't they a bigger problem than the fuel vents?"

"No sir," he said. "Our fuel tanks are filled with fire suppressant foam. We can't hold as much fuel as other Hercs, but you can empty a machine gun into our fuel tanks and they won't ignite."

"Nice," I said.

"Pilot, loadmaster. No more fuel spray right." The pilot relaxed his legs and the aircraft returned to coordinated flight.

"Fuel vents completed," the engineer said. "Flares."

"We are in the flare safe zone," the navigator said.

"Colonel Haskel," the pilot said. "You're going to want to see this. Unstrap and look out the window here." I did as requested. "Activating flares," he continued.

Though it was almost noon, straight up, the flares lit up the sky behind us. "The Fourth of July," I said to the pilot.

"It is that," he answered. "More importantly, if we get any heat seekers, the flares will direct the missiles behind us."

"Behind us is good," I agreed. The remainder of the checklist exercised the electronic detection equipment and countermeasures. The E-3A Airborne Warning And Control System (AWACS) aircraft confirmed we were on course and cleared us into the combat zone.

"Feet dry," I heard from the interphone. I could see the Croatian coastline beneath us and the Bosnian mountain ranges nearing ahead. The altimeter stopped its rotation at 10,000 feet. "We'll stay here to stay above the SAMs for as long as we can," the pilot said. "Then it will be time to hold on to your stomach."

It was a cloudless day and the winter visibility was excellent. I peered forward through the massive windows and spotted the Sarajevo airport. The United Nations had installed a temporary Tactical Air Navigation system, known as a TACAN, and I could see the counters on the pilot's instruments countdown through 10 nautical miles, 9, then 8, then 7. "Here we go," the pilot said. He pulled the throttles aft and pushed the nose forward. The airport centered itself on his windscreen.

I did some quick math. The airport was around 1,700 feet elevation, call it 2,000 feet. So we had to lose 8,000 feet in 7 nautical miles, around a 12 degree descent. Was that possible? The deck angle of the airplane became uncomfortable and I could feel myself leaning in my shoulder straps. My feet fought for purchase on the metal deck. Passing 4,000 feet I could clearly make out half the runway, but only half. In another 1,000 feet I could make out the carcass of a crashed Russian airliner, its tail blocking the far half of the runway. With barely a few hundred feet to go, the pilot pulled back on the yoke, arresting our plummet. We touched down on the first brick of the runway and were stopped in just two thousand feet and change.

"The bad guys own that half of the runway," the engineer said, pointing to a hill to our right. "They have snipers just beyond that ridge and anyone who ventures past the Ilyushin wreckage gets shot, sure as day."

We pulled off to the left and I caught a glance of the famous Sarajevo airport tower, made internationally recognizable by the 1984 Olympics. It was now little more than half a tower, much of its façade torn away by bombs and small arms fire. We were the only aircraft and the tarmac was lined with tanks and armored personnel carriers. We taxied to a point beneath the tower and turned 180 degrees.

Sarajevo Airport Delivery, 1995 (USAF Photo, from a C-17)

Flight Lessons 4: Leadership & Command

"You want to see the offload, sir?" the engineer asked.

"Absolutely," I said. I followed him aft and down a few stairs to the cargo compartment in time to see the first pallet rolled down the ramp to an awaiting ground crew. Everyone was dressed in flak vests and helmets. The noise was unrelenting as our engines were still running. After the fifth and final pallet left the airplane the ramp started back up. I looked around for the flight engineer but he had gone. With nowhere else to go I wandered forward and managed to find the cockpit. As I climbed the stairs I caught the navigator with her flight suit leg rolled up, rubbing her right calf. It was more black than blue, but it didn't look good.

"You're the nav who got hit?" I asked.

"Yes, sir," she said. "It looks worse than it feels, but it does get sore." She lowered her flight suit leg and turned to face me. "I'm supposed to give you the once over on our eekums, sir. We got a few minutes before we takeoff, can we do that now?"

"Sure," I said. "What's an eekum?"

"Electronic counter measures," she said. She pointed to one of three radar scopes with her pen and tapped the glass over three flashing icons. "We are being watched by at least three bad guys here. When we flew in I noticed four other signals but each one came up just as we were passing. I didn't have to do anything other than let the automatic system do its thing."

"Did you notice anything on the day you got hit?" I asked.

"Nothing different than what I saw today, sir," she said. "That was triple-A, just someone with a big gun and his Mark-1 Eyeball."

"Let's hope he slept in today," I said. She gave me a half laugh. The flight engineer tapped me on the shoulder and pointed at the jump seat. As soon as I sat the aircraft jerked into motion. In a few moments we were airborne.

The flight home was anticlimactic and relaxed. The pilot got out of his seat and asked me if I saw what I needed to see. "I did," I said. "Thank you for the opportunity to see real pros at work. Please be careful, it looks dangerous."

"It's not so bad, sir," he said. "As you can see we take all the necessary precautions and we do things by the book."

"I can see that," I said. "Nice work."

"Can I ask you something, sir?" he asked.

"Sure," I said.

"Are you guys hiring?" he asked. "My C-130 commitment ends next year, I'm an instructor pilot with a good record and all my professional military education up to speed."

"How long you been with 37th?" I asked.

"Two years, sir," he said.

"Well, you give your current squadron the three years they are expecting," I said. "Give us a call about six months prior and we'll see what we can do."

"Thank you, sir!" he said. "I'll do that. I just hope half the squadron doesn't beat me to the punch."

As soon as he was back in his seat and strapped in, the flight engineer took off his headset and leaned toward me. I took my headset off. "Sir, I'd like to volunteer too."

"You might find our kind of flying pretty tame compared to this," I said.

"Everyone on base knows your squadron is the place to be," he said. "Good trips, good chances for promotion, and no beatings."

"Beatings?" I said, laughing. "It can't be that bad."

"It can be, sir," he said. "But if you don't mind, I'll send my resume over too."

"Looking forward to it," I said.

"What have we got?" I asked Felix the next morning. "I'll give you a complete recap about my flight into Sarajevo but right now I need to focus on the next meeting."

"That you do," he said. "We are nominating David Ashworth and Kyle Knudson for upgrade to instructor pilots."

"Good," I said.

"You can expect some pushback from the group," he said. "Both have less than a year as aircraft commanders but both are ready."

"When you say less than a year, you mean here in Germany," I said.

"Exactly," he said. "If you get any flak, just remind them that Ashworth has four years as an aircraft commander in the KC-135 and Knudson has at least that in the C-141. They were both instructors and graduated from formal instructor pilot schools."

"Got it," I said. "What do the flight commanders say?"

"These boys are ready," Felix said. "I know you don't like to hear about popularity votes, but if there was a popularity vote, each of these guys would be voted tops by their pilots, engineers, and flight attendants."

Suitably armed, I took my seat at the Quarterly Upgrade Panel where the only controversy was in the C-130 squadron. Every C-9, C-20, C-21, And CT-43 upgrade was approved without discussion. But the C-130 squadron didn't propose any upgrades at all.

"We are just too far behind on last quarter's upgrades," Art Johnson said. "We cut the number of trainers in half to keep the combat sorties going. You can't upgrade if you don't have trainers."

"You can't keep this up for long before you break your pilots," Mayhem said. "Your senior pilots get assignments and it takes time to grow aircraft commanders and instructors. This is not good."

"No argument from me," Art said. "But if you want two combat sorties a day and if you want every flight to takeoff on time, I can only put forth as many airplanes as maintenance can give me. So what's going to give? Combat airlift or OTTO?"

"Neither," Wozniak said. "Just do the best you can." He looked at the staff outside those of us seated at the table. "I think we are done here as an upgrade panel, thank you for your hard work. I need a moment with my squadron commanders." The rest of the staff filed out, leaving Art, Maggie, Mayhem and me at the table.

"Eddie," he said once the door was closed. "How did it go yesterday?"

"Very well, sir," I said. "Art's crew did a great job getting into and out of Sarajevo without scaring me too much. They really know what they are doing and I'm glad it's them and not me." Art laughed.

"Well now it's you," Wozniak said. "General Tyson has ordered we begin VIP airlift operations into Sarajevo and Paulson has directed that you do just that, starting next week."

"What?" Art said. "This is insane!" I didn't say anything and Wozniak held both hands out, palms down.

"I trust you can do this safely," Wozniak said.

"I can't guarantee safety," I said. "But if the United States Air Force as an institution has accepted the risk of losing a VIP in a non-combat airplane, we'll do that with as little risk as possible."

"Good," he said. "One other thing, Captain Mendéz did a great job yesterday. His briefing was very thorough and it sounds like this Airlifter's Ball is going to be one for the record books."

"He's pretty sharp," I said. "Are his plans in the direction you expected?"

"Spot on," Wozniak said.

Colonel Wozniak's approval for the Airlifter's Ball went a long way in calming my unease about the event. Perhaps it was just jitters over having the rest of the wing visit our ramp. I had certainly spent enough time on their ramps to know ours were from a different genre; immaculate inside and out. It was unfair, of course. We had newer aircraft and our maintenance budget was, for the most part, unlimited due to the funding for the VIP budget versus the combat airlift and aeromedical budgets. The C-130 squadron was all blue-suit, meaning all Air Force. Our maintenance was all civilian. The ball would be held in a hangar operated by Gulfstream Aerospace under the iron hand of retired Navy Chief Robert Chambers. We rarely had problems with our birds and whenever we did, he would say, "I'll handle it, colonel." And he always did.

"I'll handle it, colonel," he said when I stopped by that evening. "You Air Force boys need your parties just like we did in the Navy. I'll have every last bit of equipment stored in safe places so that hangar will be people friendly. We are ahead of our regular maintenance checks so we can hand the place over to the ladies three days early, just like they want."

I refrained from correcting "ladies," knowing he liked the term and rarely used it in front of our flight attendants, three of which were "gentlemen" and not ladies at all.

"I can always count on you, Robert," I said as I turned to leave. "I'll never get tired of telling you thanks."

Flight Lessons 4: Leadership & Command

"Today's goal is to see how steeply a Gulfstream III will descend without gaining speed," I said to the squadron's C-20 experts. "I've found this airplane descends best with gear, full flaps, and 170 knots, the flaps limiting speed. But I'm not sure this is the best solution."

"We should try speed brakes and maximum speed," Felix suggested. "We can dish it out at the end. That gets us to the runway soonest."

"But won't that increase our exposure at lower altitudes?" Knudson asked.

"The latest intel says the SAM threat is 20 kilometers from the runway on the approach end," I said. "We are looking for the steepest possible angle, but faster speed is better. I have a drawing from the intel shop. The threat envelope is wider than it is tall. The C-130 escapes most of it with a 12-degree angle. I've never seen a Gulfstream do that."

"It can't be done," Felix said. "But I got you and Kyle up for tomorrow's trainer at a quiet time in the pattern. The tower says you own the place for an hour."

"Perfect," I said. "Is there anything else we should consider testing tomorrow?" Their silence telegraphed all I needed to know. "Kyle, let's go over the flight profile later today. Felix, I just need a little refresher on what's going on with the Airlifter's Ball."

Everyone but Felix left and after thirty minutes he left too. I sat alone at my desk, thinking about jugglers. A skilled juggler can keep five balls in the air at all times while always knowing where each ball is to the point he or she could pick out a particular ball from the group. My air combat knowledge was on the rise, to be sure, but my knowledge of the squadron's other hot button topics was on the decline. I relied on Tommy Mendéz to keep the Airlifter's Ball on target, Felix Henderson to keep OTTO in check, Susan for all the effectiveness reports, Rorie Fitzpatrick for the schedule, John Halsey for the CT-43, Eric Stumm for the C-20s, and Alan Irish for the C-21s. So I had help. But what other balls did I have in the air that I was forgetting?

The next day Kyle Knudson and I flew six approaches to Ramstein while measuring the distances and altitudes during the descent and discovered the old Gulfstream pilot's rule of thumb – best angle comes from gear, full flaps, idle – was true and the best we could hope for was a 9-degree descent.

Descending with the speed brakes, which precluded the landing gear and limited the flaps to less than full, always resulted in a shallower angle.

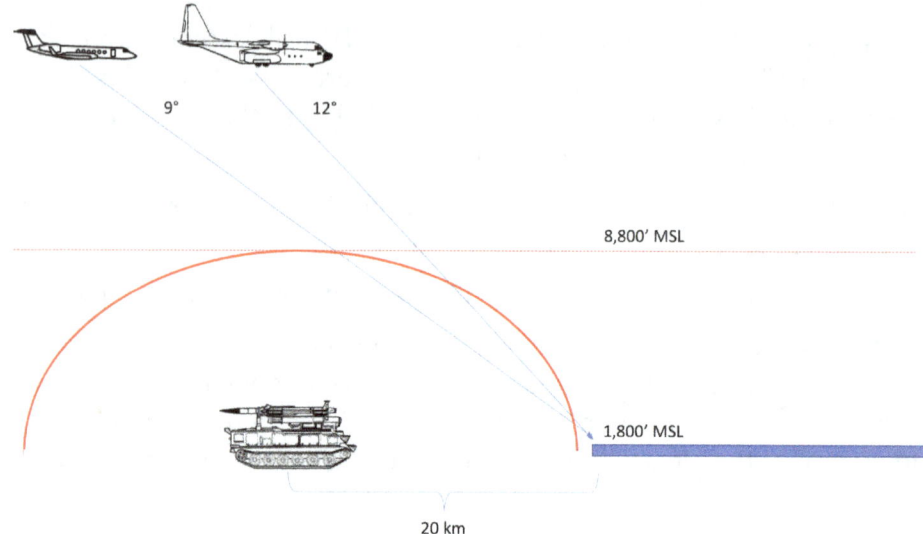

The C-20 and C-130 maximum descent rates compared

Our flight practice completed, we were scheduled for five consecutive days of classroom with the base intelligence shop, learning the local threat environment, escape and evasion techniques if shot down, requalifying on our 9-mm Beretta pistols, and memorizing local terrain maps. On the fourth day the mission was actually "fragged" – scheduled – for the day after the Airlifter's Ball. We were to pick up the U.S. Ambassador to the United Nations in Frankfurt, Germany, and fly her into Bosnia for a two hour visit before returning her to Frankfurt.

"Don't forget your blood chit," Art said the day before the trip and the morning of the Airlifter's Ball.

"What's a blood chit?" I asked.

"It's a lining for your jacket," he said. "If you are shot down and survive that, and you find a local and survive that, you can show them the chit and it will explain in all the local languages that the United States promises to reimburse them for helping you back to friendly territory. Welcome to the club, Eddie, you are now a warfighter."

Flight Lessons 4: Leadership & Command

Eddie's Blood Chit, the unclassified version (Eddie Photo)

We were issued our blood chits about 1500 and finished our last intel brief at 1600. I walked the route to our largest hangar at 1630 and was happy to see at least a C-20 and C-21 at the entrance, nose to nose. The CT-43 responded to a last-minute trip and was gone. The entrance to the hangar was suitably decked out and the sign below "86th Airlift Wing Airlifter's Ball" read, "Welcome to C-20, C-21, and CT-43 Country."

"Nice of the Learjet flight to add us to their nation," I said to Felix as I walked in.

"Those boys and girls are mighty generous," he said. "But wait till you see the spectacular job they did."

It was spectacular indeed. There was a large dance floor, tables and chairs throughout, and a very long table in the middle completely decked out with gourmet food. "I see shrimp, filet mignon, schnitzel, all sorts of brats, and the salads look great. How did we pay for all this?"

"Let's talk to the head chef," Felix said. He spotted Technical Sergeant Shields and waved her over. "Boss wants to know about finances."

"We did pretty good, sir," she said. "The ops group gave us the same budget they spent last time on catering. We bought everything from the commissary and cooked it ourselves. With the money left over we were able to get a better class of German beer and wine. I think maybe we have too much, but we arranged to send the leftovers to the base airman's club."

"Fantastic," I said. "I am very proud of all of you. Great job!"

She smiled and excused herself. Every flight attendant except the three on the CT-43 trip were manning the food stations. Most of the C-21 pilots took up stations at various parts of the venue. I spotted two C-20 pilots decked out in tuxedos behind a bar. "You guys throw a high-class event," I said to Tommy.

"We think it will be a long time before someone tops us, sir," he said.

Before too long the hangar was filled with the predicted hundreds, all dressed in flight suits and combat fatigues. The C-130 crowd easily doubled the attendance by all others combined. The ravenous herd devoured the food already on the tables and our flight attendants raced to keep the chafing dishes filled. I worried for a moment about the burners under each and knelt to inspect one. From across the table Maggie Cairns stared at me, inspecting the same burner.

"Can't you just relax?" she asked. "Your guys have done a great job here. The food is delicious, the hangar looks great, and I even like the way you parked your airplanes out front with the spot lights. You are such a show off! So leave these burners alone, they're fine."

"You're right," I admitted. "Are your people having a good time?"

"I think so," she said. "Art's squadron pretty much took the place over and I hardly see any of my guys. But of those I've seen, everyone is impressed. Speaking of which, heads up." I turned to see Colonel Wozniak approach.

Flight Lessons 4: Leadership & Command

"Congratulations, Eddie," he said while patting my shoulders. "First class, everything one would expect from the 76th Airlift Squadron."

"Should we expect the general?" I asked. Wozniak appeared surprised by the question.

"Of course not," he said. "Tonight is a night away from the brass, a night to let our hair down."

"Well before you do that, sir, let me introduce you to someone," I said. I steered him to the end of the table where Kelly Shields was replacing an empty dish of shrimp scampi. "Colonel Wozniak, allow me to introduce you to Technical Sergeant Kelly Shields, one of our lead flight attendants and for tonight, our top chef."

"Outstanding, Kelly," he said. "This spread is worthy of the finest restaurant in Germany, you have really done a top-notch job here."

"Thank you, sir," she said. "This is what we flight attendants like to do when we get a chance."

Colonel Wozniak helped himself to the shrimp and Sergeant Shields gave me a smile and scurried off with the empty dish. Every commander in the operations group, except one, made it a point to find me and congratulate the squadron for the event. I made it a point to find the exception.

"So what do you think, Art?" I asked. He was carrying a plate of sausages in one hand and a beer glass in the other.

"Nice job, Eddie," he said. "It wasn't what I was expecting but, now that I think about it, this is what you VIP types do for a living. You probably don't know this, but I was in charge of doing this three years ago when I was still a major. You've put my efforts to shame."

"Not me," I said. "We've got some talented captains running this show and we couldn't have done any of it without our flight attendants."

"Well, good job," he said as he turned to join another conversation. I stood alone, the uneasy feeling returning. Something caught my eye from overhead, but I had missed it. Then something else. It was a dinner roll. Then a falling beer bottle followed by laughter. I spun around and found a sergeant with a plate of food ready to go airborne.

"Sergeant," I said. "What are you doing?"

"Sir?" he said, as if I must have been crazy because it was all too obvious what he was doing.

"I asked you a question," I said. He lowered the plate and stood at attention.

"Just having fun, sir," he said.

"Well stop it," I said. "Somebody worked very hard to cook that food for you. You are being very disrespectful."

"Yes, sir," he said. "Sorry, sir."

He turned away but then I spotted another projectile, and then another. It wasn't a food fight worthy of the movie "Animal House," but it certainly wasn't right. Maggie Cairns caught my eye next. "I was afraid this was going to happen," she said. "I heard that's what usually happens at one of these airlifter's balls."

"Really," I asked. "I had no idea." I turned to look at the long table of food and noticed half a dozen flight attendants huddled to one side, stunned by the turn of events. I made a beeline for Sergeant Shields.

"I'm sorry about this," I said. "I wasn't expecting it."

"None of us were, sir," she said. "What should we do?"

"I don't know," I said. "I'll try to put an end to it, but keep your people from getting hurt and don't bring any more food out." I scanned the room for help and spotted Colonel Wozniak first, but then I saw Art Johnson between us. I headed for Art first.

"Art, this is unacceptable," I said.

"Unacceptable?" he said. "This is an airlifter's ball, this is what happens at an airlifter's ball."

I gave up on him and resumed my course to Colonel Wozniak, who was laughing at a collection of enlisted crewmembers drenched in spilled wine. "Pretty wild, eh, Eddie?" he said as I approached.

"It's not right," I said. "I can't get the C-130 guys to stop, I need you to exert some authority here."

"Stop?" he said. "They aren't going to stop! They are just getting started!" He pulled me to one side to avoid a conga line of captains armed with plates of sausages looking for targets. Mercifully, they were targeting only other C-130 crewmembers.

"This is conduct unbecoming officers," I said. "And it has to stop."

Flight Lessons 4: Leadership & Command

Wozniak's smile didn't miss a beat and he put his arm around my shoulders to spin me away from the center of the hangar. "Eddie, these people have been working hard all year. They need this to blow off some steam. Can't you see that?"

"This is an insult to my people who worked so hard to make this a class event," I said. "I will not allow it to continue."

"Eddie, you need to calm down," he said. I freed myself from his grasp and stood, unable to think of a retort. "Aren't you flying tomorrow?" he asked.

"Yes, sir," I said. "It's our first combat sortie."

"When do you go?" he asked.

"Takeoff at 0700," I said. "Show is 0500."

He looked at his watch. "By my math, you start crew rest in ten minutes. Why don't you go home and forget about this? I'll make sure it doesn't get out of hand." I stood my ground, still unable to come up with another word. "That's an order," he added.

I turned away, defeated. I could see Felix Henderson and Tommy Mendéz looking at us from across the hangar. Both stood with the same powerlessness I felt. I headed directly for Felix but spoke to Tommy first. "You did a great job, Tommy. I'm sorry I didn't anticipate this."

"None of us did, sir," he said. "We're just trying to hold on right now."

I looked to Felix. "I have to leave for crew rest now, please take care of this for me."

"I will, Eddie," he said. "Don't worry about it."

"Have the flight attendants take all the food and drinks away," I said. "Take anything away that can hurt anyone and make it obvious that this event is no longer fun. Maybe they'll go away on their own accord."

"You got it," he said. "We'll childproof the hangar and maybe the children will leave. Go home, we got this."

I turned to see the rest of my crew for the morning launch and motioned to the exits. I did a quick inventory: two pilots, a flight engineer, a radio operator and a flight attendant. We walked silently until we reached the parking lot. "Good night, sir," I heard from each.

I returned to the hangar the next morning at 0430 where I found Mr. Chambers pulling a chicken wing from a noise curtain alongside the corner between the large hangar door and the adjacent wall. Two technicians were knelt over what looked to be a red wine stain in the middle of the once pristine white hangar floor.

"Do you know how to remove red wine stains from an epoxy floor, colonel?" Chambers said before I could get a word out.

"No," I said.

"Me neither," he said. "In thirty-two years in the Navy and now on my eighth year with Gulfstream I never had the need to. But your flight attendants suggested white vinegar. It works like a charm."

"I'm sorry about this," I said. "I'll get my people over here to help."

"No need for that, colonel," he said. "They were here this morning when I got here at 0300. They pretty much had everything done except the wine stain on the floor and a few chicken wings here and there. They said it was a wild night."

"Anybody hurt?" I asked.

"I heard there was a broken nose when some loadmaster boltered his carrier landing," he said. "I didn't know you Air Force types did those."

"I thought we put an end to that a few years after Vietnam," I said. "When I was in pilot training enough guys got hurt bad enough where the highest levels of the Air Force said that kind of behavior would no longer be tolerated."

"There's always that five percent that doesn't get the word," he said, smiling. "You look about as upset as I've ever seen you, colonel. Don't worry about it. We don't have any lasting damage and I hear none of your people got hurt. From what I hear, you run the only sane operation on base and you shouldn't blame yourself if some of the craziness makes its way over here now and then."

"Thanks," I said. "I have to get to work." I turned to see Kyle Knudson waiting.

"Sir, we are all set," he said, handing me a mission folder. "The enlisted crew is doing the preflight and I have our flight plans, weather, and intel briefs."

"Thanks," I said while rifling through the pages as he stood.

"Wild night, huh?" he said.

Flight Lessons 4: Leadership & Command

"Yeah," I agreed. "Between you and me, I was surprised."

"I think we all were," he said. "Can I ask you about carrier landings?"

"You can ask," I said, smiling. It was an Air Force tradition during Vietnam. When the party progressed to the 'wild and crazy' portion of the festivities, the longest table was cleared and doused in red wine. Each combatant would take a run at the table and leap onto it, holding their arms and legs up so as to ensure only their chests and bellies made contact with the well lubricated table. Points were awarded for the jump, the landing, and for how far down the table the contestant could go before falling off. Extra points were given for the "spectacularness" of the crash. After enough pilots were hurt to impact the flying schedule, the Air Force put an end to the practice. Or so I thought.

We made it off the ground for another OTTO victory and to Frankfurt in time to receive the U.S. ambassador to the United Nations. About an hour later we were over the Adriatic, descending to 10,000 feet, leaving Brindisi airspace and checking in with AWACS. "Combat entry checklist," I said to the crew over interphone. We were all in flight suits, wearing flak vests. We had modeled our checklist off the C-130's, but there was far less to do. We could clear our fuel vents with yaw, but we didn't have any countermeasures to test, no flares to ignite, and certainly no Kevlar to feel reassured with. We simply turned off all external lights and ended all electronic emission except the Mode 2 "Identification Friend or Foe" transponder to let the fighters know we were one of the good guys.

"Madam Ambassador is seated," the flight attendant reported. "And I'm going to strap in too."

"IFO 20, you are cleared in," AWACS said over the designated frequency. "The reported ceiling is 600 feet with visibility at one and one-half miles. We do show multiple radar emitters but no reports of hostile fire. Happy hunting. Contact GCA."

I pulled the throttles to idle and allowed the airspeed to decay. As the speed decreased Kyle extended increasing flap settings and the landing gear. As our TACAN clicked down to 11 nautical miles our airspeed hit 170. I allowed the nose to fall of its own accord and we fell like a rock.

"On course, on glide path," the Ground Controlled Approach operator said. He had us on radar and was directing a simple Precision Approach Radar, or

PAR. It was simple except that instead of directing us on a nice, calm 3-degree glide path, he was directing us on the maximum glide path we told him we could fly. With today's winds, that came to 9 degrees. With the engines at or near idle, I had very little control of the glide path if I ended up high.

I stole a look at our weather radar. I had never used it for terrain mapping but the experts swore it could be done. I didn't see any ground returns I could make any sense of. We were descending at almost exactly 3,000 feet per minute, which meant it would all be over in less than four minutes.

"Passing five thousand feet, on course, on glide path, four miles to go," GCA reported. The Sarajevo PAR was different than most for another reason. The angle intercepted the runway not at the touchdown spot, but at the very first inch of runway. At our angle we would need about a thousand feet to arrest the descent. Touching down at 3,000 feet per minute would be an unsurvivable crash. And then there was the problem of the snipers on the other end of the runway.

"Passing three thousand feet, on course, slightly below glide path, two miles to go." That was excellent news. The headwind was helping with the descent rate so I would be able to add some thrust, giving me more control of the glide path. But more importantly, this would keep the engines above idle and reduce "spool up" time. A jet engine cannot accelerate instantaneously from idle. Our Gulfstream III's engines would take five seconds or more to produce full thrust from a prolonged idle setting. We didn't have an electronic means of keeping the engines at a higher speed, known as "flight idle." We only had a mechanical spring in the throttles themselves. Pulling the throttles back to the first point of resistance, called a "soft stop," gave us this flight idle assurance. I had been at the "hard stops," ground idle, since we started our descent. I pushed forward gently on both throttles and felt the reassuring grab of the soft stops in my right hand and the vertical velocity indicator gently nudge upward.

"Correcting to glide path," the controller said.

"Passing two thousand feet, on course, on glide path, approaching the runway threshold."

"I'm outside," Kyle said, no longer monitoring my performance inside the cockpit. "Nothing yet."

The numbers on all the gauges were good, that is to say they were unusual.

We had 30 knots too much speed and far too little thrust. But it was as we had practiced.

"Runway in sight," Kyle said. "Dead ahead."

I spotted the runway and the spot frozen in my windscreen was the first inch of pavement. I pulled back on the yoke without touching the throttles, still at the soft stops.

"Speed plus thirty," Kyle said. We were 30 knots too fast but that was expected. "Speed plus twenty." The threshold disappeared below our nose. "Speed plus ten." I pulled the throttles to their hard stops and a second later our wheels hit and then I was full on the thrust reversers.

"Whoa!" the engineer said. "Look at that!"

"Geez!" Kyle said.

I turned us left, off the runway, and they both looked right to get a better view of the crashed Russian Ilyushin-76 airliner. "After landing checklist, please," I said.

After I parked, the airplane was surrounded by army soldiers. Our passenger was whisked away by an armored vehicle, leaving us to sit and stare at the bombed-out airport terminal. Our plan was to sit for two hours, remaining inside the airplane.

"Quack," Kyle said.

"What?" I said.

"I was just thinking we are sitting ducks, sir," he said.

"Quack," I said.

"You've all gone mad," I heard from behind us. It was Staff Sergeant Cindy Turner, the flight attendant.

"How was it in the cabin?" I asked.

"Exciting," she said. "The ambassador said now she knows what it must have felt like going down Niagara Falls in a barrel."

"That's a pretty good description of what we just did," I said.

"How about some food?" she asked.

"Perfect," I said.

Every now and then I had to smile at the idea. Eating a spinach omelet in a multi-million dollar luxury jet, wearing a flak vest, surrounded by Army soldiers, sitting in a valley surrounded by enemy troops getting ready to shoot; that's what the life of a glamorous Gulfstream crew is like in the United States Air Force.

The ambassador returned on schedule and we leapt off the runway. It was a cold, winter day, the airplane was very light, and I had to pull the nose back to 40 degrees of pitch to keep our target speed as planned to evade the bad guys and their pesky radars. We returned to Frankfurt, where the ambassador thanked us for our service, and an hour later we were back at Ramstein. I returned to my office to find Felix behind my desk signing the next day's flight orders.

"I guess you made it out alive," he said. "So I have to give your desk back, don't I?"

"That's the way it works," I said. "Any fallout from yesterday?"

"None at all," he said. "The rest of the group is happy to have attended and our guys are happy to have survived. All things considered, it could have been worse."

"I guess I've forgotten about what animals you 130 guys can be," I said.

"Not me, Eddie," he said. "I left that crowd for a reason! They work hard and they play hard to make up for the work. It takes a special breed."

"Do I need to patch things up with the flight attendants?" I asked.

"No," he said. "I think the whole squadron saw it as us doing what we do best to be part of the bigger team. Everyone knows what it's like out there, in the real Air Force. Everyone knows someone in the other squadrons and knows how truly awful it can get. We're just happy we only have to be exposed to it in small doses. Don't worry about it, Eddie. You worry too much."

"So I've been told," I said. "Kyle and I will take the next combat sortie, just to be sure we know what we're doing. Then it will be you and him. Let's only use all instructor crews for these missions until we find we don't need to."

I thought I would have to spend the rest of the week mending fences with everyone in the squadron who had put so much effort into the Airlifter's Ball only to see it degrade into a college frat night, but my worries were unfounded. While the flight attendants were upset about how their food was treated in the end, they received more than enough praise before the first roll was tossed that they seemed to agree it was a successful night. Many of our enlisted crewmembers were mildly amused to see so many officers misbehave but that too was tempered with the spirit of the evening. "All things considered, it was a success," Tommy Méndez summed the night. "We're glad we did it, but we are even more glad it's over."

The next Monday I walked into the operations group staff meeting to applause. "Tell your folks that the entire group had a great time at the Airlifter's Ball," Wozniak said as I took my seat. "Art tells me his guys and gals thought it was the best they'd ever been to."

"And the food was fantastic," Art said. "I wonder what it's going to take to get stewardesses on our Hercs."

"Flight attendants," I said. "They are called flight attendants."

"Good job also on your first combat flight," Wozniak said. "Word from Headquarters Air Force is the ambassador was very happy and is recommending members of every Defense Committee in Congress come visit. I think you guys are about to get a lot busier."

"Okay," I said. "I need to start training more crews for this."

"You do that," he said. "And think about using the other airplanes too."

On Tuesday we repeated our first flight to Sarajevo with three U.S. Senators. The flight was identical except for the weather, which was CAVU, ceiling and visibility unlimited.

"I liked it better when I couldn't see the mountains," Kyle said as the surrounding terrain climbed above our winglets. I quickly looked outside and right back to my instruments.

"On course, on glide path."

"Muzzle flash!" the engineer yelled. "Just off the nose, eleven o'clock."

"Looking," Kyle said. "Didn't see it."

I landed the airplane. Two hours later we were airborne again.

"Muzzle flash!" the engineer reported. "Two o'clock, low."

"There it is," Kyle said. "It's behind us now."

Of course, there was nothing to be done about it. We were climbing as best we could and had already figured out that altitude was our best friend. As I began the process of lowering the nose in response to the thinning air I thought for the first time that in the case of small arms fire, perhaps forward velocity would be more important than vertical velocity. But then there would just be more shooters down range. There were too many variables to second guess decisions already made. The altimeter reached our proclaimed safe height of 10,000 feet and AWACS reported us feet wet. "Combat exit checklist," I said to the crew, unfastening my flak jacket.

On our return to Ramstein we were asked to stop by the base intel shop where we were met by a captain and a sergeant with a large map. "We need to know everything you saw from the ground and when you saw it."

Kyle and the flight engineer pointed to their best guesses and I verified it based on our altitude, descent and climb angles, and when they called out the muzzle flashes. "Did you see any of this for yourself, colonel?" asked the intel captain.

"No, I was heads down the entire time," I said. "But if they saw muzzles flashes, I believe it."

"Well, sir," the captain said, "so do I. A C-160 from the French Air Force departed right after you, about five minutes after you. They were hit by triple-A. We think the bad guys were surprised by your appearance, but you were moving so fast they couldn't get lock on."

"Speed is life," I said.

"The C-160 isn't nearly so fast," the captain said.

"Anybody hurt?" I asked.

"We don't know yet," he said. "They limped the airplane to Ancona, Italy."

OTTO

C-130s	2 / 10
C-9s	0 / 8
C-20s	1 / 10
C-21s	0 / 22
CT-43s	0 / 3
	lates / sorties

The next day the wing staff filed into our normal conference room and were treated with the last slide first, OTTO. It looked like a good week save three occurrences, of which I was directly involved with one. I looked at Art who returned his own, worried look. "This might be good or it might be bad," he said. I nodded. Maggie looked understandably relaxed. Finally, the general appeared and we all stood to attention.

"Be seated," he said. "As you can see from the slide, we had a pretty good week." The staff murmured, still unsure of which way to go. "Three late takeoffs isn't perfect, but I wanted to start with this slide to make an important point. All three lates were combat related. The top two all had to do with pallet loading from the Mission Support Group." All eyes darted to the Mission Support Group Commander who turned ashen. "The third late was due to the passenger terminal at Rhein-Main Air Base delaying the processing of three Senators on their way to Sarajevo." All eyes looked to me. "Colonel Haskel, how is Senator Williams doing?"

"He's doing well sir," I said. "He sends his regards."

"That's good," he said. "Paul Paulson and the senator go back many years. But the point here is this: this is a team effort. This wing is on combat footing. This isn't a nine-to-five, Monday-to-Friday, punch the clock on duty, and punch the clock off duty job. Is everyone clear on that?"

"Yes, sir," the wing staff said, almost in perfect harmony.

"Good," he said. "Let's proceed."

I relaxed in my seat and let the rest of the slides drift by. I sensed the entire wing relaxed with me for the first half of the meeting. But as the meeting drew to an end, with OTTO already taken care of, I think everyone also sensed there was more to come. As the last slide disappeared from the projector all eyes turned to Paulson.

"One more thing," he said. "We've been doing pretty good at the two-a-days and don't you forget for one minute the troops on the ground in Bosnia are counting on them. But just because we've realized our goals doesn't mean we can relax. There is a war going on. So this wing is stepping up to the plate and effective immediately, we will be doing three combat air deliveries per day. Congratulations all, let's go get 'em."

We stood at attention and as Paulson left, Wozniak turned to face Art Johnson. "I know, I know. Let's all meet in my office." We turned as a group to follow Wozniak. From the rear, I could see Art already protesting the increase in tempo. By the time we got to his office whatever decisions in combat airlift that had to be made, were apparently made.

"The combat airlift squadron is going to be under some stress for the foreseeable future," Wozniak said as we all took our seats. "The rest of us are just going to have to offer any assistance where we can. I need you four to come up with solutions to this. I've been called in to the general's office so please work this out the best you can. Oh, by the way, in the next few weeks we are starting with the usual Christmas parties. I think I'm signed up for all of them. The wing commander is going to the combat airlift squadron's party. The vice will be with aeromedical and VIP airlift. Joyce and I are looking forward to all of them."

We sat quietly until he left and then Art unloaded on Mayhem. "I know for a fact that the Air Force moved a permanent detachment of C-17s to Rhein-Main Air Base. They are doing one-a-day right now but rumor has it they are going to three-a-days."

"So they are doing what we are doing," Mayhem said. "You should be thankful for the help."

"How many pallets can you stuff into a C-17?" I asked, thinking I could set up the argument for the point Art was trying to make.

"Eighteen," he said. "One C-17 can do the work of three C-130s."

"What kind of an MC rate do they have?" Maggie asked.

"Ninety-five-plus," Art said.

"Look, none of that matters," Mayhem said. "They have a mission and we have a mission. We have to do the best with what we got."

Of course, he was right. If Paulson wanted to increase the C-130 workload by 50 percent, that was his prerogative, even if it broke the squadron. The squadron was his to break. We sat and brainstormed for thirty minutes but none of our ideas were workable. We left, defeated.

Our Christmas party was a large gathering, with almost 300 in attendance. The atmosphere was relaxed and the entertainment was light. I was seated next to Colonel Wayne Broward, a former C-5 pilot turned vice wing commander. While I had rarely dealt with him personally, I usually saw him every week behind and to General Paulson's left at the weekly staff meeting. He always nodded his head in the affirmative when called for and side-to-side in the negative when it came time for the OTTO slide. He was an unknown quantity but by virtue of his position in the wing, I considered him a threat.

"This is a pretty lively group this year," he said while making idle conversation with *The Lovely Mrs. Haskel*. "I think your husband has done a great job turning this squadron around." My first thoughts were that it must be a set up; he's trying to get her to divulge any knowledge about the secret IG complaints from Clevis Haney's tenure.

"Eddie speaks highly of his people," *The Lovely Mrs. Haskel* said, keeping her cards close to her vest. "We love it here."

At the intermission between dinner and the final gift ceremony, one where each flight presented the other flights with gag gifts, a line of pilots and their spouses formed near our table. Everyone wanted to meet *The Lovely Mrs. Haskel* and many of those to see me as well. Colonels Wozniak and Broward huddled in a corner for business of their own. After the gift session was over, dessert and coffee were served.

"How's the morale in your squadron?" Colonel Broward asked once his plate was clean. "Woz tells me it's pretty good."

"I believe it is, sir," I said. "We don't have the same pressures as the combat airlift squadron, but our workload is pretty high. Our promotions could be better and I'm not happy with the assignment process for our older pilots, but things are definitely better than they were and I think they are going to get better still."

"Well I just want you to know something, Eddie," he said. "I think you've turned the corner with the general. I know you have a history with him and it seemed at first you were trying purposely to send him right up the nearest wall at the drop of a hat. But the way you played ball on combat ops may have turned things around."

"I hope so, sir," I said. "I'm still not convinced sending an unarmed and defenseless airplane into a combat situation is a wise thing to do, but if that is the military decision we'll carry it out."

"Well wise is in the eye of the beholder, isn't it?" he said. "The decisions only get harder, but that is the nature of the business."

Pope Gregory XIII set us up in the year 1582 with a calendar that would eventually doom the 86th Airlift Wing with a single week off for the 1995 Christmas season. The combat airlift squadron would work on the Sunday that was Christmas Eve and the Monday that was Christmas Day, and hold to their promised three-a-day flights to Sarajevo. But without any trainers they were able to produce at least three mission capable aircraft each day. The aeromedical squadron cancelled all trainers and kept a crew on standby for medical emergencies. In the VIP airlift world, our passengers elected to stay home. So the last week of the year was another perfect OTTO performance.

Our first wing staff meeting of the year was scheduled for an unprecedented two hours to cover the two weeks that had passed and the year-end metrics. General Paulson gave the floor to each group commander in turn, starting with the Mission Support Group.

Colonel Heidi Vaughan spoke from her seat at the table as each successive slide revealed that comparing 1995 to 1994, the number of divorces were up by 20 percent, enlisted personnel reenlistments were down by 30 percent, and promotion rates for both officers and enlisted personnel were down about 5 percent.

"Unacceptable," Paulson said from his seat. "What's Paul Paulson's first priority?"

"People," Colonel Vaughan said.

"People, that's right," Paulson said. "Each of these metrics shows a problem and I want each of you commanders to study these slides. They are your homework." The slides reversed themselves and we got a second look at divorce rates, reenlistments, and promotions. Each slide was a graph with the percentages on the vertical axis and the twelve months along the horizontal axis on the bottom. Many on the staff scribbled hurried notes before each slide disappeared. I studied the shapes.

A new slide appeared that I wasn't expecting: deaths. Colonel Wayne Hubbard, the Medical Group Commander, cleared his throat twice and spoke uneasily. From my vantage point I didn't know if he was a doctor or a medical administrator. "Ah, deaths are something we don't like to discuss normally," he said. "But in a wing this size it is a fact of life. We classify these as deaths by natural causes, accidents on duty, accidents off duty, and suicides." There was a separate slide for each category, ending with suicides. I knew of one, a mechanic in Mark Honable's squadron. But there were apparently two others. I was again more intrigued by the shapes of the curves than the numbers along the vertical axis.

"There is no excuse for accidents on or off duty," Paulson said. "If you've had any accidents under your command, you have failed as a commander. Next."

The Security Police Group Commander stood and pointed to the next slide. Colonel Arnold Stein was a tall and husky man with a deep, baritone voice. "I know that one of our top priorities in this wing is keeping our people safe and this slide shows what should be of grave concern to us all. We've already covered deaths by accidents off duty. Well two of those are on this slide here. Our Operating Under the Influence rate is almost double what it was, year over year. Now on the next slide you will see that our security infractions have always been low and remain so. But I am very concerned about the OUIs." He sat.

"Go to the previous slide," Paulson said. As the projector cycled it hit me. The other groups showed only the year that just ended. The Security Group showed "year over year" slides that included the previous year's performance in a lighter color. The previous year did not mimic this year's pattern; the OUIs did not jump in the summer.

"OUIs are a symptom," Paulson said. "Anybody care to guess what the disease is?"

"We aren't taking care of our people," Colonel Vaughan said.

"Exactly right," Paulson said. "We have work to do. Next."

Colonel Harold Nimitz, the Maintenance Group Commander, had a single slide, the C-130 Mission Capable rate. Since the aeromedical and VIP fleets had civilian contract maintenance, our MC rates didn't count against the wing's metric. The C-130 MC rate started at 50 percent and shot up to 60% in May. At that point it gained a half percentage point each month for the rest of the year and now rested at 63 percent.

"Not too shabby," Paulson said. "But what is our goal?"

"Sixty-five percent," Colonel Nimitz said without hesitation. "We'll get there."

"I know you will," Paulson said.

And then, finally, it was Colonel Wozniak's turn. He tasked his squadron commanders with coming up with slides to sell our success stories. Maggie produced a slide reporting patient satisfaction, revealing that she came up with the idea to give each patient something akin to a customer satisfaction survey. Few of her patients bothered to mail in the survey, but those that did were apparently satisfied. Art's idea was a slide showing the metric tons delivered to Sarajevo. For my part, I gave Wozniak a slide showing the number of times we killed someone (zero) or broke something (one – a table had collapsed when a particularly large C-130 flight engineer attempted a carrier landing). In the end, we all knew, there would only be one slide: OTTO.

"General Paulson, here is the end of year on-time take off performance metric," Colonel Wozniak said from his seat. "We are very proud of the team effort put forth by the entire wing to make this dramatic improvement possible. I want to personally thank you for your support and want to say to the rest of the wing, we couldn't have done this without you."

Members of the staff started to clap and Colonel Wozniak turned in his seat to applaud his squadron commanders. General Paulson sat, smiling, and allowed the applause to die of its own accord. "Good job, Woz," he said. "Talk us through the slide."

"Well sir, we didn't actually keep an OTTO metric before June," he said while fumbling through his notes. "But we do have a resident engineer who was able to take data from the flight logs kept by the mission support squadron and tabulate the performance from previous months based on current standards to show the numbers of late takeoffs between January and June.

The numbers from that point reflect actual aircraft late takeoffs against the schedule posted at the beginning of each week."

"I see," the general said while studying the graph. "Would that resident engineer be Colonel Haskel?"

"Yes sir," he said.

"Colonel Haskel," General Paulson said while still staring at the chart, "what would an engineer call the performance of that red line in June?"

"That is an inflection point, general," I said.

"An inflection point," he repeated. "Very good. Now, can anyone else tell me what happened in June of last year?"

A few members of the staff brazenly offered "that was the month after you took command" but that was obviously not what he was looking for. "That's when we started to focus," someone said just loud enough to be heard.

"Exactly!" Paulson said. "That's the point where Team Ramstein started to focus its efforts. That's the inflection point for this wing where we started to do what we do best, and from that point, people get promoted. From that point, all other metrics will follow. From that point, Ramstein realizes its true potential. Congratulations to everyone. We are going to have a great 1996, you can bet on Team Ramstein."

There was a cheer and more applause. Paulson circulated around the room, shaking everyone's hand. He sought out the Ops Group first and shook my hand too. "We are looking forward to great things from you, Colonel."

After he moved on I looked again at the OTTO slide. I wasn't sure June really was an inflection point, strictly speaking, but it definitely presaged a change. I looked back on my notes and it hit me. Almost every slide we had seen that day showed a very large change, an inflection point, in June.

I was thinking a lot about the changes the squadron had seen in the eight short months since my arrival. I was comfortable with my role and had finally attached a name to every face. When a new person appeared, I knew they were new and not a product of my poor memory for names. I had a set speech for the new pilots from pilot training and another for those from other assignments. But I asked both to start in the "learn mode" and try to check out as quickly as possible. For those with previous instructor experience I added a second caution. "You are used to being the expert and you will find your experience in your last airplane (the C-5, C-130, C-141, KC-10, or KC-135) will serve you well here. You may disagree with how we do things here and you might be right. But hold your fire. Get checked out first. Then, once you've done that, help us to learn from you."

In a squadron of 60 pilots averaging 3 years per assignment, we had a turnover of 20 pilots a year, or one or two a month. The mathematics of ratios dictated that most of these would be C-21 pilots. In January we had our first CT-43 pilot exchange. As usual, we swapped a highly experienced instructor pilot for a newly qualified copilot.

"You've done a great job here, John," I said as Captain Halsey stopped by the office for his final farewell. "The squadron looks up to you and is a better place for your being here. I hope Shawn Timmons can accomplish half as much."

"He'll do great, sir," John said. "It's good to get another Fat Albert driver in the squadron."

"Fat Albert?" I asked.

"C-5," he said. "That's kind of an inside joke for us C-5 crew. The Air Force calls it the Galaxy. We call her Fat Albert."

"Funny," I said. "Before you go I want to give you a chance to critique anyone and anything. With a squadron this size I can't keep my eye on everything. What have I missed? What can I do better? What can the squadron do better?"

"Sir, if you asked me that a year ago I could have talked your ears off," he said. "I think the crew force is in good shape. I do worry about the combat ops. The CT-43 is from a different era than the C-20 or C-21. It is underpowered, the avionics are from the 1960's, and it doesn't have the best ground proximity system. Colonel Henderson said you fixed that when you were at the Pentagon but the fighter mafia defunded the program."

"It wasn't just me," I said. "The airlift team at the Pentagon had funded better safety systems for the entire airlift fleet. President Clinton had a series of funding initiatives that progressively took from the military and these safety systems lost in the end."

Flight Lessons 4: Leadership & Command

"That's a shame," he said.

"Yes, it is," I agreed. "But besides equipment, anything else?"

"No sir," he said. "Captain Ashworth is one of the best instructor pilots I've ever flown with. He's smart, patient, and a good teacher. Captain Timmons checked out very quickly and has some good ideas to help David going forward. Captain Nance, well, he's in his own world. But he's a good pilot."

"What about the engineers and flight attendants?" I asked.

"The best," he said. "I used to the think our C-5 engineers were maintenance experts. But these guys take it to the next level. Chief Trenchard was obviously good, but he was a bit of a pain to work with. We traded a chief for a buck sergeant in Alan Jackson but I think we did okay. Sergeant Jackson is always willing to help the flight attendants; that's something Trenchard would never do. I've never flown with flight attendants before. I'm going to miss being spoiled like this."

I wished him well and good luck going back to the C-5. He walked out the door, and in an act of poetry Captain Timmons walked in. One was only three years older than the other. But the former looked to be a wise, old, seasoned pilot with decades of experience. The latter looked every bit the novice pilot, despite having thousands of hours in one of the largest aircraft on earth, many of those hours as an instructor pilot.

As each pilot, engineer, radio operator, flight attendant, or ground support technician came and went, a little piece of the squadron changed. Of course, the same could be said of its commanders. I was starting to feel at home and, more importantly, that I was making my home a better squadron.

James Albright

Flight Lesson: Transformational Leadership

A transformational leader seeks to achieve organizational goals while helping members of the group achieve individual goals as well. The "transformation" itself suggests a move from a former, undesirable state, to a new state. Such a shift carries risks as well as potential rewards.

Transformational Leadership Defined

trans•fer•māy•shen

- A thorough or dramatic change in form or appearance

The Advantages of Transformational Leadership

Transformational leaders are seen as inspirational and will garner loyalty from followers who felt previously powerless. If the organization is coming from a stressful period or is suddenly faced with larger and newer challenges, a transformational leader can motivate followers to higher levels of performance and teamwork.

The Pitfalls of Transformational Leadership

A transformational leader walks a narrow path between achieving newer goals or repairing previously broken processes, and upsetting higher levels of leadership and the status quo. A transformational leader can become overly self-assured and therefore blind to the point where loyalty can be stretched too far.

8: The Prince

January, February, and March, 1996

The 76th Airlift Squadron, 1995 (USAF Photo)

We often began our Monday Operations Group staff meeting with the OTTO statistics at that point in the week. The numbers in December had been very good and for the first week in January were about perfect. I thought the second week would be a repeat performance until I walked in to see that the preliminary slide showed Art's squadron had already racked up ten late takeoffs in just four days. Maggie's squadron had one C-9 delay. My squadron stood alone in the perfect category. I thought for sure that would be the meeting's focus. I was wrong.

"Did your squadron make last quarter's training targets?" Colonel Wozniak asked as I entered.

"I think so," I said. "I saw them on my desk this morning but didn't have time to go through them. Let me look." I thumbed through the report, a page for each crew specialty. "Yes sir," I said. "We are at a hundred percent."

"Well at least we have some good news," Wozniak said. "Art and Maggie were not so lucky. We can't allow our training metrics to fall. The Pentagon is taking an interest in this, Air Force wide."

"Why would they care?" Maggie asked. "It sounds like micromanaging to me."

"I think it has something to do with pilot retention," Wozniak said. He left the room and returned with a stack of message traffic, sterile teletype sheets sent from one military entity to another. It was military email in the days before email. "Here it is," he said, passing the message to Maggie.

"It says too many flying units are sacrificing training events to keep up with mission commitments," she said. "They are going to do an audit of all operational units at the end of this quarter and will take corrective action as needed. That's a cute way of saying heads are going to roll."

"Take a look at the date," Wozniak said. "This came out on the second of January. General Paulson asked the base computing office for an advance look at all your numbers. You can imagine his reaction."

"Which explains why we were ordered to reinstate a full training schedule last week," Art said. "Well now comes payback. We can't continue to put forth three combat flights a day, each with a dedicated spare, and still fly trainers. Something has to give."

"Can you dedicate a single spare for all three sorties?" I asked.

"No," Art said. "The Army has a specific delivery order and they don't want to tie up the ramp with cargo they aren't ready for. The C-17s are delivering so much cargo that ramp space is at a premium."

"Which begs the question," Maggie started to say.

"The question of why we are there to begin with," Art finished.

Wozniak was thumbing through the rest of his message traffic as we spoke, only looking up once we had stopped talking. "Yes," he said. "We'll just have to give it our best shot. It's not going to be pleasant on Wednesday, but let's come up with something to fix this."

"The general already did," Art said. "He just fired the maintenance squadron commander."

"Honable?" I asked. "He fired Mark Honable?"

"Yup," Art said. "And good riddance."

"I thought he was a pretty good commander," I said. "He got the MC rate from 50 to something like 63 in just half a year."

"And he drove the squadron into the ground to do it," Art said. "After he was fired I think the troops wanted to throw a party. The general replaced him with someone from stateside and ordered they return to a five on, two off schedule."

"Five on, two off is another way of saying normal," Maggie said. "What were they on?"

"Major Honable had them on six on, two off for two weeks, then seven on, no off for the third week," Art said. "You can't treat your people like that."

"That doesn't sound like something Mark would do," I said.

"Is he a friend of yours?" Wozniak said.

"Yes, sir," I said.

"It just proves what they say about command," Wozniak said. "You don't know how people will handle the pressure when you hang the title commander on them."

"He deserved better," I said.

"We all get what we deserve in the end," Maggie said. Wozniak thumbed through his message traffic once more, punctuating our newly found silence.

"Here it is," he said, pulling the missing message from the stack. "I wanted to ask you all about this. Headquarters Air Force says we can no longer use approach plates that haven't been specifically approved by the Department of Defense."

"That's crazy," I said. "Less than a third of our locations here have DoD plates. When does this go into effect?"

"The date time group of the message says it is in effect right now," he said. "Let's see. It went into effect last July."

"So six months ago," Maggie said. "We can just stop flying to any destination without Department of Defense approach plates. That will solve our OTTO problem, we'll just stop flying."

"Yippee!" I said.

"Let's get serious," Wozniak said. "I called the Ops Group Commander at the 89th Airlift Wing at Andrews. He says they use Jeppesen plates more than DoD plates."

"The presidential wing uses Jepps," Maggie said. "That should end all discussion."

"Funny you should say that," Wozniak said. "He pretty much used those words. He told me Air Force One couldn't fly without Jepps. So this is some mindless bureaucrat spouting off about a subject he knows nothing about. Okay, that's all I have. See you on Wednesday, if not before."

As I walked out, Mayhem nodded toward his office and I followed. He closed the door behind me and pulled an unlit cigar from a coffee cup and searched in vain for something else on his desk. "Oh yeah," he said, giving up. "I stopped smoking a year ago." He fell back into his chair and I waited patiently. He looked at me.

"Your meeting, Mayhem," I said.

"You seem a little upset by the news of your friend's dismissal," he said. "Care to explain why?"

"Oh I'm not really upset," I said. "I've known Mark Honable since we were both second lieutenants and I've flown all over the world with him. But now that I think about it, he was out of his depth as a squadron commander."

"What makes you say that?" Mayhem asked.

"Whenever he was directed to increase the MC rate, he just passed the order down to his sergeants," I said. "His senior sergeants think he is great because he lets them run the squadron without interference. But Mark didn't involve himself in day-to-day maintenance. He didn't have a clue about what it was like at the bottom level of his organization. He was powerless to resist, I guess. He thought he would be fired at the first sign of resistance. Now he's fired anyway. I guess what really surprises me is that Paulson fired him for doing exactly what he wanted him to do."

"Exactly what The Prince would have done," Mayhem said.

"What prince?" I asked.

"The Prince," Mayhem said, as if repeating the words with greater emphasis would answer the question. "Don't you engineers bother with any of the classics? Does the phrase, 'the ends justify the means' mean anything to you?"

"Machiavelli?" I guessed.

"Yes!" he said. "So you aren't a literary Neanderthal after all! Your friend was just a tool used to get the MC rate up at any cost, and then he was discarded like a used bullet shell so Paulson could swoop in and rescue the troops. It's the classic Cesare Borgia technique."

"Ah, that," I said. "That explains everything."

"Okay, okay," he said. "I'll spoon feed you this one but I'm going to make you make me a promise when I'm done. Cesare Borgia was a military commander in Italy hundreds of years ago who found himself ruling over several towns of people ready to rebel on a moment's notice. He could have put a garrison of his troops in each town indefinitely, but that takes resources he didn't want to give up. So he hired mercenaries to go in and ruthlessly beat down the opposition with the standard murder, rape, pillage routine. The villages didn't know what hit them. Do you think that would work, Eddie?"

"For a while," I said. "But sooner or later the people will tire of the brutality and will rebel regardless."

"Exactly!" Mayhem agreed. "So Borgia came in with his own troops, slaughtered the mercenaries and put their heads on pikes. He showered the villages with gifts and placed only a token number of guards in each town. He ends up with what he wanted in the first place and was loved by the towns."

"So Paulson is Borgia and Honable's head is on a pike," I said. "That hardly seems fair."

"Does it surprise you?" he asked.

"It does," I said. "I've known Paulson is an unethical officer, ready to trample others for his own ends. But none of his malice ever seemed personal to me. This was malice of a targeted variety. But did that really matter? Maybe it shouldn't have."

"I had my suspicions when I saw the end of year maintenance slide," Mayhem said. "It has to be obvious to everyone that you can't raise the MC rate without additional manpower and parts without something giving. When I saw that slide, I knew it for sure. When I heard that ten mechanics got together to file a complaint with the inspector general, I knew what Prince Paulson would do next. Even reducing the work days. It's Machiavelli through and through."

"But now the MC rate is going to fall again," I said.

"Will it?" Mayhem asked. "The mechanics may end up working harder and more efficiently just out of gratitude."

"The plucked chicken," I said.

"The what?" he asked.

"Joseph Stalin said you should treat the masses like chickens," I said. "You pluck their feathers for no reason other than to gain their allegiance. After the first feather the chicken is surprised. After the second he's irritated. After the third and fourth he's mad and then really mad. But sooner or later the chicken starts to fear you. And then the chicken worships the ground you walk on when you don't pluck him."

"So you aren't illiterate after all," he said. He turned in his seat to a bookcase where he found a paperback edition of a small booklet. "Here's your homework, Eddie. If you want to survive this wing, study this book." He handed me a worn copy of *The Prince*, by Niccoló Machiavelli.

I took the book, more to humor Mayhem than to pay any fictitious debt. As I left his office Wozniak's secretary gave me her usual wink, but this time while handing me a yellow Post-It note to call Felix as soon as possible.

"We've already got two lates this morning," Felix said. "But I'm glad you called because we are working on a third. The CT-43 is due to leave in an hour to Cairo and points south. Captain Ashworth says they have a bad igniter in the left engine but can go with the remaining igniter."

"So what's the problem?" I asked.

"He's going to be in the remotest parts of Africa for three weeks," Felix said. "He would rather have the bad igniter replaced than chance being stranded. Maintenance says it will take an hour and thirty to replace."

"This is a deadhead, as I recall," I said.

"Exactly," Felix said. "They can replace the bad igniter and still make it to Cairo in time to pick up their pax."

"Sounds like a no brainer to me," I said.

"That's what I thought," Felix said. "But this will make three late takeoffs in one day and it isn't even noon yet."

"Oh well," I said. "Get them started on that igniter, I'm on my way back."

In any other wing the decisions would have been easy. We weren't inconveniencing the passengers at all and we were improving our odds of meeting their schedule for the remainder of the trip. Felix was worried about the fallout, of course. The earlier late takeoffs were less cut and dried, and the fallout would be considerable.

Flight Lessons 4: Leadership & Command

OTTO

	lates / sorties
C-130s	15 / 20
C-9s	3 / 10
C-20s	1 / 10
C-21s	1 / 22
CT-43s	1 / 3

I thought about the theatrics behind every staff meeting. The Monday Operations Group staff meeting appeared to be just Wozniak reading from his list of collected notes over the week while we squadron commanders reacted, provided answers, and received direction. My Tuesday squadron staff meetings were usually the same. But I often thought the Wednesday Airlift Wing staff meetings had to have been planned well in advance. General Paulson's behavior seemed to be the symptom of a bipolar disorder, alternating between infectious enthusiasm and a barely contained but telegraphed irritation. But no matter his mood, his performance was aimed toward motivating the staff. I thought he must have had a heads-up look at each week's OTTO. But the stunned look on his face when our worst numbers yet hit the screen belied that idea.

He looked at the slide for a few seconds and then lowered his gaze for a moment. The staff held its collective breath and I could hear a clock on the wall I had never noticed before tick. He stood, looked to Wozniak and then to us, his subordinate commanders, and said, "You four, let's have a talk in my office." Then, looking at the rest of his staff he said, very simply, "dismissed."

We followed him, like errant school children to the principal's office, as the staff looked on. He led the way into his inner office and sat behind his desk. He didn't offer us the nearby seats, so we stood at attention. He looked first to Art. "Fifteen late takeoffs out of twenty," he said. "I've done the heavy lifting for you and fixed the maintenance squadron. Tell me this won't happen again, Colonel Johnson."

"It won't," Art said. "We have our crews showing an extra hour early now to help maintenance detect problems that take a crew to discover. I think the younger pilots have the mindset that maintenance produces the airplane to fly and they fly it. They need to realize it is a team effort and we all need to think of ourselves as maintainers."

"Good," he said. He looked to Maggie, to me, and back to Maggie. "Colonel Cairns, please don't tell me your crews are still oversleeping."

"No general they aren't," she said. "We had one case of a maintenance problem that we could have detected earlier, an instructor who took too long during a prebrief, and one case of an English Channel slot time. We are going to try Art's idea of the one hour earlier show and that might have fixed all of those lates."

"Okay," he said. "I think we are making progress here. Now, for the entertainment portion of this meeting, Colonel Haskel." He looked at his copy of the OTTO slide. I could see his eyes dart up and down, trying to pick an airplane. I found myself thinking, "CT-43, please pick the CT-43."

"Tell me about the C-20 late takeoff, Colonel," he said.

"It was a trainer, general," I said. "The instructor realized at the last minute that he didn't have the right set of approach charts. He ran inside to get them and they were late as a result."

"What about the C-21?" he asked.

"One of the passengers decided just prior to engine start that he needed to rush into the passenger terminal," I said. "The passenger was a colonel and the pilot didn't have the intestinal fortitude to order him back into his seat. We've had a talk with him about priorities."

Paulson smiled briefly, and turned to Wozniak. "Anything to add, Colonel Wozniak?" It was the first time I had ever heard Paulson address Wozniak by rank.

"Yes, general," he said. "It appears the common denominator in many of these late takeoffs is the pilot. We'll see if we can analyze any failures in leadership and go from there."

"I was just thinking the same thing," Paulson said. "Colonel Haskel used the phrase 'intestinal fortitude' as he tends to use big words where small ones seem more fitting. The word you want, Colonel Haskel, is 'balls.' Your pilots don't have the balls to make the correct decisions."

My first thought was about human anatomy and then about Maggie, standing to my left. And then to the female pilot behind our C-21 late takeoff. I then thought of a sarcastic reply, "Good point, well made," but fortunately squelched that thought before it made it to my mouth.

Flight Lessons 4: Leadership & Command

"Sometimes a commander has to make tough calls," Paulson said. "I made the tough call last week when I fired that maintenance squadron commander. You will soon see a real improvement from the Maintenance Group when word gets around that their screw ups don't survive in a wing that demands perfection. Maybe your pilots need some of the same medicine. So let every pilot in this wing know this, the next pilot responsible for a late takeoff is fired. You got that? Fired!"

"Yes, sir," I heard from the three on my left.

"No, sir," I said.

"What?" General Paulson said. "What do you mean no?"

"You cannot let word get around that having a late takeoff will get you fired," I said. "You are going to have pilots taking unsafe risks for the sake of the stopwatch. That can certainly be the consequence, but you cannot make that known beforehand. It isn't safe."

I once again started to hear clocks that I had never before noticed. General Paulson normally did a very good job of disguising his anger, but for a moment I thought he was about to pop an artery. The volcano never erupted, however. Paulson leaned back in his chair. A coffee maker in the outer office completed its brew cycle and the clock resumed its tick, tock.

"Never let anyone say Paul Paulson can't admit he's made a mistake," he finally said. "Colonel Haskel, you are correct. I will not fire the next pilot in your squadron who has a late takeoff. I will fire you."

"Yes, sir," I said.

We all retreated to Wozniak's office and sat there, silently. Wozniak was unable to speak and the sound of clocks again filled my ears. Maggie finally broke the quiet. "I can't believe you said that, Eddie!"

"I can't believe you didn't," I said. "Don't we have an obligation to prevent something so stupid? You cannot issue a threat like that!"

"He didn't mean it," she said. "He was just blowing off steam."

I hadn't considered that.

"Mayhem, close the door," Wozniak said. Once the door was shut he looked at me directly. "Eddie, I'm not saying you made a mistake in there, but sometimes we need to stick together as a team. We five, in this room, are a team operating under very difficult circumstances. The general has very specific goals and we should count ourselves as lucky that he is so clear about them. But they aren't easy goals to achieve. What we need is a little loyalty to the Operations Group. We can survive this as a team. But without that loyalty, well, who knows?"

We sat again, listening to clocks. "What's next to hit the fan?" Wozniak said. "How are we doing with OTTO today?"

"Better," Art said. "The extra hour show time has already paid dividends. I'm not sure how long we can keep this up, but so far so good."

"We are perfect for now," Maggie said, looking at her watch. "At least I haven't heard of any delays yet."

"I haven't heard of any delays either," I said.

"Good," Wozniak said. "Let's get out there and ensure our people understand they are part of a team, and teams require loyalty."

As we got up I made eye contact with Mayhem, wondering if he could make any sense of Wozniak's new interest in group loyalty. He must have been having the same questions; he simply looked at me and shrugged his shoulders.

Our squadron's week was devoted to Bosnia flying, usually with the larger Gulfstream C-20 but also an occasional trip by the smaller Learjet C-21. Since we required all-instructor crews I ended up flying half the C-20 trips, so my flight proficiency started to climb for the first time in Germany. While we saw muzzle flashes now and then, only the slower C-130 and C-160 cargo aircraft were ever hit.

All three squadrons modified their training sorties so as to always leave Ramstein for German airports, eliminating any problems with diplomatic clearances crossing the border. The Operations Group rumor mill was working overtime, mostly in complaint to the added hour before every C-9 and C-130 flight.

"You want to hear something crazy?" Felix said as we sat around his desk on Friday. "Rumor has it that the general is going to fire the next pilot who has a late takeoff."

"Where did you hear that?" I asked.

"Some of our pilots heard it from pilots in the other squadrons," he said.

"And what did you say about that?" I asked.

"I told him the squadron leadership hasn't been told that, no wing commander would be so foolish," he said.

"Good," I said. "Talk like that is going to get someone hurt."

I had never mentioned the dressing down in General Paulson's office to anyone. I hadn't even mentioned it to *The Lovely Mrs. Haskel*, not wanting her to worry about it. But word had somehow gotten out.

By Monday only the C-130 squadron had a single late takeoff, all other squadrons were spared. Art, Maggie, and I sat in Wozniak's office at the appointed hour but Wozniak and Mayhem were absent. "How long do you give a full colonel?" Maggie asked.

"You give a full professor thirty minutes," I said.

"That means we give him the hour," Art said.

"Sorry I'm late," Mayhem said, closing the door behind him. "Woz is in another meeting so I need a word with you three. Let's suspend the normal agenda, I know we are doing good with OTTO, so thanks about that. I have another matter to discuss. This is close hold."

"Close hold" was an Air Force euphemism for "this isn't classified, but it should be, so hold it close to your vest."

"Colonel Wozniak has been served with an inspector general's complaint," Mayhem said, brows furrowed. "It could be serious. All four of us will have to testify. They have all of us scheduled for 0900 each day for the rest of the week. Art goes tomorrow, I go on Wednesday, Maggie on Thursday, and Eddie on Friday."

"I'll be in Bosnia," I said. "We have two instructors down, one with a sprained ankle and the other with the measles."

"The measles!" Mayhem said. "I knew you had a young squadron, but geez! Okay, I'll ask the JAG to schedule you for next week."

The next week came and went, but our Bosnia schedule never relented. The C-21 took a greater number of trips, but complaints from Congress left us with no choice but to use the C-20 more often than not. By the third week our medically grounded instructors got their wings back and I found myself walking into the inspector general's office where I found a recently departed friend.

"Nice to see you Eddie," Mark Honable said. "I wish it wasn't here, though."

"I thought you moved up to USAFE headquarters," I said. "How's life as a staff toad?"

"It's easier," he said. "I'm in an office where old majors go to die. Everyone is a passed over major going nowhere. We sit around and do special projects, but we take our time doing it. It could be worse. At least I have more time at home now."

"You aren't passed over yet," I said.

"Eddie, the board results came out this morning," he said. "I didn't make it."

"I'm sorry to hear that," I said. We sat, wordlessly. "So why are you here, back at the wing?" I finally asked.

"One of the guys in my old squadron filed a complaint against me," he said. "Said I singled him out for extra duty because I didn't like him."

"I bet there is a lot of that going on in this wing," I said. "This is probably just a formality."

"I don't know," he said. "An inspector general's complaint is never good news. What about you?"

"I don't know," I said. "Somebody filed a complaint against our Group Commander. They won't tell me who filed the complaint or even what it's about. Everyone else has already testified and I'm told it shouldn't take more than five minutes."

"Well, good luck," he said. "I never got to thank you for helping me with the promotion recommendation. It seems obvious now that Paulson wasn't going to promote me no matter what."

"You might be right about that," I said.

"Colonel Haskel?" a clerk called out. "Colonel Fielding will see you now."

I shook Mark's hand and entered the inner office. I walked to the center of the office, in front of the colonel's desk. The clerk took a seat to the colonel's left. The far wall was lined with law books, and a framed diploma on the opposite wall proclaimed that Colonel Nelson Fielding was a top graduate from Stanford. He sat at his desk, writing on a yellow pad, not noticing my entrance.

"This is Colonel Haskel," the clerk said.

"Colonel Haskel?" he said, looking up. "Ah yes, Colonel Haskel. Let's get this over with."

The clerk stood and faced me, asked me to raise my right hand, and repeat an oath. I did so.

"Have a seat," Colonel Fielding said. "This won't take long. I've already spoken to the other squadron commanders and the number two at the group. I've pretty much written the report already, but I need to speak with you just to be complete." The clerk wrote on his own yellow pad as the colonel spoke.

"Yes, sir," I said. "I don't even know the subject of the complaint."

"The subject?" he asked. "The complaint was filed against your boss, Colonel Wozniak."

"Yes, sir," I said. "That much I knew. But I don't know what the complaint is about."

"Really?" he asked. "The other commanders seemed to know."

"I guess I don't have the same network," I said. "But I don't know."

"Ah," he said. "Well this is about the Operations Group Airlifter's Ball. A number of enlisted members of your squadron filed a complaint about the conduct of some of the officers present. The charge is that Colonel Wozniak actually encouraged the mischief. Can you believe that?"

"Yes, sir," I said.

"Yes?" he asked. "What exactly do you mean?"

"I can believe some of the enlisted members of my squadron would think he was encouraging the behavior of some of the officers," I said. The clerk continued to write.

"What makes you say that?" he asked.

"Because they would have seen me try to stop the, what did you call it?" I said. "The mischief. They would have seen me try to stop the mischief and they might have also seen him refusing and ordering me to leave."

Colonel Fielding sat upright in his chair, staring at me with a pained look. "I can't believe what I am hearing," he said. "Do you want to reconsider what you just said?" He shifted his eyes without moving his head, gesturing toward the clerk. Perhaps "stenographer" was a better description of the airman.

"Let me think," I said. "No, I don't think I need to retract any of those statements."

Colonel Fielding resumed his effort to stare me into submission. I thought of Wozniak's admonition to be a loyal member of the Operations Group team. He wasn't a bad commander and he really wasn't a bad person. His goal was noble: allow his overworked people to blow off some steam. I, on the other hand, was being disloyal to the team.

"One last chance, colonel," he said.

"I can live with this," I said.

"You are dismissed," he said.

I returned to the squadron late in the day, past Susan's normal quitting time, expecting my outer office would be empty. Instead I was greeted by Major Linda Roslin, smiling.

"I don't know that I've ever seen you smile," I said, shaking the hand she had offered.

"I guess I am just happy to have so many pages turned," she said. "It's like having the weight of the world taken off your shoulders."

"Good news then," I said.

"Well, not really," she said. "I got passed over. I just found out this morning. But since we last talked I made a few phone calls and got a job offer to teach in Boston. The more I thought about it, the more I want to do this. I can hardly wait. I guess I just wanted to thank you for the talk that got me started on this new chapter of my life."

"You give me too much credit," I said. "You have served your country well and I think your students will benefit from your experiences as an Air Force officer." After she left I sat at my desk, thinking about her and Mark. If they both found out about their promotion board results this morning, then so too would have Marc Stück. Felix walked into my office, holding two beers.

"Rough day?" he asked.

"Not particularly," I said. "Have you seen Herr Stück today?"

"I did," he said. "He was mission planning for a trip tomorrow. I don't think he'll ever upgrade, but he's got the hang of being a copilot finally."

"Did he mention promotion board results?" I asked.

"No," Felix said. "Are the results out?"

"Yes," I said. "Both of his competitors were passed over."

"Which means he made it?" Felix asked.

"I think so," I said. "Strange he wouldn't mention it. This is the biggest promotion of his career and one he had no right to expect. He's an odd one."

"I believe it," Felix said. "I hear he's a cheap bastard. Figures he would keep this quiet rather than have to pay for a promotion party."

"Notch another victory for Team Ramstein," Paulson said at his next staff meeting. "The Chief called yesterday to congratulate me for the huge impact we have had at sustaining the United Nations effort in Bosnia. When Paul Paulson gets a pat on the back like that, Paul Paulson takes a bow on behalf of the entire team. Congratulations, team!"

The staff applauded. Colonel Wozniak turned in his seat to shake Art's hand, so Maggie and I followed suit. "Good job, Art!" Maggie said.

"I told the Chief we are ready for more," Paulson continued, to a hushed silence. "But the Chief has to think of the rest of the Air Force too, he can't let Team Ramstein hog all the glory!" Laughter. "So Team Charleston will be stepping up to the plate with a deployed unit of C-17s. Effective immediately, we will reduce our Bosnia operations tempo to one-a-day." Applause. "Good job everyone! Take a victory lap, congratulate your people. Go get 'em!" More applause. Paulson rose, the staff stood at attention.

After Paulson left and the staff started to leave, it hit us in the Operations Group. "No OTTO slide?" I asked aloud.

"No more OTTO," Wozniak said from his seat. "See everyone next week, Monday."

"What happened to the rest of this week?" I asked. Wozniak didn't answer and with a blink of an eye was gone.

"Eddie, let's have a talk," Mayhem said. I nodded and followed him to his office and closed the door behind us after he cast it a sideways glance.

"Do you know what just happened, at the wing staff meeting?" he asked. "Did you catch the ground shaking?"

"Well I suspect the Department of Defense got tired of Team Ramstein botching the mission five pallets at a time," I said. "I overheard the Secretary of Defense say something like that when I flew him in and out of Sarajevo two weeks ago. The Army Chief of Staff told him that our pallets are only getting in the way of the C-17 deliveries. They've pretty much relegated us to toilet paper delivery."

"Yeah," Mayhem said. "That's the gist of it. So we got told to quit. I think they gave us the one-a-day to save face."

"The Prince gets to look good, even if he isn't good," I said.

"So you've read the book?" Mayhem asked.

"Yes," I said. "It is not the best book on leadership I've ever read, but it does pretty much capture the essence of what goes on around here."

"It does indeed," he said. "But it doesn't explain OTTO. Why do you suppose the general killed OTTO?"

"I don't know," I said. "OTTO is dead. Good riddance."

"It's your doing," Mayhem said. "You can take full credit."

"How's that?" I asked.

"Colonel Wozniak has been issued a formal letter of reprimand," Mayhem said. "His fast burner career is over. He'll be permitted to finish his time here, he'll find a staff job someplace and when he is first eligible for retirement, he will be allowed to do that. He was destined for a general officer's stars, but now he's going to retire an unknown colonel."

"I'm sorry to hear that," I said. "Was it the inspector general?"

"No," Mayhem said. "It was you. The rest of his staff said things got out of hand at the Airlifter's Ball and it was all any of us could do to contain it. The IG was happy with that and ready to broom the complaints. But then you showed up and knifed us all in the back, under oath!"

"I spoke the truth," I said.

"Well I can't argue with that," he said. "But you aren't going to get away with it. Paulson now knows you can't be trusted and he can't continue to use OTTO as a threat for fear of what you might do next. The Air Force now knows you are one of those commanders who doesn't play ball and you will never be allowed to command again. You aren't going to get away with it."

I got up to leave, thinking about what I could say. But he wasn't done talking. "I want my book back."

The wing appeared to relax the next week. Without the threat of OTTO and the stress of air combat three-a-days, life appeared to be almost normal. Even our C-20 and C-21 Sarajevo trips had tapered to one a week and we hadn't seen any enemy fire in a month. The job of squadron commander was becoming, in a word, boring.

"You ready for a tough call today?" Felix asked.

"Try me," I said.

"General Paulson just promised the left seat of a C-21 to a friend of his," Felix said. "This friend is a three-star general from Systems Command. He's never flown anything other than a fighter, has never been trained in the C-21, and is outside our chain of command. If he breaks anything, heads will roll between here and the Pentagon."

"I thought you said it was a tough call," I said.

"Okay," Felix said. "Just wanted to be sure."

The next morning the first phone call was from Wozniak. "Eddie you can't do this," he said. "The general already committed us to this."

"I thought you said if General Paulson offered the seat to someone outside the chain of command we would step up to the plate together," I said.

"I think we've both used up whatever capital we have here," he said. "I don't see any harm in this as long as you have an instructor in the right seat."

"I'll think of something, sir," I said.

"I knew you would," Wozniak said. "Thanks."

The second phone call was to Felix. "Do you think Mike Hammer would have the intestinal fortitude to order a three-star general out of the seat if it became obvious he wasn't listening to a captain instructor pilot?"

"I know he would," Felix said. "Especially if he knew you had his back."

"I have his back," I said.

"I'll make it happen," Felix said.

The flight did happen and Major Mike Hammer sat in the jump seat quietly, not having to do anything at all. It was highly unusual. We usually sent a copilot along with an instructor on these general officer flights, in case the general declined the pilot's seat. Sending an aircraft commander, especially a major, was extraordinary. The general officer was polite, listened to the captain's instructions, and managed to take off and land without damaging anything other than a set of tires.

"I've never seen an airplane stop so fast," Mike said after the flight. "Was it pretty? No. Was it dangerous? No. But on the other hand, was the general happy to see a major watching over a captain watching him over? No."

I thought the episode was over until a week later when I got a phone call from someone I rarely ever heard from, the vice wing commander.

"Congratulations colonel, you are being promoted," Colonel Broward said. "You will be General Paulson's personal aide." I stared at the phone in disbelief. I had been in command for nearly a year and that was indeed the minimum time for most commanders, but two years was the normal tour.

"I'm not sure that's a promotion," I finally said. "When does all this take place?"

"One month from today," he said. "We'll have the change of command on the morning of April 1st and you can report into the General later that day. You have a month to get Colonel Henderson ready for the job."

"Yes, sir," I said.

"No pushback?" he asked.

Pushback? What good would it do? It was clearly within General Paulson's authority to pull me from my job early and "elevating" me to the wing staff was an elegant way to do that. It gave him a chance to find someone more pliable for the squadron commander's job while not hurting my career. Pushback? I suppose I had been pushing back from the day Paulson had showed up.

"No, sir," I said.

The next morning, the wing made the announcement of my "elevation" and Felix's selection to replace me. I got a series of congratulatory phone calls but the reaction from the squadron appeared mixed. A change of command is a regular event in a flying squadron and while having one every year was unusual for some, it seemed to be the norm for the 76th Airlift Squadron. I had talked myself into thinking it was just another event in a career of events, until about a week before the change of command.

"Coffee, sir?"

I looked up from my desk to see Staff Sergeant Cindy Turner with my personalized cup. "Thank you," I said. She walked into the office and lowered the cup onto my desk. She stepped back and stared at the cup. In my year's tenure in the office, only Susan made the morning coffee run for me and I normally preferred to get it myself. Cindy waited. I took a sip. "It's good," I said. "Thank you."

"You are welcome, sir," she said, still unmoving.

"Is something on your mind, Cindy?" I asked.

"No, sir," she said. "Yes, sir," she corrected herself.

"Have a seat," I said.

She pulled the chair from behind the conference table and sat, facing me rather than the table. She crossed her hands on her lap and her legs at her ankles. Finally, her eyes met mine. "We are worried," she said. "We are worried that things are going to return to the way they were. I'm not going to feel safe anymore."

"Who is 'we' and why do you feel that way?" I asked.

"We is," she started but stopped. She drew in a loud breath and held it. Her shoulders slumped as she exhaled. "We is the flight attendants, but I think it probably includes most of us who have been here for a while. You don't know what it was like before."

"Under Colonel Haney?" I asked.

"Yes, sir," she said, voice trembling. "But it was that way long before him. And I hear it was that way with the previous commander too."

"Colonel Henderson will be great," I said. "He and I see eye-to-eye on safety. You shouldn't be worried."

"Yes, sir," she said.

"Give him a chance," I said. "He deserves that."

"Yes, sir," she said, smiling for the first time. "Thank you, sir."

A few other squadron members stopped by with less emotional goodbyes and that evening *The Lovely Mrs. Haskel* and I were treated to the largest squadron farewell party we had ever attended. I felt, for the first time in my life, like a rock star. I had a smile on my face as we drove home.

"They are worried," *The Lovely Mrs. Haskel* said.

"Why is that?" I asked. "And who is 'they'?"

"The squadron," she said. "They are worried about Felix. Many of the wives and some of the squadron members came up to me and said so. They said things are going to go back to the way they were."

"Ridiculous," I said. "Felix feels the same way I do on just about everything. He has backed me up every step of the way. I couldn't have asked for a better second in command."

"I know you've always said that," she said. "And I believed that too. But I heard something today I never heard from you. About Felix."

"I can't imagine," I said. "I think the world of him. He has had my back every step of the way."

"Well you might be right," she said. "But consider this. He was also Clevis Haney's second in command and he allowed that madman to run all over the squadron. Those inspector general complaints? Felix had to have stood idly by and let all that happen. He didn't have the guts to stand up to him."

"We don't know that," I said.

"Eddie, I know you like him," she said. "But that is just like you. You grow attached to people and can't see the bad in them."

I let her words drift into space as I pulled into our driveway. She gathered the farewell gifts we had received and I busied myself paying the babysitter and making sure our children were in bed asleep. *The Lovely Mrs. Haskel* tossed and turned through the night, almost in perfect rhythm to my own unsettled movements. I thought back to Alton Gee's last words to me, six years ago. "I predict you will fail."

Alton said that I had a blind spot for my friends and that I was predisposed to not trusting those above me in the chain of command. Felix was a kind and generous gentleman who went out of his way on day one to make me feel at home in my new surroundings. He never questioned an order and was my most enthusiastic supporter.

Flight Lessons 4: Leadership & Command

"What does 'shut up and color' mean?" *The Lovely Mrs. Haskel* said, after an hour of trying but failing to fall asleep.

"That's what some commanders will tell subordinates when they run out of argument," I said. "If they fail to persuade you they'll just say 'shut up and color' as if they were talking to a five year old. Why?"

"Cindy Turner told me that was something Felix used to say when defending Clevis Haney," she said. "Haney would come up with some kind of cockamamie order and they would rush to get Felix's take. He would say, 'sometimes you just have to shut up and color.' Can you believe that?"

"I've never been a second in command," I said. "It can't be easy."

"There you go again," she said. "You do have a blind spot for your friends. You always have."

"Sir, I relinquish command." The words stung as I spoke them. General Paulson returned my salute. One salute later Lieutenant Colonel Felix Henderson was the new commander of the 76th Airlift Squadron and I was General Paulson's personal aide.

"What's the first thing you want to do?" General Paulson asked.

"Take a month of leave," I said.

"You can have a week," he said. "We have too much to do. One week from today, I want you in my office ready to work."

Five days later I was in a hotel room in Amsterdam when I saw the news. Our CT-43 had crashed on the hills of Dubrovnik, Croatia. Everyone onboard was killed.

Flight Lessons 4: Experience

Flight Lesson: Machiavellian Leadership

Niccoló Machiavelli (3 May 1469 to 21 June 1527) was an Italian Renaissance philosopher who may have been best known for his work, "The Prince." The book theorized that a new prince who comes to power through means other than heredity must command by a different set of rules. Often summarized by sayings such as "the ends justifies the means," Machiavellian leadership is often broken down as follows:

1) It is better for a leader to be feared than loved.

2) A leader must stabilize his command and build an enduring structure.

3) Brute force and deceit to exterminate external and internal threats is justified since it brings a positive good to society.

4) Princes should delegate the difficult tasks to others while keeping the popular ones for themselves.

5) The Prince does not need to be or do good, only to be perceived as good or doing good.

6) Enemies should be treated kindly (so as not to be hungry for revenge) or utterly crushed (so as not to be capable of revenge).

Machiavellian Leadership Defined

A Machiavellian leader is one who utilizes the techniques espoused by "The Prince" to achieve organizational and personal goals. Subordinate levels of leadership are often sacrificed to achieve goals at minimum cost to the higher levels of leadership.

The Advantages of Machiavellian Leadership

A Machiavellian leader can accomplish many difficult tasks very quickly. In a military environment, where promotions can be rapid, a Machiavellian leader can reap many rewards and then leave the mess for successors to clean up.

James Albright

The Pitfalls of Machiavellian Leadership

A modern day Machiavellian leader seldom operates in a vacuum and news of ruthless behavior can travel quickly. Few large organizations can tolerate such leadership before the organization itself becomes threatened.

9: The Process
April and May, 1996

CT-43, 4 April 1995 (Photo: US Army)

"Who?" I asked.

"Captains Ashworth and Timmons," Susan began. "Sergeant Jackson was the engineer, and the flight attendants were Sergeants Shields, Ferris, and Turner."

"Oh no," I said.

"It's terrible," she said. "Can you come back?"

"Right away," I said.

I had never flown to any part of Croatia before coming to the 76th Airlift Squadron. The country declared itself independent from the Socialist Federal Republic of Yugoslavia in 1991 and in the years since had become a thriving country. Geographically, Croatia surrounds Bosnia, another former socialist republic. But economically, the Croats were leaving the Bosnians in the dust. The two countries were officially at war until February of 1994. As the Bosnians retreated, more and more of Croatia was open for business. My first trip to the country was to Zagreb, the Croatian capital, a year after the official cease fire. But I could still hear gunfire and bomb explosions while standing on the tarmac at the airport. Three months later I flew to Split, Croatia. And once again the sound of bombs in the distance was always present. The last major city to be liberated was Dubrovnik. I had never heard of the city until the day our CT-43 attempted and failed to land at its lone airport on the coast of the Adriatic.

We managed to find a British newspaper on our drive south back to Ramstein but the details remained sketchy. "The weather was terrible," *The Lovely Mrs. Haskel* read as I sped along the A61 *autobahn*. "A local resident said it was the worst storm in decades. A local official says the airplane was not where it was supposed to be. It flew along the valley but should have flown along the coast. Recovery is difficult because the area is still laced with landmines from the Bosnian war. This is awful." She cried softly as the children slept in the back seats of our Volvo.

Six of them, all dead. Their faces kept appearing before me, obscuring the lines of the road ahead. I had pushed so hard for Ashworth's upgrades. I remember feeling relieved at the sight of Timmons' flight record, knowing we were getting a new great pilot to replace a seasoned great pilot. Jackson showed up at our doorstep looking for a job and both the C-20 and CT-43 flight commanders lobbied to get him, he was good enough to fight over. Shields was my "go to" flight attendant for the big jobs, but Turner was the steady hand that kept our flight attendants on track. Ferris was the always jovial "flight stew," as he called himself. The last time I had seen them all was at our farewell party. Each went out of their way to say goodbye. Goodbye.

"Here," *The Lovely Mrs. Haskel* said while handing me her box of tissues. My cheeks were soaked.

Once we returned to our home in Hütchenhausen, just a few kilometers west of Ramstein, we turned on the television to the local military station. The Stars and Stripes was a six days a week newspaper published for U.S. military personnel throughout Europe and the Pacific. They also had a television station which showed American television and a news program tailored for the U.S. military. The news progam was consumed with the crash. The aircraft was carrying the U.S. Secretary of Commerce – a personal friend of the President – and 34 others. "An anonymous source reports that the aircraft's squadron commander, Lieutenant Colonel Edward Haskel, was ousted from his position for objecting to these types of VIP flights in hazardous conditions. General William R. Paulson, the commander of the 86th Airlift Wing, was unavailable for comment."

I picked up the phone and called the squadron. "What can I do?" I asked Felix.

"Come on in," he said. "The squadron is in shock and we just need some moral support."

The shock was palpable, but I wasn't sure how much good I could do. Felix handed me the morning copy of the Stars and Stripes, where the crash dominated the front page.

"Haskel's boss tells his side of dismissal"

April 7th, Ramstein, Germany. Was Air Force Lt. Col. Edward Haskel a cowboy who operated outside the chain of command, or a pilot who was so opposed to shuttling VIPs through the former Yugoslavia in unsafe conditions that he was willing to lose his command over it?

It depends on who you believe when trying to sort out why Haskel was relieved of command five days before this tragedy.

Both sides agree that prior to the crash, Haskel had raised concerns about the safety of shuttling VIPs throughout the region. Hostile fire, bad weather and ground-based navigational equipment were among the issues discussed in meetings that included Haskel and his boss, Brig. Gen. William R. Paulson.

Paulson said he and Haskel had reached an agreement on safety issues and that he had relieved Haskel for "discipline reasons" and Haskel's problems with working within the "chain of command."

According to Paulson, Haskel had permitted pilots under his command to land between the hours of 1 and 3 a.m. Normally, such activity is banned because German neighbors are disturbed by the noise. "That is why I relieved him."

"I wonder if Paulson believes that?" I asked.

"Of course he doesn't," Felix said. "As soon as I read that I checked the base regulation and it shows the Stage III exception just as we were told. He's lying and we can prove it."

"I think he's fighting a public relations battle," I said. "The story talks about 'both sides.' I wasn't aware there were sides to this."

"The wing is in full lockdown mode," Felix said. "Paulson wants to control the message but somebody's been calling the press. The Air Force has an accident investigation team down there right now and they've appointed a brand new one-star to lead the AAIB."

"That's usually a colonel's job," I said.

"The Secretary of Commerce was a personal friend of the President," Felix said. "This one's going to be political."

An Aircraft Accident Investigation Board is charged with finding probable causes with the aim of preventing a recurrence of the "accident." They are given first rights to the wreckage and are supposed to remain free from any political or military influence. Even so, politics did sometimes muddy the process, although the politics were never of a Presidential level.

Two days later the Dubrovnik airport maintenance chief committed suicide. The Croatian Interior Ministry said the maintenance chief was not working the day of the crash and did not have any connection to the crash. The president of the AAIB immediately issued a statement that "we're satisfied with that."

"How can he know that without investigating," *The Lovely Mrs. Haskel* said after reading the news story. "Have you ever heard of Brigadier General Charles H. Crowley?"

"I haven't," I said. "I've never met the man."

"Poor equipment, procedures cited"

April 29th, Ramstein, Germany. Captain David Ashworth and his copilot, Captain Shawn Timmons, had good reasons to forget about trying to land in the pouring rain at Dubrovnik. The captains had never seen the Dubrovnik airport.

Croatia Airlines will not let its own crews land there if both the pilot and copilot have never done it before.

Flight Lessons 4: Leadership & Command

The Air Force directed pilots based in the United States never to land there in anything but clear weather. However, these restrictions applied only to pilots from the Military Airlift Command and did not restrict USAFE pilots based in Europe.

So Ashworth, 35, and Timmons, 33, pressed on with Flight IFOR 21. Nearly 12 miles out, heading southwest, their military Boeing 737 passed over a navigational beacon. They were right on course. But sometime during the next four minutes something went terribly wrong. They veered way off course.

The correct flight path to Dubrovnik's single runway was a course of 119 degrees. But the pilots, flying on rudimentary instruments, followed a course of 109 degrees--straight at the highest mountain for miles around. Seconds later, the plane slammed into the peak and exploded, killing all 35 people aboard.

It was 98 feet shy of clearing the summit. Air Force officials declined to comment until the results of the ongoing investigation are released. The investigation is said to show:

- The plane that crashed could not have flown commercially in the United States because it did not meet civilian safety standards. So the planes that carry Cabinet secretaries, lawmakers, and the President lack safety innovations afforded to the general public.

- The pilots were navigating with a compass and radio receiver. Air Force generals called this equipment "primitive."

I was due to report in for my new job as Paulson's aide but was told to "lay low" until summoned. I had nothing to do but read the Stars and Stripes and learn as much about Dubrovnik as I could. I discovered how Lieutenant Colonel Dillon May managed to pass the hours without a high stress job; he spent those hours at the base library.

"Want some company," I asked.

"Sure," he said. "How are you doing?"

"I'm just laying low, as I was told," I said. "I seem to get a phone call from one reporter or another a few times a day. I was just invited to fly to New York, all expenses paid, for an interview on 'Good Morning America.' That seems a bit odd."

"So what did you say?" he asked.

"What did I say? What could I say? I told them to call the base public affairs office," I said. "It's not like I have any choice."

"You are allowed to talk to the press, Eddie," he said.

"I don't trust the press," I said. "Vermin."

"Well, you are allowed to do it," he said. "Paulson's been talking. Did you hear about 'The McLaughlin Group' news show?"

"No," I said.

"One of the panel reporters said Paulson had lied about the noise issue and couldn't be trusted," Mayhem said. "Another reporter said that he had it from the highest source that you were fired because of a Tail Hook incident."

"Wow," I said. "So someone is saying the Airlifter's Ball was something like the Navy Tail Hook party?"

"You got it," Mayhem said. "You might want to reconsider that interview."

"I think I'll pass," I said. "The facts will come out eventually. I'm still not sure why the airplane crashed."

"The board has been leaking to the press too," he said. "General Paulson spent two days with them last week and Wozniak is there all day today. I hear you have to testify tomorrow, be careful. That AAIB general isn't to be trusted."

"Explain what has to happen prior to allowing a general officer to fly one of your C-21s," General Crowley said after introducing the members of the AAIB. "Take us through the process."

"What?" I said. "What does this have to do with the CT-43?"

"We're asking the questions here, colonel," he said. "There is apparently a leadership issue in this wing and much of that starts with general officers flying your C-21s. Explain it for us."

I spoke at length and the board members listened, occasionally taking notes. The same clerk who swore me in sat at a desk, typing everything as I spoke. They were all dressed in their Air Force blue uniforms, most had removed their jackets but the general kept his on. He listened intently as I spoke, rarely interrupting other than to say, "go on."

"So this would not have been allowed under the old rules with the Military Airlift Command, sir," a board member asked. "But they are now?"

"Under the old MAC rules the general officer would have to attend a training course first," I answered. "The rules also specified there had to be an operational need for the general to do so and that was widely interpreted to mean the general had to be in the chain of command."

"Who's interpretation is that?" the general asked.

"I don't know," I said. "But I have never witnessed that interpretation violated until it happened here."

"Anecdotal," the general said. "We cannot consider your uncorroborated opinions."

"Is this an accident investigation or a court of law?" I asked. "Under Air Force safety regulations you aren't constrained by those kinds of rules."

"I know the rules," the general said. "Let's take a break for lunch, back here at 1300. Let me remind you colonel that you are under oath and may not discuss anything we've covered here today."

After lunch I was reminded that I was still under oath and asked about the C-21 noise issue and on time takeoffs. By the time the day was complete, we hadn't talked about the CT-43, its crews, or Dubrovnik.

The next morning I was asked about manpower shortages, pilot training, and what I thought about General Paulson.

"I'm not sure what that has to do with the crash," I said.

"I am growing weary of reminding you that your job here is to answer our questions, colonel," the general said.

"Yes, general," I said. "General Paulson has a very sharp focus on the mission and has placed his wing on a wartime footing to accomplish that mission."

"And you do not agree with that?" a board member asked.

"I'm not sure it is my place to agree or not," I said. "I think in the end we had the same goals. My squadron's mission was a small subset of the wing's mission. We both wanted to meet our mission goals, support our people, and keep things safe. We drew the line between the mission and the other two items a little differently."

"And who has the official responsibility for drawing that so-called line," Crowley said.

"We all do," I said.

The "so-called line," as General Crowley put it, consumed the rest of the morning. When I got back from lunch the table I normally sat behind had a copy of the Dubrovnik, Croatia Non-Directional Beacon Runway 12 approach plate. "At last," I said to myself.

"Colonel Haskel," a junior member of the board said once everyone was seated, "are you familiar with this approach?"

"I am," I said. "I read this was the approach in the news and have studied it at length."

"You shouldn't have done that," General Crowley said. "We want to get your reaction to it from the perspective of a pilot seeing it for the first time."

"Well I guess you aren't going to get that from me then, sir," I said.

"Humor us," he said.

"My first thought would be that it is an NDB approach and that alone deserves a fair amount of caution," I said. "I would also be worried about the MSA, but the fact it is according to PANS OPS is a mitigating factor. That would be my first reaction, but there is much more to worry about."

"Hold on," General Crowley said. "You are talking way too fast and using way too much jargon. With a few exceptions, we are all pilots here. So let's try that again."

I was seated behind a small table, perhaps two by three feet on top. Each board member had their own tables arranged in a semicircle around me. The general was flanked by six pilots, ranging in rank from captain to lieutenant colonel. There was a colonel with a maintenance badge and two more with judge advocate badges.

"An NDB approach deserves special attention just by virtue of the ADF," I said.

"Back up," he said. "Explain NDB and ADF."

"A non-directional beacon is a simple radio," I said. "Well, there are two of them on this approach. The ones marked KLP and CV are NDBs. They broadcast a signal, something like what you would get from an AM radio station. The aircraft is equipped with an Automatic Direction Finder radio that has a needle that simply points to the NDB."

"Just like a VOR," General Crowley said. "Yes, we know this."

"No sir," I said. "It is nothing like a VOR. The NDB sends out one signal and the ADF tries to figure out where that signal is strongest and points the needle. It is subject to weather, electronic interference from the ground or the airplane, and can be unpredictable. The VOR sends out two signals, one of which is calibrated and the other is timed. You end up with a magnetic bearing and not just an approximation of direction. VORs are much more accurate and reliable."

The general looked to his left where one of the captains was nodding his head. "Regardless," he said, "continue."

"The next thing that would catch my eye, right off the bat, is the MSA," I said. Crowley opened his mouth and leaned forward in this chair, but hesitated. "Minimum Sector Altitude," I added. "The MSA is usually drawn around the airport but in this case it is around the first NDB. These are safe altitudes within 25 nautical miles, usually, around that point."

"Why would that alarm you, sir," one of the board members asked. He was a major with pilot wings and should have known the answer. Or perhaps he was asking for the benefit of the non-pilots.

"The MSA is very high in relation to the field elevation," I answered. "So, you are either going to need a significant portion of the approach in visual conditions or the approach is going to have to get you down low on instruments. This MDA is substantially lower than the surrounding terrain. The Minimum Descent Altitude, I mean. The pilots will normally descend to the MDA while looking for the runway. They cannot descend below the MDA until the runway is in sight. But this particular MDA is thousands of feet lower than the surrounding terrain."

"That isn't unusual in mountainous terrain, though, is it?" the board member asked.

"No, you will see approaches like this in Colorado and parts of California," I agreed. "But I think it is unusual for an NDB."

"Let's not waste any more time," General Crowley said. "Somebody ask the question about, what was it called?"

"Cross-tuning," another pilot said.

"Yes, cross-tuning," he agreed. "Ask that question."

"Sir," the captain board member continued, "as you testified, this approach has two NDBs. Can a CT-43 legally fly this approach?"

"Yes," I said.

"How do you know that?" Crowley asked. "Have you ever flown the CT-43? Do you know how many NDBs the airplane has?"

"I have flown the airplane," I said. "The airplane does not have any NDBs but it does have one ADF receiver and that is what you need to fly this approach."

The general appeared dumbfounded. He looked to the captain on his left who rose to the challenge. "But sir," the captain said, "don't you need two ADF receivers to fly an approach with two NDBs? You cannot cross-tune on the approach, after all."

"You can," I said. "Section six of the Air Force instrument manual permits cross-tuning so long as it is done before the final approach fix."

The pilots at the panel diverted their eyes downward, most of them writing. "Is that Air Force Manual 51-37 you are referring to?" one asked.

"Yes," I said.

"Let's adjourn for an early lunch," Crowley said. "Colonel, you are dismissed until 1300."

Crowley and the other board members remained seated. I stood, turned, and left. I walked across the street toward the officer's club, checked the path behind me and diverted to the library. I picked up a phone in the entryway and dialed. "Is Mike Hammer around?" I asked.

"He is, standby," the voice said.

"Major Hammer," he answered.

"Mike, do you have a copy of 51-37 nearby?" I asked.

"In my hands right now," he said.

"Really?" I said.

"Yes, sir," he said. "You wouldn't believe what the Stars and Stripes is reporting this morning."

"Try me," I said.

"An unnamed source is saying the CT-43 illegally flew that approach because they only had one ADF," he said. "An Air Force official told the reporter that cross-tuning is illegal."

"But it is allowed up to the final approach fix," I said. "That's in section six, I think."

Flight Lessons 4: Leadership & Command

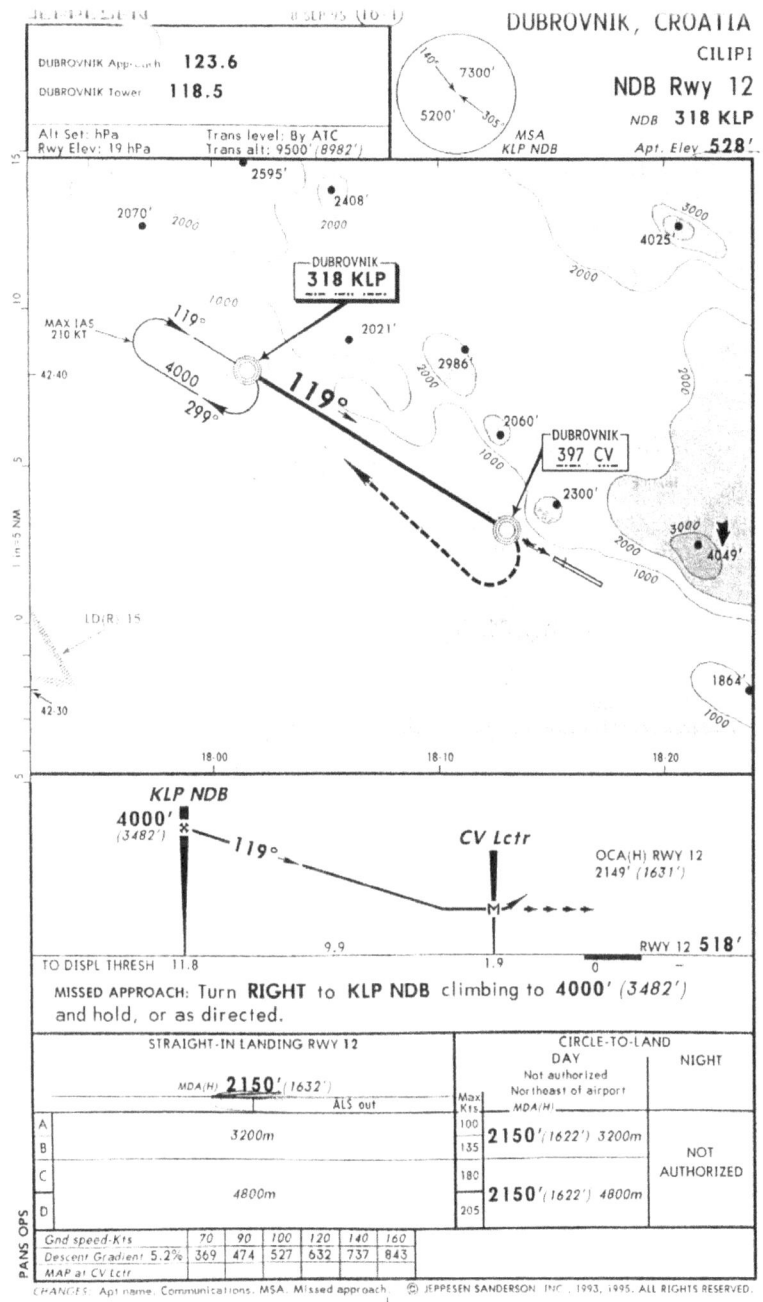

The infamous approach

"Chapter six, actually," he said. "Paragraph 6-16, if you need that. Good luck, stranger."

"Thanks," I said. Of course, I wasn't permitted to make the call while under oath. Mike certainly recognized my voice and was providing me cover.

The board reconvened, the general reminded me I was still under oath, and one of the captains resumed the questioning. "Sir, can you take us through how you would fly this approach?"

"Certainly," I said. "Assuming I had the required weather I would shoot the holding pattern off of Kilo Lima Papa at least once, to be certain I had the 119 degree course nailed inbound and had the drift figured out."

"Would that take more than one turn?" he asked.

"Probably not," I answered. "But I would leave that as an option just to be sure. So tracking 119 inbound, once the Kilo Lima Papa needle swings, I would dial in Charlie Victor and switch the needle so I could track it inbound and then descend to the MDA."

"But that's because you have two ADFs," he said. "The CT-43 would have to cross-tune."

"Yes," I agreed. "So in their case they would have to wait for the needle to swing, indicating they were overhead Kilo Lima Papa. At that point they could dial in Charlie Victor. This would mean they had to delay their descent until that was done. In either case, you then descend to the minimum descent altitude and look for the runway or go missed."

"The ADF receiver in the aircraft you now fly is digital, is it not?"

"If you mean digital in that we can input the exact frequency, then yes," I said.

"Are you familiar with the ADF receiver in the CT-43?" he asked.

"Yes," I said. "It has a dial you have to rotate while looking at a signal strength meter. It isn't as easy to use."

"So wouldn't it take a long time to cross-tune from one frequency to another?" he asked.

"Three seconds," I said. "Tops."

"Are you speculating, colonel," General Crowley asked.

"No sir," I said. We had the same ADF in one of the airplanes I used to fly. That airplane also only had one ADF and we did this all the time." He was at a loss for words, again. "As permitted by AFM 51-37, chapter six, paragraph 6-16, I believe."

"I find that hard to believe," he said.

"There is a CT-43 unit in Panama," I said. "Perhaps you should ask them."

"Don't presume to tell us what to do, colonel," he said. He looked to his left, nodding to the captain who seemed to be their instrument procedures expert.

"When do you go missed?" the expert asked.

"When Charlie Victor swings," I said.

"Could you time?" he asked.

"No," I said. "The approach doesn't include a timing block."

"Why can't the pilots just do the math?" the captain asked. "Don't some pilots keep a distance versus speed table for just this purpose?"

"I think any pilot who does that doesn't understand the risks," I said. "This approach is very close to hazardous terrain. Not only do you have to keep your airspeed constant, but you need to have a good idea of what the winds are doing."

"So is it your opinion that you would have to fly Charlie Victor inbound and you cannot shoot this approach using Kilo Lima Papa outbound?"

"Yes," I agreed.

The captain finished his notes and looked to the general. "I think we're finished with you, colonel," the general said. "You are dismissed."

"Sir, if I may," I said. "I'm not trying to tell you how to conduct your investigation. But this approach violates a host of PANS OPS rules and you haven't mentioned PANS OPS. I am a graduate of the Air Force Instrument Instructor Course and can help you with those."

"That would be highly inappropriate," the colonel with the lawyer's badge said.

"I'm not sure I see why that is," I said. "But taking that as a given, I think you need an instrument procedures expert to look at that approach."

"You are right," General Crowley said. "You are right that you are not here to tell us how to conduct our investigation. I will not repeat myself. You are dismissed."

"Guess how long it takes to cross-tune an ADF receiver on a CT-43?" Mayhem asked the next time we met at the base library. "Three seconds, that's how long. They had the airplane from Panama fly the approach and they timed it."

"You heard," I said.

"I did," he said. "Nobody on that board seems to think they have to keep silent about their proceedings. I hear you made Crowley look pretty foolish. Good job."

"That wasn't my intent," I said.

"Eddie, you probably believe that," he said. "But I've noticed you don't think much of pilots who don't know what they should know. General Crowley is a command pilot with less than 2,000 hours. He needed a waiver to get his command pilot wings. The only airplane he's ever flown is the KC-135 and he did that back in the days when that airplane wasn't allowed to fly anywhere except to an Air Force base."

"Does he have any background in safety?" I asked.

"No," Mayhem said. "In fact, only one board member does, and he's a captain."

"Figures," I said. "This has a political feel to it."

"Well they turned in their report this morning," Mayhem said. "It's all done. My sources say you are completely exonerated and there is a faction at the Pentagon that wants to pin a medal on you."

"Now you are joking," I said.

"No, really," he said. "The investigation revealed just how screwed-up this wing has become. Paulson has been ordered to make sure you are taken care of."

"Taken care of?" I asked.

"Taken care of, in a good way," he said.

"Good," I said. "That can't make him happy."

Flight Lessons 4: Leadership & Command

"Just be careful," Mayhem said. "Think of how The Prince would handle this. Paulson is backed into a corner, he is still dangerous."

"Why have you always been so helpful to me?" I asked. "Someone fudged OTTO numbers for my squadron, and I think it was you. I've seen you go to bat for me more times than I can count. I can't remember ever doing anything for you."

"I'll tell you someday," he said. "But not today."

In the month following the crash I was starting to think of myself as unemployed. I was officially attached to General Paulson's office as his personal aide, but was ordered to stay away and continue to "lay low." I tried to remain clear of the squadron as well, not wanting to get in Felix Henderson's way. So I became a regular at the base library where squadron members who wanted to find me could.

"I got your messages for you, sir," Rorie Fitzpatrick said. "I think everyone is doing well and we want you to know you are invited to a party we are having this weekend."

"Thanks," I said. "I'll try to make it."

The top message said, "Call Colonel Gibbs." I recognized the name as a friend from pilot training and the number as one from the Pentagon. The librarian agreed to give me her office and a long-distance line and with a few button presses I was talking to the Air Force executive assistant to the Secretary of Defense, Marke Gibbs.

"The Secretary has been following the investigation," he said. "He ordered the Air Force Chief of Staff to make sure the AAIB spreads the blame around first, and then to fix what is broken at Ramstein."

"How do you spread the blame around?" I asked.

"That's not why I wanted to talk Eddie," he said. "The Secretary thinks the way the Air Force picks general officers needs a relook, and your wing commander is the poster child of that effort. But they want to make sure you are taken care of before that happens."

"Taken care of?" I asked. "That can mean many things."

"Protected," Marke said. "They need to give you a good assignment. You cannot be seen as being punished after having tried to stop that lunatic in so many ways. You name your assignment. Call me when you have a good assignment. I'll let the Secretary know and we can all get this thing behind us. Do it quickly."

I debated that for all of one hour. Another squadron? No, the politics were more than I wanted to face ever again. The Pentagon? No, my kids were approaching the age where they needed a full-time dad. Another flying job? No, same argument as the Pentagon. My mind was made up.

"Good to see you Eddie, we have some business to discuss." General Paulson pointed to two comfortable chairs around a coffee table and invited me to sit. He smiled warmly and poured coffee into two cups. It would be my fifth cup of the morning, but he was being so extraordinarily polite it would seem rude to decline. It was my first time in his office since the day he threatened to fire me if any of my pilots had late takeoffs.

"I just want you to know the Chief is very impressed with the way you've handled yourself," he said. "He asked me to personally tell you that. This has been a very nasty situation and, unfortunately, far too public. But the Chief realizes you've not talked out of school and he appreciates it. Soon the report will come out and it will be obvious this was one of those things none of us commanders could have prevented."

"I don't know, general," I said. "I don't have any idea what the report is going to say. From my time in front of the board, it seems they were clueless about what happened in Dubrovnik."

"The Chief assures me the report is quite thorough and that they used quite a bit of your knowledge as an instrument pilot," Paulson said. "So it is time for you and me to move on, don't you think?"

"Yes, sir," I said.

"So I just need you to contact someone in the press, and finally make a statement," he said. "Our public affairs office will help you with this. You just need to say something that tells the world that Team Ramstein is a strong team, a team that has gotten it done and will continue to get it done. If you do that for me, I can guarantee you a good assignment. You name your next assignment."

"I would like to move to Illinois," I said. "Someplace quiet and safe to raise my kids. There is an opening for a budget programmer at the United States Transportation Command. They might be reluctant to hire me, given all this notoriety."

"USTRANSCOM," he said. "That's a fine choice. I'll make that happen. Now what about that statement to the press?"

"I can't do that," I said. "I'm still not sure what happened in Dubrovnik. I'm not sure who is to blame, or even if it is me. I want to hold my silence for a bit longer."

Paulson looked at me and then at his coffee. "I see," he said. "Colonel Haskel doesn't budge for the good of the team." We sat silently. He finished his coffee and stood. I stood, leaving behind my half-filled mug. "Good luck Colonel," he said. I left his office.

Late that night I got a call from the Air Force Military Personnel Center. "We know it must be late in Germany, sir, but we were told to let you know as soon as possible."

"No problem," I said. "What's up?"

"We are cutting a rush set of orders for you," the personnel officer said. "You are to report to Scott Air Force Base, USTRANSCOM, as soon as possible. We are authorizing air shipment of all your personal goods. How soon can they expect you?"

"Our kids just finished the school year," I said. "We can do this quickly."

I immediately called Marke Gibbs. "It's done," I said.

"Good," he said. "It will hit the fan tomorrow."

The news did hit the fan the next morning at 0800, Washington, D.C., time. By 1500 Germany time, both Paulson and Wozniak were escorted from their offices, never to return.

"2 Commanders fired over CT-43 crash"

May 31st, Ramstein, Germany. The Air Force relieved two high-ranking commanders in Europe over the April 3 crash of a military transport plane near Dubrovnik, Croatia.

Brig. Gen. William E. Paulson was dismissed late Wednesday as commander of the Ramstein Air Wing. Also relieved was Colonel John E. Wozniak, operations group commander.

The officers were relieved by Major General Samuel T. Foster, commander of the 17th Air Force headquarters, after Foster was briefed on the soon-to-be-released findings of the CT-43 accident investigation.

A spokesman for the 17th Air Force insisted the firings were "unrelated" to the dismissal on March 29 of Lt. Col. Edward Haskel, a popular former commander of the 76th Military Airlift Squadron. Haskel had voiced concerns about the safety of flying VIPs in the former Yugoslavia, and Paulson relieved him of command five days before the CT-43 crash.

One Air Force official said the report is "just about complete."

Flight Lesson: Bureaucratic Leadership

A bureaucratic leader seeks to achieve organizational goals by following strict procedures while seeking to avoid ad hoc measures not covered by written rules or accepted protocols. The leader tends to be more worried about pleasing upper levels of leadership (or avoiding angering them), than meeting organizational goals.

Bureaucratic Leadership Defined

bu•reau•crat•ic

Relating to the business of running an organization or government.

Overly concerned with procedure at the expense of efficiency or common sense.

The Advantages of Bureaucratic Leadership

Bureaucratic leaders are seen as reliable and steady; they are especially valued in organizations where the tasks are set and innovation is seen as a threat to order. Bureaucratic leaders can be easily trained and, in the right environment, can be left without supervision for long periods.

The Pitfalls of Bureaucratic Leadership

A bureaucratic leader may struggle to adapt to changing circumstances and can be blind to innovation or situations where thinking "outside the box" is required. Subordinates can find the environment stifling and may be inclined to flee to where career progression is more assured.

10: What Really Happened

At the end of several months, the board released a 7,000-page report that gave the instant impression of thoroughness by virtue of its ponderous mass. The conclusions of the report were summarized in a 94-page volume which cross-referenced the remaining pages in an intimidating array of footnotes.

Initial reaction from the press was favorable. The report spread the blame around to the usual suspects and included portions of the Air Force itself:

1) The command (USAFE) failed to comply with an Air Force Instruction, prohibiting the use of approach plates other than those published by the Department of Defense, unless they had been reviewed by the command itself.

2) The pilots made errors executing the approach, including failing to realize the approach could not be flown with only one ADF receiver, flew the approach 80 knots above final approach speed, flying a course 9 degrees left of the correct course, and failed to identify the missed approach point.

3) The government of Croatia failed to ensure the NDB Instrument Approach Procedure was correctly designed and computed the minimum descent altitude several hundred feet below where it should have been.

The report summary concludes "this mishap resulted from the combination of the three causes listed above – any one of which, had it not existed, would have prevented the accident."

The report got two out of three wrong. It took me three months to read all 7,000 pages and a second reading to really comprehend what had happened. It took a third reading to understand why the findings were written the way they were: to protect the Headquarters of the United States Air Force itself. I've included copies of the pertinent pages from the Accident Report in the Appendix.

An improperly designed approach.

Of the three listed causes, only the third is correct. In Dubrovnik's cold war heyday as part of the Socialist Federal Republic of Yugoslavia, the airport had modern Instrument Landing System (ILS) and VHF Omnidirectional Range (VOR) approaches. Both types of approaches are far more accurate than an NDB approach and not prone to electromagnetic interference. When Croatia and Slovenia declared their independence from Yugoslavia in 1991, Dubrovnik lay under siege for nearly seven months from armies supported primarily by Serbia. As the Serbs finally retreated, the ILS and VOR equipment was stolen.

The airport was either left with the two NDBs or installed both as the cheapest way to get an instrument approach up and running. Approach designers failed to consider the nearby terrain and the excessive distance between the two NDBs. The published Minimum Descent Altitude (MDA) was 2,150 feet and the aircraft impacted the mountain at 2,175 feet. The MDA should have included an additive for the terrian and been listed as 2,822 feet. Had the approach listed the MDA correctly, the crash would not have occurred.

USAFE failed to comply with an Air Force Instruction.

The United States Air Forces Europe (USAFE) is a "Major Command," a subordinate command to Headquarters United State Air Force (HQ USAF), also known as the "Air Staff." In the early 1990's, the Air Force Chief of Staff decided Air Force Regulations were too restrictive and instructed the Air Staff to replace them all with something that gave commanders much more latitude. These Air Force Instructions (AFI) were at first understood to be guidelines, not regulations. I always accepted them as mandatory but perhaps that belief wasn't held by everyone in the Air Force. After the CT-43 crash, all AFIs had the following statement added on their covers:

COMPLIANCE WITH THIS PUBLICATION IS MANDATORY

A 1995 change to AFI 11-206 required that "any instrument-approach procedure not published in a U.S. Department of Defense (DOD) or [U.S.] National Oceanic and Atmospheric Administration (NOAA) flight information publication be reviewed by the major command terminal instrument procedures (TERPs) specialist before it can be flown by [U.S.] Air Force crews." There is an exception within the AFI that allows U.S. Air Force crews to use a non-DOD/NOAA approach chart if the weather conditions meet the minimums required to conduct a visual flight rules (VFR) approach and landing.

USAFE, for its part, delayed releasing the change to the AFI until 1996, when it could do so with its own supplement to that instruction. The 86 Operations Group requested and was granted a waiver via an email exchange with USAFE. The Air Staff denied the waiver was ever approved and in 1996 informed USAFE of just that. The 86 Operations Group Commander asked his squadron commanders for an opinion. I called the leaders of three stateside squadrons and found all were operating as before, using non-DOD/NOAA approach charts without review. This included my former squadron at Andrews Air Force Base, the 99th Airlift Squadron which is a part of the 89th Airlift Wing. My fellow squadron commanders reported back with similar results. Based on this, the 86 Operations Group Commander elected to keep the waiver in place until USAFE put together a mechanism to provide the required reviews.

What is missing from this picture was the necessary manpower and funding to allow the Major Air Commands to fulfil the AFI's mandate. At the time of the crash, the restriction had been in effect for over eighteen months and not a single unit in the entire Air Force was in compliance. It is doubtful any Major Command had any TERPS specialists on staff at the time. (Did the investigators know this? Yes. I told them.)

The pilots failed to correctly fly the approach procedure.

The report says investigators looked for evidence of where the instruments indicated the aircraft was at time of impact and pointed to a report that said no data was obtainable from the aircraft's Radio Magnetic Indicator (RMI). The report then went to great lengths to extrapolate the aircraft's radar plot from an Airborne Warning and Control System (AWACS) E-3A aircraft and winds from Brindisi Italy to hypothesize the crew was flying 9 degrees in error, exactly where the aircraft ended up. That would have been over a mile and a half north of course. They also used this extrapolation to say the crew crossed the final approach fix 80 knots too fast. The report leaves no doubt in its executive summary: these pilots flew a sloppy approach. But the evidence pointing to them flying 9 degrees north of course and 80 knots too fast was all made up.

Buried in the appendices of the report, on page O-28/3, the company that provided the initial finding that no data was recoverable from the aircraft's RMI wrote back to say they got the data after all. The RMI was reading 115, just 4 degrees north of course and less than half the deviation claimed by the executive summary. This puts into doubt the report's usage of Brindisi winds to extrapolate the winds over the KLP NDB and therefore the speed of the aircraft. Brindisi is 103 nautical miles away from KLP. It would have made much more sense to use Dubrovnik's reported wind, only 12 nautical miles away.

So we cannot believe the report's assertion that the crew navigated 9 degrees north of course and flew 80 knots too fast. But the airplane ended up on a mountainside, 9 degrees north of course. How can that be, when the pilots were looking at an RMI showing them within Airline Transport Pilot standards of plus or minus 5 degrees? The answer is buried in the appendices.

Croatian Airlines pilots (report page V-233), air traffic controllers (report page V-523), and the Croatian government's flight department chief (report page V-168) all agreed the NDB was prone to forcing airplanes to the north under weather conditions present the day of the crash. But the report ignored this fact, the fact that the Croatian maintenance chief responsible for the NDB committed suicide three days after the crash, and that an electrical power line wasn't tested for interference under conditions identical to the night of the crash. While acknowledging the presence of an electrical power line which ran "from the power plant up the face of the mountain in the general direction to the accident site" (report page J-3/7), the investigators did not follow through with realistic tests of possible interference to the NDB's signal.

So what really happened? The General in charge of the investigation was interviewed years later and said, "perhaps we'll never know." And yet countless books and magazine articles have been published since, using his report to say the pilots were "rogue" and the Major Air Command was operating outside of the rules and regulations of the Air Force. Allow me to provide a more plausible explanation using the evidence in the report itself.

1. The pilots made a mistake by flying the KLP NDB outbound instead of the CV NDB inbound.
2. Their chronometers were running at the time of impact and it appears they attempted to use timing to determine the missed approach point.
3. After crossing the KLP NDB, their ADF pointed along the power plant's powerline instead of the weaker NDB. This is a known flaw of ADF receivers and a probable cause of the effect noted by pilots from Croatian Airlines and the Croatian government's chief pilot, as well as the local air traffic controllers.
4. Because the approach MDA was designed 647 feet too low, the aircraft impacted terrain.

Flight Lessons 4: Leadership & Command

A final question remains, however. Why would the report go out of its way to paint the pilots as sloppy and perhaps reckless, rather than simply say they expertly flew the wrong NDB using a timing method that wasn't allowed? I believe it was to protect the Air Force itself.

If you say the pilots flew 9 degrees north of course and 80 knots too fast, the cause and solution is easy. The cause was sloppy and reckless pilots. The solution is purge the ranks of sloppy and reckless pilots.

If, on the other hand, you say the pilots made two mistakes in planning the approach, the error trail doesn't stop there. Why did the pilots think flying the KLP NDB outbound using ad hoc timing was okay? Because they were improperly trained. Of the pilots I surveyed at the time, only Mike Hammer and I knew this wasn't prudent. Most Air Force pilots aren't trained to analyze an approach plate to the extent we were taught to do at the Air Force Instrument Instructor's School. The cross-tuning technique was allowed by the Air Force instrument procedures manual in effect at the time. That same manual was silent on the matter of ad hoc timing to determine a missed approach point.

The change to the AFI required the Major Command to assign a TERPS specialist to review each approach plate because pilots were taught to trust the approach plates given to them. Any approach plate with the acronyms TERPS or PANS OPS were assumed to be properly designed. The Dubrovnik approach plate had PANS OPS, the internationally approved "Procedures for Air Navigation Services, Aircraft Operations" printed on the side. But they didn't need outside approval from anyone to do that, and no agency regularly checks these approaches for PANS OPS compliance. (Croatian pilots knew by word-of-mouth to add a few degrees to the course centerline.) Any Air Force pilot without the specialized training of the Air Force Instrument Instructor School would have assumed the approach was properly designed.

All Air Force pilots are instrument rated when they get their wings. At each aircraft qualification course, they are taught the intricacies of flying instruments for their particular aircraft types. And at the squadron level, pilots are given continuing training based on the Air Force manuals, which are silent on the subject of multiple NDB approaches.

Given all this, I would rewrite the list of causes as follows.

1) The Croatian aviation authorities failed to properly design the NDB approach into Dubrovnik. This caused the accident aircraft to fly a

Minimum Descent Altitude (MDA) that was too low to safely clear terrain during its missed approach.

2) The Headquarters United States Air Force staff failed to immediately enforce restrictions against flying non-DOD/NOAA instrument approaches without Major Air Command validation, and to fully fund and provide manpower to enable the Major Air Commands to do so. Such a review could have alerted the accident crew that the MDA was too low.

3) The Headquarters United States Air Force staff failed to adequately provide its pilots with the necessary training to analyze an approach plate and determine the correct methods for determining a missed approach under a variety of circumstances.

Postscript
Two Years Later, 1998

United States Transportation Command Emblem (Drawing: US Army)

"This should be your name, sir," she said as she fastened the new tag on the door. As our office secretary, she would be working very closely with the new boss. But she needed time to adjust.

"The CINC deserves his top pick," I said. "Colonel Szabo will be good for us."

"It still stinks," she said. "Sir."

That seemed to be the consensus. I was assigned to the United States Transportation Command as the leader of an office of budget programmers, but was quickly taken away by the chief of legislative liaison to be his deputy. We worked directly for the CINC, pronounced "sink." As the Commander In Chief of the United States Transportation Command, USTRANSCOM, General Roger Craft was responsible for the wartime roles of the Army, Navy, and Air Force components of the military transportation system.

As the office deputy chief, my job was to corral the efforts of officers from each service to provide the CINC with the advice he needed to lobby Congress and members of the President's staff. It was a fun job that required a "big picture" focus of all things transportation. After playing second fiddle for two years everyone thought I would take over when the chief retired. I knew that would never happen and I knew why; but I had to keep that a secret. It was the only fair thing to do for the new boss.

Lieutenant Colonel Daniel Szabo was the CINC's favorite pilot from a past life and appeared to have everything I lacked. He was an accomplished KC-135 tanker pilot, flying a major weapon system owned by our command. By comparison, my flight log only included passenger type airplanes that did not have war-fighting roles. At six-foot-three his stature was not apparent until he stood next to me. He wore those extra three inches well. He greeted everyone with a broad smile and clear blue eyes that placed a laser lock on you and made you feel important.

"Eddie, I've been looking forward to meeting you," he said while boring his eyes into mine. "Everyone says you know the command's business like nobody else and the Congress like the back of your hand."

"I suppose," I said.

"Frankly, I am surprised you didn't get the job," he said. "I thought maybe it had to do with the CT-43 crash," he said. "So I read the accident report. It doesn't mention you at all."

"Then you didn't read the whole report" I said.

"Well no," he said. "Just the executive summary."

"The accident report was filled with errors," I said. "It failed to identify a primary causal factor and because of that failed the most important tenet of the Air Force Flight Safety Program. It will not prevent recurrence."

"Okay," he said, "I'll bite. What was the primary causal factor?"

"The approach was designed incorrectly," I said.

"The report says that," he said. "It blamed the approach design, the command, and the pilots."

"It blamed the approach plate design," I said. "The approach plate was designed with a 600-foot error, that's true. But the approach itself was designed incorrectly. In the heat of battle the pilots made a mistake, but that mistake should not have been fatal. The pilots flew the first NDB outbound when they should have switched to the next NDB."

"There you go," he said. "Pilot error."

"Yes," I said. "But they flew that outbound NDB with enough precision to miss the mountain. The report ignored a teardown analysis of the instrument to pin the blame on them and make them the primary causal factor.

Flight Lessons 4: Leadership & Command

They were not."

"Then why did they end up on the side of that mountain?" he asked.

"There was a powerline from the city that pointed right up to that mountain," I said. "The ADF receiver on the airplane followed it right to the crash site. The only time the powerline was a factor was at night with high power plant output. The Croatian pilots knew about this and routinely flew the needle five degrees to the south. The appendix of the report says as much. But all that was ignored in the conclusion."

"It's too bad they all died in vain," he said.

"Maybe some good came of it," I said.

"How so?" he asked.

"The Air Force cut all funding for enhanced ground proximity warning systems just over a year before the crash," I said. "I was at the Pentagon at the time. They used the money to help pay for a Clinton health care initiative. After the crash all those programs were restored. Now we just need to replace all those ancient aircraft."

"Well, we're not here to dwell on ancient history," Szabo said. "Whatever the report says, the CINC says you've done a great job. Why don't you bring the rest of the staff in here and do the introductions."

I left his office and returned to the trenches where the other three officers waited. Major Michael Houghton was an airlift pilot and was probably the smartest person I had ever met. It would only be a matter of time before he outranked me. Lieutenant Commander Richard Grafton was a Navy officer with a variety of shipboard experiences that made him pretty smart about all things sealift. He was a clever officer who could latch onto concepts but may have been a bit lazy in execution. A Navy lieutenant commander has the equivalent rank of an Air Force or Army major. Grafton was up for promotion, but his chances were only average. Finally, Army Major Steve Christ was our class clown. He started his career driving the M1A1 main battle tank but took a detour to the quartermaster corps. Unlike the rest of the office, he wrote poorly but could hold his own in a conversation. The three looked at me. I held both hands upward with index fingers aimed skyward. With a flick of both wrists I pointed to the boss's office and we four marched in, followed by our secretary.

Szabo greeted everyone warmly and with a firm handshake. He devoted a minute to each, in turn, about family, career, and life in general. Once everyone was made to feel suitably warm and fuzzy, we all sat. He gave us a peek into the future, saying every Monday morning we would start with a staff meeting and the first Monday of each month would be special.

"The CINC says he relies on this office for coming up with things the rest of the headquarters can't," Szabo said. "He says Eddie has a knack for thinking 'outside of the box' and that I should encourage that. So, Eddie you can take a break while the rest of us try to revolutionize transportation. On the first Monday of each month, one of us will present an idea that comes from left field. You will explain your idea with some detail and nobody else can speak until you are done. And then we can all punch holes in the idea to really flesh it out. Since I am the leader, I'll take the first Monday. And lo and behold, that's today! What are you thinking, Eddie?"

"I am thinking this is a promising start," I said.

"I think so too," he agreed. "Here's my out of the box idea. We in the Air Force are wasting a tremendous amount of money on the C-21 Learjet fleet," he said. "I think we can better put that funding into a major weapon system."

Szabo spoke at length and in great detail about the cost of running the 70 Learjets the Air Force used throughout the world versus using the local airlines to do the same job. He said the number of pilots used by the program would go far in answering the shortage of pilots in our airlift and tanker fleets. The rest of us sat patiently as he pontificated.

"So, what do you think?" he asked finally. The two majors and the lieutenant commander looked at me, perhaps with a bit of deference. Or perhaps they knew what I knew and wanted me to catch the spear surely to come to anyone daring to mention the new emperor's lack of clothing.

"The idea certainly appears to have its merits," I said. "But the airlift provided by the C-21 is not the purpose of the program but a side benefit. The original and continuing purpose of the program is to season pilots. It takes four to five years to bring a brand-new pilot from copilot to aircraft commander in a tanker or airlifter. Then he or she only has four or five years left before possibly jumping to the airlines. Putting them in a C-21 first gets them to the left seat of the bigger airplane in half the time."

He sat silently as I spoke but at my first pause jumped right in. "Yes, but we need copilots too. You might as well season them in the big airplane."

"When the program was first proposed, they went through the numbers," I said. "We don't have a shortage of copilots, in fact we have too many. We just can't get them ready for upgrade soon enough because training in the big birds is expensive. The C-21 is a bargain."

"Well, then!" he said. "Good discussion. You all have work to do and I have a meeting with the CINC. Commander Grafton, how about you come up with an out of the box idea for next month?" Grafton shot him a thumbs-up. "Good! Everyone dismissed; except you, Eddie. Stick around a few minutes."

Everyone filed out and Szabo closed the door behind us. He aimed his normally friendly eyes and spoke, leader to follower. "One of my cardinal rules about leadership, Eddie, is that loyalty is critical. It never helps to badmouth the boss, especially in front of others."

"What happened to everyone can punch a hole in the idea?" I asked.

"You have a special role as the number two in this office," he said. "They all look up to you. You should never criticize me in public."

"I suppose that's true," I said. "I'll try not to take you so literally next time."

"You do that," he said. "Dismissed."

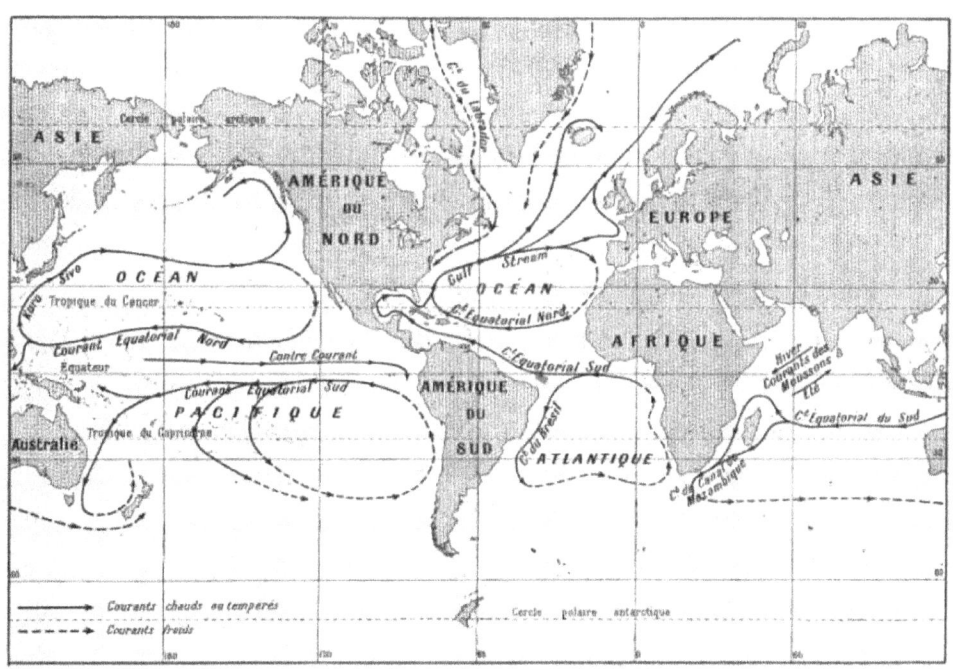

Map of the oceans as they were known in 1910, A. Sauvaire-Jordan

I returned to my desk to see Rich Grafton hovering in a holding pattern.

"How can I be of assistance?" I asked.

"I wanted to bounce my 'out of the box' idea off you, sir." He just couldn't give up the "sir" routine and I had given up asking that he call me Eddie. He pulled the nearest chair toward my desk and spread an ancient mariner's map in front of me.

"I've heard brown shoes talk about flying faster in a headwind and slower in a tailwind to improve fuel consumption and was wondering if I could apply that to our container ships."

"You've heard brown shoes talk, Rich?"

"Sorry, sir," he said. "That's navy slang for navy pilots, who wear brown shoes. Us surface guys wear black shoes."

Rich went on to say most of their sealift ships cruised at 25 knots because they could. "It's always been done that way," he explained. But he had heard their fuel consumption would drop 25 percent if they simply pulled it back to 22 knots. "If it works for airplanes, why not ships?"

"Truth is, it doesn't," I said. "For most jets you cannot vary the speed enough to make up for the difference in wind speeds. Most jets can only vary their speeds at altitude by ten or twenty knots. Since the winds can vary by as much as 200 knots, the percentage difference is very small. We would almost never see a 25 percent drop in fuel consumption at our flyable speeds."

"So if the percentage of the speed variation is higher relative to the wind, you could do it?" he asked.

"Sure, what kind of current speeds are we talking about?"

"Usually only one or two knots," he said. "But if you get into the Atlantic gulfstream, it could be as high as 6 knots."

I saw where he was going with this. I pulled out a blank sheet of paper and started to scribble. "What's the distance between a typical port in the east coast of the United States to one in Europe?"

"Four thousand nautical, give or take," he answered.

"So at 25 knots, we get there in 160 hours," I said. For the next bit I needed my pocket calculator. "At 22 knots, that makes 182 hours; that's 22 hours or just under another day at sea. What about fuel burn?"

Rich opened a book he had been holding and turned to a dog-eared page.

Flight Lessons 4: Leadership & Command

The chart showed a burn of 350 tons per day at 25 knots and 250 tons per day at 22 knots. I realized we had the information we needed but to convince our aviator bosses, we would need to translate everything to aeronautical speak. "So that comes to 14.6 tons per hour fast, and 10.4 slow. That's even better than 25 percent. What's a ton of fuel cost?"

Rich turned a few more pages. "Four hundred, fifty dollars a ton, give or take."

So that came to 160 x 14.6 x 450 = $1,051,200 for the fast trek, or 182 x 10.4 x 450 = $851,760 for the slow. "Arriving a day later saves you almost two hundred thousand dollars."

"Now what if there is no change in current at all?" he asked.

"In the aviation world we have a way of thinking about this," I said. "Most flight manuals give us numbers for maximum range for when we want to go as far as we can go."

"Our destinations are pretty much set in stone," he said.

"Well, us too," I admitted. "But knowing those numbers gets you to the destination with the most fuel in reserve and you can work that backwards to determine taking less fuel."

"It takes fuel to carry fuel," he said.

"Exactly," I said. We refigured the math for a constant current, a "tail current," and a "head current." In every instance we ended up with significant fuel savings.

We sat back and basked in the glory of his idea. I had worked with Lieutenant Commander Grafton for nearly two years and knew he faced long odds on his upcoming promotion board. He needed some kind of zinger for his recommendation and this just might be the idea that gets him promoted. "Well done," I said, handing him my notes.

The next few weeks were consumed with preparing for the next session of Congress and I all but forgot about the first of the month ritual. Szabo did not. "So now it is time for out of the box thinking," he said. "Commander Grafton, the floor belongs to you."

Rich got up and handed us each a hand drawn map of the Atlantic with a course from Charleston to Antwerp and my calculations. He finished with the bottom line he had come up with just a week prior. "We delay the containers by a day, we save two hundred thousand dollars. With our current deployment schedules, that saves the U.S. taxpayer nearly seven million dollars a week, over 300 million dollars a year."

"That is brilliant," Szabo said. "Commander Grafton that is exactly what we are looking for. Let me see how far I can take this."

Rich beamed a smile and the rest of us took turns shaking his hand and patting him on the back. Szabo dismissed the staff and asked me to stay behind. "Let's talk about promotions," he said.

"That would be great," I said. "Rich is up for promotion in November and Steve in December. I wrote their last effectiveness reports and am concerned for them both. Steve will probably make it. I'm not so sure about Rich. He has another effectiveness report due in June. If we get somewhere with his 22-knots idea, we might have what we need. This is the kind of idea that gets officers promoted."

"Oh, yeah," Szabo said. "That's a good thought. But what I had in mind was our promotions. You and I are both up for full colonel next year and the definitely promotes will be written next January. Now I am a pretty good writer but the CINC tells me you are even better. I think we are both guaranteed promotion but let's not take any chances. Start thinking about our promotion recommendations."

"Okay," I said. "But let's not forget about Grafton's idea. If we get some traction on that soon, we can get him promoted."

Szabo soon forgot the "out of the box" idea program, except for whenever Commander Grafton asked about the 22-knot idea. "I'm working it," Szabo said each time. "These things take time."

USTRANSCOM is a "Joint Command," meaning it is comprised of members from more than one military service. Besides the CINC, each service would provide a flag officer to act as the senior representative of that service. Because the CINC happened to be an Air Force general, a four-star general, the Air Force also provided a lower grade flag officer. Our legislative liaison office worked directly for the CINC so I never paid much attention to the other Air Force general. But all that changed when he was replaced by a new flag officer: Major General Charles H. Crowley, who had parlayed his work on the CT-43 accident investigation into a second star. Crowley's job was to head the command's operations center. He dealt only in day-to-day operations and had nothing to do with future acquisitions, my office's focus. I carefully planned a confrontation, but had to find the right moment.

I thought I had my moment a few weeks later, when Szabo was attending a legislative liaison training session in Washington, D.C. That left the weekly CINC meeting for me to attend. Before Szabo's arrival I would attend every week and each subordinate general officer would show up fifteen minutes early and chat before the CINC showed up. I took my seat early but Crowley only appeared seconds before the CINC. Crowley ignored me, though we were seated right next to each other.

After a few words from the CINC, each flag officer normally took a turn. The Admiral's normally dour countenance was missing and he seemed eager to speak. When his time finally came, he spoke rapid fire.

"We have the results of our study and it is fantastic. Yes, everything is confirmed. We can slow the ships from 25 to 22 knots and only lose an average of one day transit time while saving a butt load of fuel. Sure, we have to pay the crews for another day and there are some insurance costs, but that is chicken feed compared to the cost of fuel." The CINC shot him a double thumbs-up. "And it's not just the fuel. Maintenance costs are expected to drop as well. We estimate annual program savings at half a billion dollars!"

The flag officers broke into enthusiastic chatter, which the CINC ended with a raised hand. "Colonel Haskel, please pass on to Colonel Szabo our thanks and a well done. It figures that an Air Force tanker pilot would come up with a way to save the Navy gas money!"

Once the meeting ended everyone rose until the CINC was gone. I turned to Crowley. "General I would like a few minutes, if I may."

"I'm too busy, colonel," he said. "Call my office to get on the schedule."

USNS Bob Hope Container ship, (Photo: US Navy)

The following Monday, after Szabo's return, I entered his office without asking and closed the door behind me. "The Navy is pretty happy with your 22-knot container ship idea," I said. "The CINC was singing your praises all week."

Szabo looked up from a stack of paperwork and briefly smiled. "That's good. Anything else."

"Did you stop to think, for even a moment, it would have been a good time to credit the inventor of the idea?"

"Commander Grafton works for me," he began. "All of his ideas belong to me. If it weren't for me asking for out of the box ideas, he would never have had it in the first place."

"Rich is up for promotion and this could have made the difference," I said. "Instead he is going to end up demoralized that his idea was stolen and he may eventually be passed over."

"Don't lecture me about morale," he said. "I am responsible for everyone's morale. When the office receives recognition, everyone benefits. As the leader, my achievements are reflected by all who follow me."

"I think you have that backwards," I said.

Flight Lessons 4: Leadership & Command

"You are being overly dramatic," Szabo said. "He works for a great office and the glory I collect on our behalf is shared by everyone. Even you."

"I have my own rules about these things," I said. "A true leader passes along credit where it is due and does so generously, while at the same time accepting responsibility for his actions and those of his subordinates. I doubt you get any more out of the box ideas worth a damn once your subordinates figure out you don't give a damn about them personally."

"Well, colonel," he said. "You are wrong. That's why they put me in charge of the office instead of you. It seems I have better instincts on these things."

"You are probably right about that," I said. Szabo returned his gaze to the papers on his desk, my sarcasm lost on him.

I returned to my desk and found Rich sitting in my chair, reading a Military Sealift Command newsletter. The lead title said it all, "Three Knots Saves Millions."

"I've asked around," he said. "The sealift staff said this revolutionary idea came from Colonel Szabo. Nobody sees my fingerprints on any of this."

"I know," I said. "I can't explain it; the boss must have his reasons."

"I should have gone through Navy channels," he said, tossing the newsletter into the trash. "Air Force officers are just too political." He lifted his gaze to mine. "Sorry, sir. Not you. I'm just pissed."

"I don't blame you," I said.

As the afternoon turned to evening I lost track of the time while working on the CINC's next speech. His previous speech writer fell ill the previous year and by volunteering to be a temporary fill in I had in effect inherited a new duty. I remained in my own world until the phone jarred me back to reality. "In the zone?" *The Lovely Mrs. Haskel* asked. I looked at the clock, it was past seven.

"Oops," I said. "On my way." I stuffed my brief case and turned out of the office. Szabo looked up from his desk.

"Before you go I want to ask you about this," he said, handing me a letter. I recognized the first paragraph and flipped the pages to the signature block.

"I wrote this about two years ago," I said. "I've never heard back."

"And you won't," Szabo said. "While I was in D.C. I visited a friend of mine in the Chief's office. When I mentioned your name he gave me this. He said he stopped it before it ever got to the Chief. You should be grateful that he did."

"I don't know about that," I said. "The system that allowed the Air Staff to levy a requirement on air wings without the necessary funding and personnel still exists. Maybe two years ago he could have used this as the impetus for change."

"Eddie I have to tell you something," he said. "In all my years in uniform, this letter is the greatest example of insubordination I've ever seen."

"High praise," I said.

"Take it," he said. "Shred it."

"Okay," I said.

I added the letter to the stack in my brief case and went home. I thought about the anger I felt after having read all 7,000 pages of the CT-43 accident report. The anger that inspired me to write the letter. Now, two years later, the letter reignited the passion. But the passion didn't have a direction.

I bypassed my office the next morning to sit in on an Army briefing about the Afloat Prepositioning Program, or simply, "Prepo." The Army had several battalions' worth of tanks, armored personnel vehicles, ammunition, and spares sitting on ships all over the world. It was one of their sanest programs designed to ensure they could take the fight to any place on earth in minimum time. I grew up during the Vietnam War thinking the U.S. Army could do no right. But now, witnessing their metamorphosis since the 1990 Iraq War, I was a convert.

I returned to my office around 10 a.m. and found a stack of messages, including one from Major General Crowley's office. The general didn't have an opening in his schedule for the foreseeable future. After handling the other messages, I thought about my planned confrontation. The letter I had written to the Air Force Chief of Staff sat beside my computer, taunting me with facts fading in my memory. It was a good letter. I changed the salutation and the rest of the letter rewrote itself.

Major General Crowley,

It has been two years since you signed the Air Force CT-43 Accident Investigation Report and the systemic problems made evident by the accident still exist. Just as importantly, the shadow cast on the families of the deceased crewmembers has not been removed. We have a chance to correct all that

Flight Lessons 4: Leadership & Command

before the crash fades from memory. I will not rest until this is done and would appreciate your help.

The report cites an improperly designed approach plate, command failures, and pilot error as the three causes of this crash. I will address each.

The approach plate design. As the report notes, there is no doubt this approach procedure was improperly designed. I certainly agree. It was designed for an Instrument Landing System (ILS) where the long spacing between (Non Directional Beacons) NDBs and the Minimum Descent Altitude (MDA) made sense. When the retreating Bosnians took the ILS and the Croatians substituted the NDB-only approach, the MDA should have been raised by 647 feet to meet international approach design standards, the Procedures for Air Navigation Services (PANS OPS).

Command failures. I heard you address this item at a news conference right after the report was released. You asked "How can we have a major air command ignoring Air Force directives?" This was the reason General Paulson and Colonel Wozniak were given Article 15s.

No major air commands who had planes using Jeppesen approach plates had instituted the review process mandated by recently changed Air Force directives. Not a single one! When the regulation was changed, no commands were given the additional funding or manpower to accomplish these reviews. On the day of the crash, the Air Mobility Command--the Air Force's biggest user of Jeppesen approach plates--was flying using these non-DoD approach procedures without review.

By giving Article 15s to Colonel Wozniak and General Paulson, we have punished the only group and wing commanders in the entire Air Force who were dealing with the problem. Your accident investigation board ignored this fact. This suggests Wozniak and Paulson were "scapegoats."

When the Air Staff agreed to place restrictions on non-DoD approach plates, they should have publicized the changes and given each major air command the people and funding needed to carry out the new rules.

Pilot error. Volume 1 of the report says the pilots flew a course nine degrees in error, directly contradicting evidence in the body of the report itself. Allow me to point out my review of the evidence.

(1) The report clearly acknowledges the airplane's NDB bearing pointer was pointing to 115 degrees--only four degrees off course. (Page 0-28/3) This

is not only better than what the report admits are Air Force standards (ten degrees) but also bests the tougher Airline Transport Rating standards (five degrees).

(2) The report ignores this fact and then uses a dated wind prediction of 180 degrees/30 knots to hypothesize a 6-degree drift was needed on final. (page W-3/1). This wind is based on an extrapolation from Brindisi, Italy and is hours old.

(3) The report ignores previous pilot reports that there was no drift at all on final, and it had been that way all day. (page V-170).

(4) The report says the pilot's heading bug set on 116 must have indicated his intended heading, based on four separate references in the body of the report. (page 78).

(5) And yet, when you read each of these references, three disagree with the statement, (pages V-245, V-1265, V-1632) and the remaining is non-committal (page V-1010).

(6) Several Croatian officials acknowledged the Kolocep NDB was prone to inaccuracies during the weather conditions present on the day of the crash. (pages V-233, V-523, V-580)

While Volume 1 paints an inaccurate picture of the pilots flying nine degrees off course, the rest of the report proves the pilots flew well within the toughest standards. The report clearly implicates problems with the NDB which the investigators ignored. The report notes the Dubrovnik power plant was operating at very high output and the powerline to the city was highly energized. The accident aircraft flew a line along that powerline right to the crash site. While the report mentions this, the subsequent flight tests were done five days after the crash, in dissimilar weather conditions, and during lower power plant output. The investigators also failed to look into the airport maintenance chief's suicide, accepting the Croatian claim of innocence at face value.

The report is heavily flawed and should be corrected. The system that allowed one part of the Air Staff to levy a requirement on another without funding still exists. The Headquarters Air Force Director of Operations can again issue a written edict and consider it "job done" without the necessary follow through. This can be unsafe and it is up to us to fix it.

Edward Q. Haskel, Lt Col, USAF

Flight Lessons 4: Leadership & Command

C-17 at night, (Photo: Adrian Vargo)

Once the next congressional term began our focus turned to the CINC's next visit. The headquarters staff would build hundreds of pages of issue papers, thinking their work would be read by the CINC. In fact, only the legislative liaison office staff read the papers which we would use to brief the CINC during his walks between one Senate or House office and the next. We sent an officer a day early to practice the route we would have to walk and to meet with the senator's or representative's staff. On the day of the CINC's visit, we repeated the process for real. Since Szabo had never done this before, I played the role of instructor.

"The senator is going to push hard for the next C-17 simulator," I said to Szabo. "I think his state's Air Guard wants to get their hands on it to cement their role as the premier Guard C-17 base."

"Nothing wrong with that," he said.

"It takes a year to build a simulator," I said. "We only have one. We can train Guard pilots but they refuse to train ours. We don't have enough C-17 pilots because we can't train them fast enough. Giving them the next simulator sets our manning back two years."

"Got it," he said. "Next topic."

We spent about six hours walking the route and talking with staffers and then repeated the walk just to make sure Szabo had it down. We went over the pertinent issues during the walk and it appeared Szabo had a handle on all the Air Force issues and was starting to get familiar with the Army and Navy hot buttons. "Give me that issues book and I'll burn the midnight oil."

The next day Szabo and I walked with General Craft from office to office with Szabo providing a heads up about what to expect from the Senator or Congressman in the next meeting. As we got to each office, I continued to the next office to confirm everything was in readiness, and then doubled back to take notes as the general got out of his closed-door meeting.

As he exited the first senator's office, the General faced me and started talking as Szabo led the way to the next office. "The senator has agreed to the C-5 engine funding," he said. "In exchange, we are going to earmark the next C-17 simulator to his state."

I knew this would be a problem. But what could I do?

"That's a big mistake," I said. The general stopped. "General, we only have one C-17 simulator now and it is maxed out. The Guard will only use their simulator to one-tenth of its capacity and will not train active duty pilots. They are scheduled now to take delivery of simulator number 5 in six years but do not face any delay in their pilot production. Giving them simulator number 2 pushes our program back two years."

"Well, the engines were a good trade, and the C-5 program is short on engines," he said.

"That's what the engine manufacturer is saying, but your Air Force staff says it isn't true," I said.

Szabo stepped in. "We need to get moving, general. Eddie, we'll talk about this later."

In the next four hours "we" made more trades and the list of phone calls I had in front of me was becoming daunting. I was going to have to explain to the staff the disaster that I had witnessed. As the general's limousine pulled up he turned to Szabo and extended his hand. "Great job today, Danny. I couldn't have done this without you." He gave me a nod and turned to the opened limousine door.

I looked at Szabo who kept his gaze on the limo until it was gone from our sight. "We did good today," he said. "I think I've got the hang of this and I'll go solo next time around."

"That's good," I said. "I don't think I can take another bloodbath like that."

"Bloodbath?"

"We started with a list of ten items we needed to accomplish on behalf of USTRANSCOM," I said. "Of those we got one. One out of ten. I need about an hour with a phone. This isn't going to go well with the staff."

"I'll leave you to it," Szabo said. "See you back at the hotel for dinner. Call my room."

That night at dinner Szabo was in the mood for career counseling. "Eddie, you need to learn a few of my leadership techniques if you expect to go any further in the Air Force. I was thinking about the way you talked back to the CINC today; very bad form."

"I am always in learn mode," I said.

"You need to learn to time your protests," he said. "The CINC had already made those deals. It does you no good to bark at him like that after the fact."

"There are a lot of issues and a lot at stake," I said. "We need to be tenacious in getting him to understand what his staff wants him to know. He's going to come home to a headquarters staff that is going to be in shock and will look to him for answers. He needs to understand the ramifications of his actions."

"And you need to understand that it is better to keep your powder dry for when you really need it," Szabo said.

"We are underutilizing our newest airlifter by a factor of ten because we can't train pilots fast enough," I said. "The situation calls for the courage to tell the boss he is cutting the legs from underneath his troops."

"You are too invested in the airlift fleet," Szabo said. "You need to keep the big picture in focus."

The next day I was cursed with the seat next to Szabo on our TWA flight back to St. Louis. I carried a novel with me during check-in and boarding. As I sat I opened the novel and started to read. Szabo didn't take the hint.

"Do you know how many full colonel eligibles we have next year?" he asked.

"No," I said.

"Seven," he said. "There are seven of us at the very top of the airlift world all competing for only two definitely promotes. How unfair is that?"

General Craft could guarantee two promotions by bestowing "Definitely Promote" recommendations on his top two lieutenant colonels. He was duty bound to make the decision himself without outside influence. If a review board detected any delegation of this responsibility or that the definitely promote recommendations were given to lesser deserving officers in a move to game the system, the general himself would be subject to rebuke. Everyone in the Air Force part of the USTRANSCOM staff assumed the definitely promotes would be awarded to the two lieutenant colonels in his legislative liaison office.

"That may very well be a problem with the system," I agreed. "But it is the system. Not much we can do about that. Odds are we'll promote one more officer. Three out of seven is above the Air Force average."

"It will be a damned shame if only three of us get promoted," Szabo said. He was my rating official but my performance report and promotion recommendation would both be signed by General Craft. Of course, I wasn't concerned at all. After seven months together, Szabo was still unaware of my secret.

"General Crowley has a plan," Szabo said. "It's going to get us one more colonel."

"I'm surprised Crowley can tie his own shoes," I said. "Any plan of his should be avoided. I hear he was an incompetent tanker pilot who somehow survived a tour as a training squadron commander and then again commanding a leadership school. He botched the CT-43 accident investigation. Over the years, his personal staffs have had to work overtime to keep him from looking like an idiot. It has been a losing effort."

"No, that's not true," Szabo said. "He's a good officer. General Craft is having him write the definitely promote recommendations. General Crowley figures he can give your definitely promote to another lieutenant colonel. Since your last two performance reports were signed by a four-star, your promotion is guaranteed and we get one more colonel promoted. That's pretty good thinking, don't you think?"

"No, I do not," I said. "First of all, he is not allowed to delegate the selection. Secondly, four general officers have been reprimanded in as many years for trying to game the system. Leave it to Crowley to do something so blatantly unethical."

Flight Lessons 4: Leadership & Command

M1 Abrams tanks on US Army Railcars (Photo: BNSF War Machines)

We got back to the office the next day and the news was the Army had solved a problem that had stymied USTRANSCOM for years. During the Iraq War the Army couldn't get its tanks to ports because the necessary flatbed railcars were otherwise devoted to lower priority cargo. Other bases, including Air Force and Navy bases, refused to give up rail cars in fear they would never get them back. USTRANSCOM, the biggest player in the problem, could not come up with a solution.

Then, out of the blue, a lowly Army major submitted an idea through a suggestion program that allowed any officer to simply submit any idea on a postcard. That major's name was Steve Christ.

The note on my desk was written with an angry hand. "See me, ASAP!"

I rapped my knuckles on his open door. "Get in here," Szabo said. "Close the door."

"Talk to me about flatbed railcars and how it is one of my majors solves a problem through a suggestion program and gets his name plastered all over the news without any mention of our legislative liaison office! Talk to me about that."

"Steve's idea is brilliant," I said. "The way he describes it, we just flip a switch when we mobilize. We rewrite every railcar contract to say the individual base owns it until mobilization, and then we own it. When mobilization is over, they get their railcars back. When he told me about this I wondered why I never thought of it!"

"So you knew about it?" He asked.

"Yes," I said.

"And did you tell him to stab me in the back by going outside the chain of command?"

"No," I said. "I simply encouraged him to develop the idea and do his best to get it implemented. I am surprised he went through the Army suggestion program. I would have counseled him against that. It is unethical to do something like this for personal gain when it is part of your job to come up with ideas."

"You are damned right it's unethical!" Szabo said. "He's made an enemy of his own boss!"

"He's not your enemy," I said. "He's a young staff officer who just needs a little counseling. I'll talk to him. Exacting a pound of flesh from him sends the wrong message to the others."

"Do you remember what I said about loyalty?" he asked.

"Something about it being critical," I said.

"That's right," he said. "So why is that Army major so disloyal?"

"Perhaps you need to expand that rule," I said. Szabo slumped into his chair, somehow defeated by one of his subordinate's successes. "Loyalty works both ways. Leaders can only earn their follower's trust and loyalty by showing them an equal amount of trust and loyalty."

"That's horseshit," he said. "Loyalty is given up the chain because that's the military way. Leaders earn that loyalty through credibility."

"Leaders must be credible," I said. "But credibility is earned through actions."

"You give him a good ass chewing," Szabo said. "He's dug himself a hole and I'm out of shovels." Szabo slumped back in his chair, defeated. I withdrew to the main office area where everyone found an excuse to be anywhere else, everyone except Major Christ.

"Colonel, I hope I didn't get you in trouble," he said. "That was never my intention."

"I know, Steve." I sat at my chair while the major remained standing. On the one hand I felt a small measure of vindication that Szabo's knife in Grafton's back was so swiftly repaid. But on the other hand I felt I had let everyone down. I should have counseled the Army major better.

"Do you know why he is so upset?" I asked. "Can you see the situation from his side, Steve?"

"Yes, sir," he said.

I waited for the "but" that often follows in these situations but it never came. It appeared Major Christ understood his sin.

"We all saw what happened to Commander Grafton," I said. "It seems unfair but in the end the Navy gained a great technique, the office looks good, and maybe we can make this work out for Rich too. It is too soon to tell."

"Yes, sir."

"Now you have solved a long-standing problem," I said. "And that makes you look good, no doubt about it. But it could also gain you a reputation as an officer willing to sabotage the greater good for individual gain. You don't want that."

"No, sir," he said.

"I am betting you will never do that again," I said.

"You can count on that, sir."

 Our office braced itself for a winter of personnel changes, promotions, and pass overs. Any officer passed over for promotion would immediately be replaced, its service not wanting to waste a position with such close ties to the CINC. The Navy would release its results for Commanders in November, the Army its results for Lieutenant Colonels in December, and the Air Force its definitely promote list to Colonel in January. My secret was still a secret, but my decision wasn't yet firm.

On the second Monday of November, Lieutenant Commander Grafton learned he would never be promoted to Commander and that his next assignment would be aboard a frigate in the Atlantic as a supply officer. It was the first pass over suffered by the legislative liaison office in anyone's memory.

Four weeks later the Army's list of brand new lieutenant colonels included Steve Christ. He wasn't due an assignment for two years and the Army seemed eager to let him remain for additional seasoning.

And that left us two Air Force lieutenant colonels in the breech. General Craft had to make his definitely promote decision by the first week in January and the promotion board would meet in February. Seven lieutenant colonels become two colonels, three if we got lucky.

General Craft asked all seven of his lieutenant colonels to spend an hour with Major General Crowley for background information used to write the promotion recommendation. That meeting would be followed up with a briefer meeting with Craft himself. I called Crowley's office, who had no choice but to finally schedule the meeting.

"I got your letter," he said as I sat in the chair opposite him at his desk. "I'm not going to hash over history to soothe your hurt feelings. We have a specific list of things to cover here and that's all we are going to cover."

"Yes, sir," I said.

"You have a very good record, Colonel Haskel," he continued. "It is my considered opinion that you are going to be promoted with or without a DP. It will be my recommendation to award that DP to another officer."

"Thereby getting the command another promotion," I said.

"Exactly," he said. "That's the smart way to do this."

"If by 'smart' you mean 'unethical,' I would have to agree," I said.

"I think we are done here," he said.

"One final question, sir," I said. "Is it true that General Craft is allowed to bestow a DP on two officers by virtue of the fact we have seven eligibles, the factor being 24 percent?"

"Yes," he said. "I think it's 24 percent rounded to the nearest whole number."

I returned to our office where Szabo had already returned from his meeting with Craft. "The general's ready for you, Eddie," he said. "He's pretty confident about our promotions."

I walked into the general's office and his secretary waved me right in. General Craft rose from behind his desk and offered his hand, which I shook. We both sat at a window table, overlooking the headquarters building front entrance.

"It looks like you have full colonel in the bag," he said. "You've been here for three years, which is a long time for a full colonel, so we need to think about your promotion in terms of the next job. I just need to know where you want to go next. I am thinking you should return to the Pentagon where you can spearhead our efforts to procure more C-17s. That airplane is the key to airlift in the next century. What do you think, Eddie?"

"I don't mind going back to the Pentagon, general," I said. "But I'd rather not have anything to do with the C-17."

"Why is that?" he asked.

"The airplane is a compound mistake. It was designed to carry two M1A1 tanks. Two M1A1s will fit, but will place the airplane out of center of gravity so it can only carry one. Meanwhile the Army has given up on the idea of heavy tanks. So the reason itself is gone. The resulting shape of the airplane makes it a flying speed brake, too slow and without sufficient range. We should cut our losses and buy a fleet of cargo Boeing 747s for a quarter of the cost and ten times the lift capacity."

General Craft looked at me for a minute, silent. "Colonel Haskel, always the contrarian," he said. "I admire your guts and confidence. But your outspoken nature will cost you in the end."

"Yes, sir."

"Sometimes we can't pick our issues," he finally said. "Sometimes we have to assume the Air Force position over our own."

"And sometimes, we need to take a stand," I said. "We can't all be unthinking automatons; there will always be a need for critical thought."

"There is a line to be drawn," he said. "Eddie, you tend to straddle that line more than most. You will make a great colonel and with your mind for facts and numbers I think you will do great things for the Air Force. I do, however, have something I've been wanting to ask you."

"Sir?"

"When the chief of legislative liaison job came open, everyone assumed you would be a natural. But you never volunteered. Why?"

"It was the right thing to do," I said. "When it comes to legislative matters, you need to have someone on the same frequency as you and that certainly isn't me."

"Well I hope you find a place in this man's Air Force," he said. "And even if you don't, best of luck, Eddie."

I left the general and stopped by my office to retrieve my hat. Szabo looked up from his desk as I walked out, not saying a word. The walk to the base personnel office took about ten minutes and gave me a chance to reflect on decisions made a year ago and only recently solidified. It was the right thing to do. With the stroke of a pen, my Air Force career would officially end exactly 20 years after it had begun.

My last day in the office was set and I declined the formal ceremony, which was my right. I thought it best given that I had just torpedoed the promotion odds for several officers. I set my retirement date to guarantee that I had 20 years on active duty. Because that date fell before the definitely promote math was computed, the command's allotment of DPs decreased from 2 to 1. That DP went to Szabo.

I showed up for my last day in uniform and was surprised to see several faces from past assignments. General Craft entered the room with another flag of-

Flight Lessons 4: Leadership & Command

ficer, retired Brigadier General Lesley Remington, the last wing commander at Ramstein before it turned from a fighter air wing to a C-130 airlift wing.

It wasn't much of a ceremony, as these things go. Lieutenant Colonel Szabo read the retirement orders, General Craft shook my hand, and I was officially retired. We stood around awkwardly until Craft excused himself, asking Remington to follow. I stood at the front of the room as members of the USTRANSCOM staff stood in line to shake my hand. I kept looking at the back of the room, wanting to ensure two old friends didn't leave.

Once the last of the current staff had left, retired Lieutenant Colonel Dillon May stepped forward. "Eddie, when are we going to see you in an airline uniform?" he asked.

"Never," I said. "I hope. But you are with Southwest, I hear."

"And loving it," he said. "Free airline trips, you know. The minute I heard you set a retirement date, I knew I had to come here."

"I got so wrapped up in the closing days in Germany I never got a chance to thank you," I said. "You always seemed to be able to protect me from my own mistakes, even to the very end."

"I don't think you made many mistakes," he said. "You turned around a dysfunctional squadron and protected that squadron from a dysfunctional wing. We all make mistakes and none of yours could have prevented the crash."

"I'm not so sure about that," I said. "I think I would have recognized that bad NDB approach. I should have spent more time teaching instrument procedures than worrying about promotion recommendations." Dillon thought for a moment.

"Remember what you said to me about Remmy and the Black Hawk shoot down?" he asked.

"Not really," I said.

"You said the only thing he could have done to prevent it was to fly every sortie himself," Dillon said. "There comes a point where you have to trust the Air Force has trained its people well and that your people will live up to that training. Don't beat yourself up over it."

"Regardless, you were always a secret wingman," I said. "I asked you a while ago why. You told me you would answer some day. That some day is today."

"That it is," he said. "Did you ever hear how I got my call sign?"

"Mayhem? You hardly seem to fit that," I said.

"I was a T-38 instructor pilot at Williams Air Force Base in 1979," he said.

"Really?" I said. "I was there in 1979."

"I know that," he said. "We never flew together and we never met. But the year before you got there I got mad when the wing commander forced us to join the officer's club, against all regulations about it being purely voluntary. So I sabotaged the drink station at one of the bars. Free beer for anyone ordering a lemonade."

"That's pretty good," I said.

"The O'Club manager went nuts trying to figure out why beer sales fell but their beer taps started running dry more often. Only my squadron mates knew it was me and that's how I got the name," he said. "At the time, I thought I was quite the maverick for doing that. The next year I heard about what you did."

"Oh," I said. "I wasn't the lead dog, but I had a role."

"That's not what I heard," Mayhem said. "You turned the wing commander in to the Air Force inspector general and he was forced to apologize to all you lieutenants. That had to be humiliating. After you left he was forced to retire. You took down a colonel as a second lieutenant."

"We had a captain who knew the system but didn't know how to write," I said. "So I wrote the complaint. That's all I did."

"Well, you made a reputation for yourself early on," Mayhem said. "I recognized your name when you got orders to Germany and did some calling. Looking at your twenty years I think you deserve the name Mayhem more than I do. Remember I was going to come up with a call sign for you? At first Woz and I started calling you 'The Professor' behind your back. And then we settled on 'Doctor No.' I think that one fits pretty good. Eddie, congratulations. You had an impact every place you've been. If you change your mind about the airlines, give me a call."

"I will," I said. Dillon's place in line was taken with another face from the past, retired Lieutenant Colonel Alton Gee. "Good morning, Ed-you-el," he said. "Do you remember me?"

"I will never forget you, Alton," I said. "I am very honored that you would make the trip out here for me."

"Well there's not much else for a retired navigator to do," he said. "Besides, I owe you an apology."

"What do you mean?" I asked.

"The last time we ever spoke I gave you two predictions," he said. "I predicted you would one day command a squadron of your own, and by golly you did. But I also told you I thought you would fail."

"The jury is still out," I said.

"No it's not," he said. "I've read everything there is to know about you, your squadron, and the crash. You did good Ed-you-el. I am proud to have known you."

Alton gave me a hug. "The feeling is mutual, Alton," I said.

I looked up to see the last remaining face in the crowd I needed to speak with. "General Remington, I'm honored you could make it out here. Surprised, but honored."

"I actually live just down the road," he said. "I knew you got assigned here and promised myself I would see you when you retired. I was hoping we could have a long chat."

"My pleasure," I said.

It was a cold day outside and the general seemed to be content standing in the front foyer at our headquarters building. We spoke about family, the Air Force, and lost comrades. When I thought we were all talked out he finally asked. "From everything I've read about you it seems you learned the secret of command better than just about anyone else. But I would like to hear it from you, Eddie. What is the secret of command?"

"When you first hinted at this I thought about leadership styles," I said. "I spent a lot of time looking for the perfect leadership style and tended to find more bad than good. I finally realized there is no ideal leadership style. Leadership is situational, you need to adapt. But you didn't ask about leadership, you asked about command."

I was formulating the answer as I spoke. I knew what I wanted to say, but had never articulated it before. But then it came to me.

"I'm not sure this is what you are looking for," I said. "But I think it is that all commanders need to learn about the two directions of loyalty. A commander will automatically have a certain level of loyalty from the troops just by virtue of the title. But you cannot expect enduring loyalty from your troops if they don't sense the same from you."

"Bingo," he said. "That's about as well said as I've ever heard it. But that makes sense, coming from you."

"I'm not so sure," I said. "Years after the crash people are still talking about how dysfunctional that wing had become under General Paulson. And it could be that given his personality, that was a foregone conclusion. But I think I could have shown him a little more loyalty and maybe that would have changed things."

"You are too hard on yourself," Remington said. "From the minute I met that psychopath I knew he was trouble."

"Yes, sir," I said. "But I had a gift for winding him up and maybe I even tried to wind him up. I should have cut him some slack, met him halfway, or just part of the way. The more I pushed back, the more he pushed harder each time. I ended up spending so much time protecting the squadron from him that I didn't spend enough time looking over operations."

"That was your ops officer's job," Remington said. "You can't do it all."

"Well I should have found the time," I said. "I could have taught my pilots to recognize a bad approach plate. I could have been a better commander for my people if I were a better subordinate to my commanders."

"You might be right," Remington said. "A good commander does indeed apply loyalty up and down the chain of command. But a great commander is one who sticks up for his people and isn't afraid to face the consequences."

The general, in civilian clothes, stood at attention and saluted me. I returned the salute.

A Few Thoughts

A Few Thoughts About "Expert Pilot Consultants"

As I've related, I was invited to appear on several television programs following the crash of our CT-43 and declined. It always amazes me when "expert pilots" flock to the nearest television camera to pontificate about something they could not possibly know anything about, even if they were qualified in the same type of aircraft. Within a day of our crash, several of these so-called experts bemoaned the fact our pilots were not able to stand up to the unreasonable demands of their Very Important Passengers. In fact, these pilots had a good track record of doing just that. The next day the pundit pilots were on again to talk about the dangers of ducking under a Minimum Descent Altitude (MDA); when in fact nothing of the sort happened.

Good intentions or not, these pilots are defaming the characters of some very fine pilots. The only thing our CT-43 pilots were guilty of was not being able to detect a bad approach plate and not understanding the nature of the two beacons on that approach. Very few of us are capable of the former and many of us could have been guilty of the latter. Had the approach been properly designed, flying the wrong beacon would have just resulted in a late missed approach.

A Few Thoughts About the Accident Investigation

The Air Force rarely gives in to public pressure to knowingly color the results of an accident for military or political reasons. When I attended the Air Force Flight Safety Officer's Course we studied the crash of the Thunderbirds, caused by the lead pilot flying his T-38 into the ground and the rest of the team following him in. The initial report blamed a non-existent stabilizer problem but didn't make any attempts to fix the stabilizer on the surviving fleet. The Air Force, wisely, fixed the report. In the case of our CT-43, it is clear the U.S. government was unwilling to put the blame solely on the Croatian government. They were going to blame the pilots no matter what.

Most of the accident reports I've studied from the National Transportation Safety Board and other civilian entities have been very good. They do, occasionally, get it wrong. We pilots need to study these reports with the thought, "how can I prevent this from happening to me?" With that mindset, you will be prepared to understand what really happened.

James Albright

A Final Thought About Leadership

I've held several leadership positions during my 20-year Air Force career and several more to follow as a civilian. The biggest challenge for me, in both worlds, has been and continues to be getting honest feedback. It pays to have a second-in-command who is willing to tell you to your face that you are making a mistake. But even with that advantage, you have to be willing to listen.

You can see these lessons in action in the fifth and final volume in this series, Flight Lessons 5: People. It deals with crew resource management for pilots and people management for leaders.

Appendix: Accident Report Extracts

The 7,000-page accident report starts with a 96-page executive summary that references the remaining pages, imparting the idea that those 96 pages are authoritative and the investigators were thorough and fair. Nothing could be further from the truth. The report sets out to paint the pilots as reckless so as to deflect the blame from the Air Force itself and Croatia. If the pilots were reckless, the solution is to simply purge reckless pilots from the ranks. But, as I contend, the pilots were conscientious and methodical, the blame lies with their training. I've included extracts of the pertinent pages to show that the pilots were not reckless; rather, they were conscientious and methodical.

So how do you paint the pilots as reckless? First, you have to say there is no evidence they flew the airplane within the tightest pilot standards.

1. Pages O-28/1 and O-28/2 of the report contain a letter from Allied Signal, the manufacturer of the Radio Magnetic Indicator (RMI), dated 3 May 1996, that says they could not determine where the RMI was pointed at time of impact but used a simulation technique that resulted in a bearing that was obviously wrong. The report uses this initial letter to justify going to great lengths to determine the course indication the pilots were flying.

a. They started with the position of the heading bug on the Horizontal Situation Indicator (HSI), not the instrument the pilots would have been using for the NDB approach. They would have been using the Radio Magnetic Indicator (RMI) to fly a heading since this is the instrument with the ADF needle.

b. They then used old winds from Brindisi Italy to make an adjustment to the heading bug (wind drift) to hypothesize the aircraft was on a course 9° left of course, precisely where it had crashed. This wind could also be used to say the crew flew 80 knots too fast.

2. Page V-245 of the report interviews a pilot of a CT-43 used to test the approach. He was asked, "Would you fly the heading off the RMI or would you fly the heading off the HSI that you derived from the RMI heading." He said, "I would fly the RMI heading." Investigators got the same answer from each of the other CT-43 pilots interviewed. Their hypothesis that the accident crew relied upon the HSI heading bug was wrong and not supported by the testimony of other CT-43 pilots.

3. Page V-170 of the report has testimony of a Croatian pilot who had flown into Dubrovnik earlier in the day. He was asked about the drift on

final, to which he said, "Almost nothing, not more than 3 degrees I would say because the wind was pretty much in line with the runway." He was asked about the difference between his indicated and ground speeds. "The difference was about 10 knots if I recall." Even if the heading bug theory was true, the use of Brindisi winds used to calculate the drift was wrong. This calls into question the report's assertion that the crew flew 9° left of course and 80 knots too fast. But the theory was called into question before this . . .

4. Page O-28/3 of the report contains a second letter from the RMI manufacturer, dated 7 May 1996, that says they did determine where the RMI was pointed at time of impact: it was indicating 115°, just 4° north of course and well within the U.S. Airline Transport Rating standard of 5°. You cannot say these pilots flew 9° left of course when their indicator shows they were just 4° left of course. So if the pilots flew within airline pilot standards, why did the airplane end up 9° left of course? The accident report contains the answer, if only the accident board members were willing to see it.

5. Page J-3/7: "An electrical power plant with associated distribution power lines is located in Plat, Croatia. A power line to serve the small community of Velji Do, Croatia runs from the power plant up the face of the mountain in the general direction to the accident site." Could the powerline have misled the aircraft's avionics? Investigators studied this possibility . . .

6. Page J-3/131 of the report notes that "the effect of PLC [powerline communications] signaling on NDB receivers has been previously measured and documented." (In other words, it has been previously proven to be true.) But then the report says, "The PLC emissions are not predicted to cause any response in the NDB receiver at distances greater than 800 m (~ 2624 ft). Of course, the aircraft never got higher than 2,150' as it flew right over that powerline. With the shape of the terrain, it is likely the aircraft flew within a few hundred feet of the powerline. Accident investigators dismissed the effect of the power lines because a flight test using another CT-43 on a clear VFR day did not duplicate the accident aircraft's ground track. But this test flight was not flown under the same weather conditions and at night, which could have impacted the amount of electrical power in those power lines. We will see that Croatian pilots and air traffic controllers were well aware of the possibility . . .

7. Page V-233 of the report interviews a CT-43 pilot used to test the approach. He says he heard that Croatian pilots fly the approach "three radials to the south." You might say this is hearsay. But there is more . . .

8. Page V-523 of the report has testimony of a Dubrovnik area air traffic controller, who was asked about the NDB's performance under the conditions present on the night of the crash, known as "Jugo" storm fronts. After he alluded to NDB performance issues, he was asked, "And that when this phenomenon Jugo takes place, the pilots that you have spoken to are cautious because they feel that there is some effect to the Kilo Lima Papa NDB which causes the aircraft to drift left of course . . . and that would have taken them into the mountain." To which he said, "Yes."

In my opinion, the Air Force Accident Investigation ignored evidence that the pilots flew within U.S. Airline Transport Pilot standards and failed to properly investigate the likelihood that the aircraft's ADF receiver followed the power plant's distribution power lines up the mountain. The pilots did make a procedural mistake: they flew the KLP NDB outbound when they should have flown the CV NDB inbound. This was an error in their training, not their skills as pilots.

James Albright

AEROSPACE

AlliedSignal Inc.   616 582 6526
Government Electronics Systems
Counter Operations
375 N. Lake Street
Boyne City, MI 49712

TECHNICAL EVALUATION OF CT-43A, 73-1149 MISHAP
3 MAY 1996

I. INTRODUCTION

The purpose of this report is to provide the results of the analysis conducted on the Radio Magnetic Indicator, part number 36154-1AJ25B1, which was removed from CT-43A, 73-1149.

II. RADIO MAGNETIC INDICATOR FUNCTIONAL DESCRIPTION

The Radio Magnetic Indicator (RMI) is a multi-purpose navigational instrument that displays an aircraft's magnetic heading and magnetic bearing to two radio navigation stations - VOR and / or ADF. The indicators are integrally lighted and incorporate warning flags. The face of each indicator consists of an azimuth ring with lubber-line indexes fore and aft and 45 degree markings through 360 degrees. A compass-off flag is located at the fore lubber-line index. An inner rotating compass dial is graduated from 0 to 360 degrees in five-degree increments. The compass dial is read against the fore lubber-line index for aircraft heading as transmitted by the compass system. A narrow pointer and a wide pointer pivot concentrically with the compass dial and are independently controlled by bearing information received from ADF and VOR navigation aids, as selected by rotary switches on the front of the indicators. When read against the compass dial, a pointer indicates the direction of a radio navigation transmitter. When read against the lubber-line, a pointer indicates the direction of a transmitter relative to the aircraft's heading.

III. EVALUATION

The RMI unit was received on May 2, 1996 and opened in the presence of the local government officials.

 a. <u>Removal of Unit from Packaging</u> The unit was separated into 3 bags. One bag contained the rear case which was obviously cut away from the unit near the mounting area and detached from the rear cover which showed removal of 2 screws after the heat damage and shearing of a third screw. The second bag contained screws and miscellaneous components which had fallen off as debris from the unit. The third bag contained the remains of a mechanism which had been charred under heat high enough to burn the Teflon coating off all internal wires.

 b. <u>Visual Analysis</u> Due to the excessive heat damage, all unit identifications (serial number, part number and component identification) had been destroyed. Visually the front aluminum diecast bezel and glass were missing with the remains of the bezel pieces around the attachment screws. The heat and impact that destroyed the bezel also was extensive enough to completely destroy and eliminate the plastic dial compass card, the diffuser, lighting PC board and the pointers. The Pointer Knobs are completely missing with the exception of the stainless steel shaft and lighting wire ends. Although the warning flag itself was missing due to the

O-28/1

Page 2

excessive heat, the flag shaft and solenoid were visually noted to be in the upward normal operating position.

The mating connector wire harness had been cut off, and the mating connector was left attached to the unit. The unit was received with the mating connector intact. When the mating connector was removed, it was noted that pins 25 and 26 of the unit connector were bent. Under examination of the mating connector, there is evidence of wear from pins 25 and 26 in the mating pin locations.

As evidenced by the position of the pointer knob gear location, both pointers were in the ADF receiving mode. Although the compass card is completely missing, the location of the two screws which mount the dial will indicate only 2 possible readings which are 180° apart. Comparing the location of the screws to an intact unit using a tooling protractor, it was determine that the dial reading was either at West 25° North (North 65° West) or at East 25° South (South 65° East).

c. Investigation to Determine Synchro Angular Position Since the pointers were missing as a result of the extensive heat damage, the team attempted to determine pointer and bootstrap transmitter locations from the synchros angular position. The insulation damage prevented wire color identification. We were able to trace most of the synchro leads to their electrical assembly location to identify stator wire color. Due to the excessive heat damage, the BTR1 and BTR2 synchros had shorted stator and/or rotor wires and were unable to be energized to determine phase angle location. BTR1 drives the narrow pointer. BTR2 drives the wide pointer.

The team was able to remove the synchro rear covers and identify the stator lamination slot relationship to the rotor lamination location. We were able to simulate this condition in a functional synchro with an attached digital angle indicator. The angular indication will indicate only two possible readings which are 180° apart. The pointer position of BTR1 is at approximately 245° or 65°. The pointer position of BTR2 is at approximately 210° or 30°.

SECTION IV. SUMMARY

Since the returned Radio Magnetic Indicator was severely fire damaged, we were unable to obtain complete information about the unit's history and functional test capability.

The team was able to visually determine that both pointer knobs were in the ADF position. The dial compass card was either in the West 25° North (North 65° West) position or the East 25° South (South 65° East) position. The pointer position of BTR1 is at approximately 245° or 65°. The pointer position of BTR2 is at approximately 210° or 30°. The warning flag was in the up or normal position. This information was determined solely by visual examination of the components' positions on the returned unit.

Don Kincheloe, DCMC QAR   Alice Schaub, Engineer

O-28/2

ADDENDUM TO
TECHNICAL EVALUATION OF CT-43A, 73-1149 MISHAP
7 MAY 1996

AlliedSignal Inc
Government Electronics Systems
Courter Operations
375 N. Lake Street
Boyne City, MI 49712

616 582 6526

In reviewing the data for closure of this project we discovered an error in the reported angular readout of the position of the BTR1 Pointer. The synchro angle from the BTR1 Pointer was measured with a digital angular indicator which read in a reverse angular direction (clockwise synchro rotation caused decreasing angular readings). When taking into account that clockwise synchro rotation causes increasing angular readings, BTR1 was remeasured to show a corrected angular reading of either 115° or 295°. The BTR2 Pointer was reverified at the same position as previously measured.

The bootstrap synchro transmits the dial position to an external receiver. The bootstrap synchro is mechanically linked through the gear train with the compass card position. The bootstrap signal has been measured at either 118° or 298°, which confirms the correlation of the compass card position to the bootstrap angular position.

In the course of confirming the above readings, the team had also noted that the monitor amplifier had the component side toward the front of the indicator. Although the repair manual doesn't specify position of the component side, the prints show the component side should be toward the rear of the unit. Since the monitor amplifier is connected only to the J3 connector with its wire lead, it is insensitive to its assembly position.

In summary, these findings correct the BTR1 pointer from a readout of either 65° or 245° to a readout of either 115° or 295°. The BTR2 pointer readout remains at either 30° or 210°. The bootstrap readout is at either 118° or 298° which correlates with the compass card position of either 115° (East 25° South) or 295° (West 25° North). This data shows that the compass card, flag, and bootstrap remained in correlation throughout the crash. There is no evidence in the gear train mesh of any broken teeth or mesh loss. The pointers which are in the ADF position show no evidence of any mechanical anomalies which would have prevented them from functioning normally. Even though the unit was severely heat damaged, the physical evidence shows that the unit appeared to have been mechanically intact and functioning.

Don Kincheloe, DCMC QAR

Alice Schaub, Engineer

O-28/3

shown in Attachment 7 and References 5 and 10 (No correlation has been possible between the PEDs for which measured data is available and any specific PEDs that may have been present on IFO 21.) However, measurements of several PED devices with liquid crystal displays (LCDs) have shown a margin of protection of approximately 25 dB in the frequency range of NDBs, as shown in Attachment 7. For the case of the ADF not being tuned to a NDB (i.e. not KLP 318 or CV 397), the possibility of a bearing error increases slightly since there is no desired signal present. It may be noted from Attachment 7 that some notebook personal computers and cellular telephone operational modes produce emissions in the frequency range of NDBs, while others do not.

One investigative test for spurious emissions from an available PED was performed at the Dubrovnik Airport on 16 April 1996 by staff of the DoD JSC. A DANCALL Logic Type HP 1111 Nordic Mobile Telephone (NMT) 450 cellular telephone was borrowed from US Army IFOR Security Staff at the airport. The telephone was then tested in OFF and STANDBY/ RECEIVE modes while placed near the ADF antenna of CH-47 88-00099 while the CH-47 AN/ARN-89 ADF receiver was monitored for reception of spurious emissions from the DANCALL internal circuitry. Separation between the DANCALL and ADF antenna was minimized. No emissions were detected at any of the frequencies monitored using the ADF (neither audio or RMI needle movement). Frequencies checked were: 318, 330, 340, 350, 360, and 380 kHz. ADF operation was confirmed by reception of CV 397. Refer to Evidence TAG Number 487, 6 developed photos of billboard reflector antenna, and cellular telephone used for CH47-ADF ground test.

The CT-43A AIB members conducted additional ground and flight tests of aircraft ADF performance in the presence of PED spurious emissions in frequency ranges including 318 kHz. The Ground Test Plan and Report is Attachment 8. The PEDs Flight Test Plan and Report is Attachment 9. The composite Flight Test Report is contained in Tab O. All applicable test results support the finding that EMI from sources inside the aircraft did not contribute to the IFO 21 accident.

External Interference Source - Electrical Power Plant/Distribution System - General:

An electrical power plant with associated distribution power lines is located in Plat, Croatia. A power line to serve the small community of Velji Do, Croatia runs from the power plant up the face of the mountain in the general direction to the accident site. See 1:50,000 scale map DUBROVNIK, 2780 III M709 Edition 3-DMA, Defense Mapping Agency, Army Map Service, Tab R. The distribution system is both 220 and 110 KVAC, three-phase and includes power line carrier signals to control down-line switching stations. These signals are in the 120-124 kHz and 216-220 kHz frequency range, well below the frequency range of NDBs. The system was constructed in 1965 and has experienced no electrical interference generation complaints or corona discharge during high humidity. See Tag 606, verbal testimony of Vinko Basich.

J-3/7

graph three curves are used to relate field strength to the horizontal distance separation from the HVPL. These three curves correspond to flight altitudes of 500 ft, 1000 ft, and 1500 ft above the HVPLs. Separate graphs were prepared for each of two undesired radiated frequencies, 200 kHz and 500 kHz; and four power line voltage levels, 345 kV, 500 kV, 765 kV, and 1100 kV.

Based on this data, the maximum field strength predicted for power lines with any of the four voltage levels analyzed was a field strength of 35 dBuV/m. This equates to a field strength of 56 uV/m. Thus, the field strength of the corona discharge at a horizontal distance separation of 100 feet from the power line is below the minimum specified sensitivity of the AN/ARC-83 direction finder.

Corona discharge is not predicted to have caused interference to the NDB receiver onboard this aircraft.

POWER LINE CARRIER INTERFERENCE

The effect of PLC signaling on NDB receivers has been previously measured and documented[1]. The conclusions made in this report are based on the assumption that the injected PLC power is 1 W and that the aircraft is located 400 m (~1312 ft) above the transmitting substation. The conclusions are based on testing done with only two types of NDB receivers and only a single circuit, three-phase, horizontally disposed power line.

For the measured cases in this report, typical field strengths seen from PLC transmitters were 30 to 35 dBuV/m. The worst case field strength measured was 40 dBuV/m. The AN/ARN-83 receiver sensitivity equates to an interference threshold of 37 dBuV/m. To reduce the PLC emissions to the interference threshold would require a distance separation from the HVPL to the NDB receiver of 800 m (~2624 ft).

The PLC emissions are not predicted cause any response in the NDB receiver at distances greater than 800 m from the HVPL.

RE-RADIATION OF THE NDB SIGNAL

Both Reference 1 and Reference 2 addressed the subject of HVPL re-radiating the NDB signal. Both references concluded that the reradiated signal is on the order of 30 dB below the direct signal. Therefore, the re-radiated signal would not cause interference to the NDB receiver.

---

[1] Kissik, W.A.; *Power Line Carrier Radiation and the Low Frequency Aeronautical Radio Compass*, Dept. of Transportation, Federal Aviation Administration, Report No. FAA-RD-80-31, May 1980.

Flight Lessons 4: Leadership & Command

51.Q   What did you actually see?
51.A: Yeah.

52.Q   So you saw what was reported?
52.A: Basically, basically it was pretty close.

53.Q   How about your preflight briefing, the weather when you took off from Zagreb, did they report thunderstorms in the area?
53.A   They did, and I had--I took the last METEO report on the hour, which was the same report as I told you right now.

54.Q   On the hour?
54.A   Yeah. When I say the hour, the last time I could have a report before taking off.

55.Q   Oh, I'm just making a note because my question would be which hour at Zagreb? About what time did you receive that report?
55.A   I think it was around noon, but I'm not sure. I have to, you know, check my book. I can't actually recall that data.

56.Q   Did you have your GPS on that day?
56.A   Yeah, programmed.

57.Q   And programmed--did you happen to recall the winds on the final?
57.A   No, I didn't. I didn't do the wind parameter because it's a little bit difficult to do. I have to change a lot of pages to get it. On the front page, I can read my bearings and my deviations and now, I also have a ground speed data. That's, basically, what I need to fly the approach. I was listening to the winds that was reported by the tower and, you know, just making the normal wind correction that you see flying the--purely an ADF approach.

58.Q   Do you recall just what that drift angle or what drift correction--quite minimal?
58.A   Almost nothing, not more than 3 degrees I would say because the wind was pretty much in line with the runway.

59.Q   How about your ground speed reference here, the difference between your ground speed and
59.A   Yeah, the ground speed was--the difference was about 10 knots if I recall, 10 knots plus--to start with the approach and then end the approach, minus -about that data.

SARINIC

	the missed approach point, the point where you would abandon the approach and . . .
52.A.	Okay.
53.Q.	. . . and basically go somewhere else.
53.A.	Yeah, looking at the approach plate here, the copy that you guys are giving me, this is a – I've never seen an approach like this. I don't think I've seen it quite, you know, in this – this kind of manner, but basically it looks like you can hold off of Kilo-Lima-Papa, which is the initial – call that the IAF, which is an NDB. You could hold off of that. You penetrate inbound on the one-one-nine, in bound. It's a black line. The – the approach is depicted as though you would stay on Kilo-Lima-Papa and have to be forced to cross tune on Charlie-Victor using another radio. Basically, what – what most people have said when they look at this, and what I kind of said was that it's an illegal approach to do. That was the first thing that I thought. However, after hitting Kilo-Lima-Papa inbound and going off of the one-one-nine, it looks like it's possible to dial up three-ninety-seven off of Charlie-Victor and then fly the one-one-nine inbound from that. That would be the only way you could really do it with our setup in our airplane.
	Fifty-one-thirty-seven – fifty-one-thirty-seven really, I don't think, covers this type of scenario that well. I don't think fifty – fifty-one-thirty-seven is an instrument regulation that the Air Force uses, taking into account FARs – Federal Aviation Regulations, that kind of thing. So I might elect to do – to fly the one-one-nine inbound to Charlie-Victor, which is the second locator here, or which is the locator here after Kilo-Lima-Papa. So sometime after getting on course, I would dial that up and fly it. That's the only way I could define the missed approach point.
	Is that the best idea in the world? No. The – the problem I have with it is you lose your course guidance when you have to switch over. You lose course guidance once you have to – to switch over to Charlie-Victor. This – I've heard, since the accident, that 7-3-7 pilots, the Croatian Airways, they will pass Kilo-Lima-Papa inbound and they'll – basically they'll dial up Charlie-Victor on their NAVAIDS, because they have the same setup that we do, and they'll fly a one-one-six inbound which gets you three radials to the south. So – but your – your missed approach, you would have to go at Charlie-Victor locator . . .
54.Q.	And what are they concerned about? Why do they do that?

Flight Lessons 4: Leadership & Command

	Maybe in general or even in specifics, if you could remember the way either of those guys flew typically with – fly an NDB approach. Would they set the – the course they intended to fly, sometimes they would set that in the course select window in their Horizontal Situation Indicator even though they couldn't use that indicator; would that – would they set the – their course in there like, in this case, I think the Dubrovnik course is one-one-nine.
106.A	That's correct.
107.Q	Would they typically dial that in the course select window?
107.A	That's conjecturing on their part. I – I do it.
108.Q	You do it.
108.A	I do it.
109.Q	So that's a – a way they could have maybe done that?
109.A	Sure. I mean, that's, you know – that's a fifty-fifty chance they could have done that. I mean, I don't know what the NAVAID is just prior to – to Kilo-Lima-Papa. I'm not sure what it is up there, but, you know, a lot of times guys will – will leave that last one in – that last navigational aid, you know, in case it's part of the missed approach procedure, which it isn't in this one. That – that was my personal technique – I like doing that.
110.Q	When you fly an NDB approach, would you typically – in your – in your instrument cross-check, would you fly the heading actually off the RMI or would you fly the heading off the HSI that you derived from the RMI?
110.A	Right. I would fly the RMI heading.
111.Q	So you would essentially take the HSI out of your cross-check and – and rely on the RMI?
111.A	I wouldn't take it out of the cross-check. I would use it as a backup, just to make sure the headings are right and, of course, dialing that course in there is one way to kind of back yourself up on that in the HSI, that is. But no, I wouldn't let it go out of my cross-check at all.
112.Q	Would you use the – the heading bug in the HSI for anything in particular?
112.A	I'd put it on runway heading – put it on runway heading.

289

and emerge out of clouds. The nose of the plane was in direction to the mainland. I cannot say how many degrees was the inclination, but obviously we were headed into the hills and, of course, he took the correction and everything was safe when you are out of clouds and you see the ground and when you have the ground contact, it is quite a different situation and you can take the correction.

44.Q. You stated that this is associated with a weather phenomenon that you know to be Jugo?
44.A. Yeah.

45.Q. My understanding, and correct me if I am wrong, Jugo is a storm front generally moving from the southwest to the northeast?
45.A. That's it.

46.Q. And is always accompanied or most often accompanied with some type of precipitation, rain or thunderstorm activity, is that correct?
46.A. Yes.

47.Q. And that when this phenomenon Jugo takes place, the pilots that you have spoken to are cautious because they feel that there is some effect to the Kilo Lima Papa NDB which causes the aircraft to drift left of course, and on the particular occasion that you mentioned, you riding, observed that your aircraft was tracking in a direction that would have taken them into the mountain?
47.A. Yes.

48.Q. I just want to be clear. This is on an approach from Kilo Lima Papa to Charlie Victor on an approach into runway 12 at Dubrovnik Airport?
48.A. That's it.

49.Q. On that occasion, was the pilot utilizing Kilo Lima Papa as the nav aid, principal nav aid for course guidance, or was he tuned to Charlie Victor?
49.A. He was using Kilo Lima Papa.

50.Q. With reference to Kilo Lima Papa, did you happen to notice if he was maintaining his course accurately?
50.A. I can't say precisely because when we flew there, Dubrovnik was liberated only two or three days before that. So at the time, the procedure was not

LAZIC

V-523

Flight Lessons 4: Leadership & Command

James Albright is an average pilot with average stick and rudder skills, but has an above average desire to learn and instruct. He spent twenty years in the United States Air Force as an aircraft commander, instructor pilot, evaluator pilot, and squadron commander. After retiring as a lieutenant colonel, he went on to fly for several private and commercial operators as an international captain, check airman, and chief pilot. His logbook includes the T-37B, T-38A, KC-135A, Boeing 707, Boeing 747, Challenger 604, and the Gulfstream III, IV, V, and G450.

His website, www.code7700.com attracts over three million hits each month and his articles have appeared in several magazines, most notably Business & Commercial Aviation.

While he claims to be devoid of ego, that can hardly be true of someone willing to write a five-volume set of flight lessons based on his own experiences.

www.ingramcontent.com/pod-product-compliance
Lightning Source LLC
Chambersburg PA
CBHW050626300426
44112CB00012B/1673